The Playboy of the Western World—A New Version

Irish Studies
Kathleen Costello-Sullivan, *Series Editor*

The Playboy of the Western World

A New Version

A Critical Edition

BISI ADIGUN AND RODDY DOYLE

Edited and with an introduction by
Jason King and Matthew Spangler

Syracuse University Press

For a listing of books published and distributed by Syracuse University Press,
visit https://press.syr.edu.

ISBN: 9780815638339 (hardcover)
9780815638346 (paperback)
9780815657057 (e-book)

Library of Congress Cataloging-in-Publication Data
Names: Adigun, Bisi, author. | Doyle, Roddy, 1958- author. |
King, Jason (Jason Francis), 1970– editor. | Spangler, Matthew J., editor. |
Synge, J. M. (John Millington), 1871-1909. Playboy of the Western World.
Title: The playboy of the western world—a new version : a critical edition / Bisi Adigun
and Roddy Doyle ; edited and with an introduction by Jason King and Matthew Spangler.
Description: First edition. | Syracuse, New York : Syracuse University Press, 2024. |
Series: Irish studies | Includes bibliographical references.
Identifiers: LCCN 2023046222 (print) | LCCN 2023046223 (ebook) |
ISBN 9780815638339 (hardback) | ISBN 9780815638346 (paperback) |
ISBN 9780815657057 (ebook)
Subjects: LCSH: Ireland—Drama. | Synge, J. M. (John Millington), 1871–1909.
Playboy of the western world. | Literature and society—Ireland—History—21st century. |
BISAC: DRAMA / European / English, Irish, Scottish, Welsh | HISTORY /
Europe / Ireland | LCGFT: Drama. | Literary criticism.
Classification: LCC PR9387.9.A343576 P57 2024 (print) |
LCC PR9387.9.A343576 (ebook) | DDC 822/.92—dc23/eng/20231128
LC record available at https://lccn.loc.gov/2023046222
LC ebook record available at https://lccn.loc.gov/2023046223

Manufactured in the United States of America

Contents

Acknowledgments

The editors of this book would like to thank the Irish Research Council as well as the Research Foundation and College of Social Sciences at San José State University for grants that made this research possible.

The support of our colleagues has also been pivotal, especially that of Charlotte McIvor, Patrick Lonergan, Myles Dungan, Kellie Hughes, Charlotte Headrick, Brian Singleton, Philip Mullen, Colleen Hamilton, and the editorial team at Syracuse University Press: Kathleen Costello-Sullivan, Deborah Manion, Kelly Balenske, Miranda Baur, and Jessica Bax. We would also like to thank our families and friends for their roles in this process, especially Eliot Spangler, Crystal Smith-Spangler, Aislinn King, Nathalie King, Fergus King, and Kerry West.

Chronology of Major Productions and Adaptations of John Millington Synge's *The Playboy of the Western World*

1907	First production at the Abbey Theatre in Dublin.
1911	First professional US production by the Irish Players on a tour of the United States.
1946	Cape Playhouse production on Cape Cod, Massachusetts, starring Gregory Peck.
1958	Musical adaptation, titled *The Heart's a Wonder*, by Nuala and Mairin O'Farrell, presented at the Gaiety Theatre in Dublin, Lyric Theatre in Belfast, and Westminster Theatre in London.
1962	Film adaptation starring Siobhán McKenna and Gary Raymond.
1971	Lincoln Center production in New York City for the centenary of John Synge's birth.
1975	Druid Theatre production in Galway, directed by Garry Hynes.
1975–1976	National Theatre production at the Old Vic Theatre in London, starring Stephen Rae.
1982	Druid Theatre production in Galway, Edinburgh, Dublin, and throughout Ireland, directed by Garry Hynes.
1984	Mustapha Matura's *Playboy of the West Indies*, produced by the Oxford Playhouse.
1998	Steppenwolf Theatre Company production in Chicago.

2001	Peacock Theatre production in Dublin, directed by Niall Henry of Blue Raincoat Theatre Company and starring Mikel Murfi and Olwen Fouéré.
2004	Mustapha Matura's *Playboy of the West Indies*, revived by the Nottingham Playhouse and Tricycle Theatre in London.
2004	Druid Theatre production in Galway, directed by Garry Hynes and starring Cillian Murphy.
2005	Presented as part of DruidSynge, in which all of Synge's six plays were presented over the course of consecutive days; first presented at the Galway Arts Festival.
2006	Pan Pan Theatre's Mandarin-language production at the Beijing Oriental Pioneer Theatre, directed by Gavin Quinn.
2007, 2008–2009	Bisi Adigun and Roddy Doyle's adaptation at the Abbey Theatre in Dublin.
2011	Old Vic production in London, starring Ruth Negga, Robert Sheehan, and Niamh Cusack, directed by John Crowley.
2022	Solas Nua production of Bisi Adigun and Roddy Doyle's adaptation in Washington, DC.

The Playboy of the Western World—A New Version

Introduction

Jason King and Matthew Spangler

Bisi Adigun and Roddy Doyle's centenary adaptation of John Millington Synge's classic *The Playboy of the Western World* (1907) had a sold-out run when it was first produced at Dublin's Abbey Theatre in 2007. It was brought back by popular demand the following year. The play takes the story out of Ireland's rural west at the turn of the twentieth century and places it in a Dublin pub at the turn of the twenty-first century and features a Nigerian asylum seeker in the co-lead role. Under the authorship of Adigun—artistic director of Arambe Productions, Ireland's first African theater company—and bestselling, Booker Prize–winning author Roddy Doyle, perhaps best known for his novels about working-class Dublin life, *The Playboy of the Western World—A New Version* represented an intercultural artistic collaboration and adaptation of an Irish theater classic. It is far and away the most commercially successful theater production to date on the themes of interculturalism and migration in contemporary Ireland.

But despite the play's popularity and the increasing importance of its subject matter related to race and immigration over the last two decades, it has only seen three productions: the two at the Abbey Theatre in 2007 and 2008–9, and a more recent US production at Solas Nua Theatre in Washington, DC, in November 2022. This short production history, unusual for a play of its popular success, is largely due to the crumbling of the relationship between the principal artists involved, marked by a series of lawsuits initiated by Adigun against Doyle and the Abbey Theatre. Following the second

1

production in 2008–9, Adigun claimed his moral rights[1] to the play had been violated, due to textual changes made in rehearsal without his consent. The legal battle was resolved by an Irish court in 2013, largely in Adigun's favor, with Adigun receiving €200,000 from the Abbey and full ownership of the play. It is fair to say that few contemporary Irish plays have been as commercially successful, and yet have generated as much controversy offstage as Bisi Adigun and Roddy Doyle's *The Playboy of the Western World—A New Version*. The production is nearly as well-known in Ireland as Roddy Doyle's bestselling books and the works of Ireland's most successful playwrights, such as Martin McDonagh and Conor McPherson, in spite of the fact that the play had a limited production run and its script has never been published. In fact, we believe *The Playboy of the Western World—A New Version* remains the most important unpublished play in twenty-first-century Ireland.

This volume publishes the play script for the first time, along with a series of critical essays by leading experts in the fields of Irish studies and intercultural theater who examine the text and the issues it raises concerning adaptation, interculturalism, migration, and race in contemporary Ireland. The specific topics considered by the essays collected here include the value of the play text as a teaching tool in the classroom; the nature of adaptation and its relationship to source material and so-called originality; the way in which adaptation of a canonical text can function both as a strategy to challenge and rearticulate dominant narratives of Irish identity, as well as, and perhaps at the same time, reaffirm existing, dominant-hegemonic self-perceptions a community has of itself;[2] the wider contemporary Irish

---

1. Moral rights are an aspect of international copyright law and refer to the right of an author to prevent unauthorized alterations to a copyrighted work, and to be given appropriate credit as the creator of such work.

2. In this sense, this collection illustrates what Simone Murray calls the "sociology of adaptation," a view toward studying adaptation that goes beyond textual considerations—or the mere noting of similarities and differences between the source material and adaptation—and instead considers a wide range of cultural,

cultural framework over the last two decades, during which Ireland has witnessed a dramatic increase in so-called inward migration; the inevitable challenges that come with intercultural collaboration in performance, challenges that are not new and not unique to an Irish context;[3] the history of the play's creation, including the working relationship between its principal creatives; and the legal case and fallout between Adigun, Doyle, and the Abbey Theatre during and after the play's initial production period. As such, this volume also seeks to build on past research on the topics of interculturalism, migration, and globalization in the context of Irish theater.[4]

The Playboy of the Western World—A New Version has continued to resonate over the years on both sides of the Atlantic, even in

---

commercial, legal, industry, and even political forces that contribute to the making and reception of an adaptation in the broader extratheatrical world. See Simone Murray, *The Adaptation Industry: The Cultural Economy of Contemporary Literary Adaptation* (London: Routledge, 2012), 4, 6.

3. See Charlotte McIvor, *Migration and Performance in Contemporary Ireland: Towards a New Interculturalism* (London: Palgrave Macmillan, 2016), 39–84, for a wider discussion of Irish immigration and other adaptions of John Millington Synge's *The Playboy of the Western World* between 2004 and 2011, such as DruidSynge featuring the Irish-Ethiopian actress Ruth Negga as Pegeen Mike in Perth, Australia (2005), and at the Old Vic Theatre in London (2011), Pan Pan Theatre's 2006 Chinese adaption of *The Playboy of the Western World* and subsequent intercultural collaborations, as well as Adigun and Doyle's *The Playboy of the Western World—A New Version* (2007, 2008–9).

4. See Charlotte McIvor and Jason King, eds., *Interculturalism and Performance Now: New Directions?* (London: Palgrave Macmillan, 2019); McIvor, *Migration and Performance in Contemporary Ireland*; Charlotte McIvor and Matthew Spangler, eds., *Staging Intercultural Ireland: New Plays and Practitioner Perspectives* (Cork: Cork Univ. Press, 2014); Pilar Villar-Argáiz, ed., *Literary Visions of Multicultural Ireland: The Immigrant in Contemporary Irish Literature* (Manchester: Manchester Univ. Press, 2014); Patrick Lonergan, *Theatre and Globalization* (London: Palgrave Macmillan, 2010); Loredana Salis, *Stage Migrants: Representations of the Migrant Other in Modern Irish Drama* (Newcastle: Cambridge Scholars Publishing, 2010); Karen Fricker and Ronit Lentin, eds., *Performing Global Networks* (Newcastle: Cambridge Scholars Publishing, 2007).

its unpublished form and despite the fact that its last performance in Ireland was well over a decade ago. In this book's opening chapter on identity, audience, and power dynamics in Adigun and Doyle's play, Kelly Matthews makes an impassioned argument for the relevance of the script to contemporary viewers and readers around the world. As Matthews shows, multivalent cultural and linguistic markers make *The Playboy of the Western World—A New Version* "a perfect text to center questions of social engagement and Irish identity in a contemporary context." The play's crosscurrents of class consciousness and immigration create a racially and socially charged atmosphere that speaks as clearly to American college students today as it did to the audiences who first saw it in the Abbey Theatre in 2007–09.

In making the "Playboy" a Black man and transposing the setting from the wild coast of Mayo to contemporary suburban Dublin, Matthews argues that the playwrights "shift the power dynamics of Synge's original tale." Moreover, Adigun and Doyle's fidelity to key lines and stage directions from Synge's 1907 script allow them to interrogate assumptions about identity that are as central to our contemporary global society as they were to the Celtic Revival of a century ago. In tune with Adigun's emphasis on interculturalism, Matthews's students examined the intersecting social groups represented in the script: working-class Dubliners, gangland crime bosses, starstruck teenagers, and Nigerian immigrants. As she explains, the resulting hullaballoo and humor in the play provide a lens for contemporary students to gain a clearer focus on their own society as issues of patrimony and privilege rise to the fore.

Matthew Spangler also explores the play's transatlantic influences and resonances in his close reading of the script and its adaptations. His chapter, *"The Playboy of the Western World—A New Version* in Adaptation Practice and Theory," situates Adigun and Doyle's work within the broad concerns of contemporary adaptation practice and examines the text of the new play relative to Synge's source material. Spangler argues that while Adigun and Doyle's adaptation may be temporally second, it is by no means unoriginal either as a work of art or in the themes it raises. Spangler further argues, citing Homi Bhabha's notion of "surveillant culture," that the performance of this play onstage creates a visual metaphor for the ways in which minoritarian identities are "seen" within dominant culture, especially as these identities pertain to race and immigration. In this respect, Spangler contends, Adigun and Doyle have written what adaptation theorist Linda Hutcheon calls a "transcultural adaptation,"[5] one in which the setting, historical era, or characters of the source material are re-presented in the adaptation in such a way that the new work engages intercultural or political themes not present in the source text. Spangler also provides a chronology of major adaptations of Synge's play throughout the century from its many musical adaptations—*The Heart's a Wonder* (1958), *Christy* (1975), *Black Country* (1978), *Golden Boy of the Blue Ridge* (2009)—to Mustapha Matura's widely celebrated *Playboy of the West Indies* (1984), and Pan Pan Theatre's Mandarin-language production at the Beijing Oriental Pioneer Theatre and Project Arts Center in Dublin (2006). Synge's play has proven remarkably popular for adaptation over the years. Spangler concludes this popularity is likely due to the play's use of a simple, widely used, and yet engaging storytelling device—"a mysterious stranger walks into a bar"—linked with three of the most popular themes in theater: sex, violence, and comedy.

The Playboy of the Western World—A New Version stood on the shoulders of an exceptionally robust theatrical movement focused on themes of race and immigration in Ireland that marked the first decade of the twenty-first century. This collection of work took a variety of artistic forms, including modern dance (the Irish Modern Dance Theatre's *Fall and Recover*, 2004); one- and two-person shows (Mirjana Rendulic's *Broken Promise Land*, 2013; Donal O'Kelly's *The Cambria*, 2005); performance art as in the work of Polish Theatre Ireland; audience-immersive performance (ANU Productions' *Vardo*, 2014); community-based work (Upstate

5. Linda Hutcheon, *A Theory of Adaptation* (New York: Taylor and Francis, 2013), 45.

Theatre Project, from 1997); street theater (*The Parable of the Plums*, 2004); more straightforward examples of narrative theater (Charlie O'Neill's *Hurl*, 2003; Paul Meade's *Mushroom*, 2007); and entire companies whose purpose it was to engage the topics of race and migration (Calypso Productions, 1993–2008; Adigun's own Arambe Productions, 2002–13).[6]

Being the largest, most widely seen, and commercially successful of all these projects, *The Playboy of the Western World—A New Version* is the defining theatrical work of Celtic Tiger Ireland, an era in which the country was grappling with questions of immigration almost a full decade before the topic would fuel the United Kingdom's Brexit vote and the election of President Donald Trump in the United States. Driven by the Celtic Tiger economic boom that began in the mid-1990s (lasting from roughly 1994 to 2008) and the enlargement of European Union member states in 2004, historically high numbers of immigrants were settling in Ireland during the years that Adigun and Doyle wrote the play and saw it through its first production. The foreign-born population in Ireland had increased from 5 percent of the total population in 1996 to nearly 17 percent by 2011. Galway City had Ireland's highest proportion of foreign-born residents at nearly 20 percent; the foreign-born population of Dublin was 17 percent of the city's total population.[7] This rapid population increase of immigrants in Ireland led to a backlash from certain parts of Irish society. For example, in 2004, the divisive Citizenship Referendum, championed by Minister of Justice Michael McDowell, changed the Irish constitution so that children born in Ireland were no longer automatically Irish citizens. That the referendum passed with nearly 80 percent support was a distressing outcome to those in Ireland's immigrant-serving communities—a sign, it was perceived

6. For more on this work see McIvor, *Migration and Performance in Contemporary Ireland*; McIvor and Spangler, *Staging Intercultural Ireland*; McIvor and King, *Interculturalism and Performance*; Fricker and Lentin, *Performing Global Networks*; and Salis, *Stage Migrants*.

7. McIvor and Spangler, *Staging Intercultural Ireland*, 4–5.

at the time, of Irish xenophobia—though one effect of the referendum was to further highlight conversations about race and immigration in the public sphere. While immigration has slowed and even reversed somewhat in the post–Celtic Tiger years after 2008 (in 2016 the foreign-born population of Ireland was 11.6 percent[8]), there is no doubt that present-day Ireland is host to a sizeable multiethnic, foreign-born population, and immigration will likely be a persistent theme in not only Irish theater, but society at large for the foreseeable future. The question of how immigrants adapt and integrate into their host societies, and how those societies adjust to the immigrants in turn, has become one of the most topical and urgent issues not only in Ireland but also the European Union and North America.

In this volume, Sarah L. Townsend situates *The Playboy of the Western World—A New Version* in the context of Ireland's ostensible Celtic Tiger prosperity and increasing cultural diversity. She argues that while the play may appear to challenge received notions of race and immigration in Ireland, it actually reaffirms them as markers of short-lived Irish affluence. She claims that Adigun and Doyle's adaptation largely confirmed what audiences in 2007 wanted to believe about the stability of an upswing whose days were already numbered. Celtic Tiger–era narratives about Ireland's new arrivals, she contends, often double as narratives about the Irish themselves. This self-reflective quality is especially apparent in literary and theatrical works that, like *The Playboy of the Western World—A New Version*, celebrate pluralism in order to perform the permanence, even nonchalance, of Irish prosperity. More specifically, she situates Adigun and Doyle's play within a recurring subgenre in Celtic Tiger and post–Celtic Tiger fiction and drama, the multicultural sequel or adaptation, in which immigrants assume the homes, jobs, rituals, and literary and theatrical roles formerly occupied by the native Irish. This tendency to return to familiar narrative territory is, she argues,

8. "Census of Population 2016—Profile 7 Migration and Diversity," Central Statistics Office, 2016, https://www.cso.ie/en/releasesandpublications/ep/p-cp7md /p7md/p7anii/.

more than a gimmick. Rather, the very process of adapting or sequelizing reinforces—and in some cases, challenges—the ideological work of what Gargi Bhattacharyya has referred to as "feel-good" multiculturalism.[9] By tracking the production of a form she calls the immigrant-as-sequel through the Celtic Tiger and the subsequent recession, her chapter considers both the congratulatory and critical narratives about Irish society that are unleashed through the act of envisioning the immigrant as a variation on the same.

Emer O'Toole's chapter frames *The Playboy of the Western World—A New Version* within the long-running theoretical and global debates surrounding the ethics of intercultural theater practice. This chapter provides a well-rounded gloss on intercultural performance theory as it was influenced by Peter Brook's controversial production of the Indian epic *The Mahabharata* (1985). This chapter also offers something of a warning for how even well-intentioned intercultural collaborations in the arts sometimes go awry. O'Toole argues that, while interculturalism in the Irish context has the potential to destabilize exclusionary fixities of cultural identity, the Abbey Theatre production of *The Playboy of the Western World—A New Version* fell short of its intercultural, offstage potential. She contends that the Adigun/Abbey controversy shows that not only was the outcome of their intercultural collaboration not a utopian cross-cultural fertilization, but it provided yet another example of those disempowered by structural oppression being marginalized once again. Her chapter describes the challenges of intercultural collaboration in the arts and is a must read for anyone, inside or outside Ireland, who wishes to engage in such collaborative work.

In chapter 5, Jason King focuses on the impact that the global and Irish economic crises had on contemporary Irish theater as revealed in this adaptation of *The Playboy of the Western World*. He

9. Gargi Bhattacharyya, "Riding Multiculturalism," in *Multicultural States: Rethinking Difference and Identity*, ed. David Bennett (London: Routledge, 1998), 252–66; Paul Gilroy, *Against Race: Imagining Political Culture Beyond the Color Line* (Cambridge, MA: Harvard Univ. Press, 2000), 21.

contends that the legal controversy surrounding the second production in 2008 provides a case study of how professional theater productions that dramatized stories of immigrant empowerment during the Irish economic boom were profoundly inhibited and undermined by the bust that followed. King claims that the breakdown in the creatives' relationship and ensuing legal dispute is more symptomatic of Celtic Tiger Ireland in economic collapse than the content of the play itself, or most other productions mounted in the period. He argues that this dispute did not simply reflect, but also reinforced, the social effects of the economic crisis, through its prolonged litigation, enormous expense, and especially, the missed opportunity that it represented to position the multicultural and migrant-themed *The Playboy of the Western World—A New Version* within the Irish theatrical mainstream. More broadly, his chapter contends that the economic crisis has been marked by the disappearance of immigrants from the professional Irish stage.

Bisi Adigun has the last word in this book. In chapter 6, he reflects on his own practice of adaptation in the context of his collaboration with Roddy Doyle and the ensuing controversy. For many years, Adigun and his theater company, Arambe Productions, were at the forefront of using adaptation as a form of migrant reclamation—what Ric Knowles calls "strategic reappropriation . . . of the symbolic capital of the dominant culture, as canonical texts are rewritten and reconfigured through difference."[10] Arambe recuperates Irish cultural icons, such as the figure of Christy Mahon, as immigrant predecessors who help redefine the place of the migrant at the heart of Irish culture. In this chapter, Adigun provides a detailed history of his inspiration for the adaptation, his method of intercultural collaboration with Roddy Doyle in writing the script, and negotiations with the Abbey Theatre to produce the play on Ireland's national stage. He offers an inside, intimate, and on-the-ground

---

10. Ric Knowles, *Performing the Intercultural City* (Ann Arbor: Univ. of Michigan Press, 2017), 32.

look at the creative and production process of a new play, of which one is rarely afforded a glimpse. Adigun also addresses the play text and describes how specific moments in the play came about through the process of adaptation and cowriting. We would note that the play text included in this volume is the 2007 performance text of the play.

This publication, coming well over a decade after its onstage, theatrical premiere, also takes place in a unique and even fraught cultural moment. The resurgence of the Black Lives Matter movement in the United States, after police officers killed George Floyd on May 25, 2020, created heightened consciousness of racial disparities and structural inequalities on both sides of the Atlantic, as well as a reckoning within various theater communities in which people in power have been encouraged to step aside and make room for those who have been traditionally left out or delegitimized in the creative process. Within the Irish context specifically, recent years have seen the development of new Black-led cultural and political organizations, such as the African American Irish Diaspora Network in the United States and Black and Irish in Ireland.[11] This heightened consciousness has exposed (once again) the relative lack of racial diversity in Irish theater and performing arts. Since the controversy surrounding this play, no migrant- and minority-themed production of comparable stature has found its way onto Ireland's national stage. The publication of the Irish Arts Council's landmark report *Cultural Diversity and the Arts*[12] in 2009, when reviewed today, underscores this lost decade.

In some respects, Adigun and Doyle's *The Playboy of the Western World—A New Version* represents one of the great missed opportunities of Irish theater history. As Charlotte McIvor observes, it brought "to an end any fast-tracked hopes for the integration of

---

11. See https://www.aaidnet.org/ and www.blackandirish.com/.

12. Daniel Jewesbury, Jagtar Singh, and Sarah Tuck, *Cultural Diversity and the Arts: Final Report* (Dublin: Create—The National Development Agency for Collaborative Arts and Arts Council, 2009).

minority-ethnic and migrant artists into the institutionalized professional Irish theatre, represented at its zenith by the Abbey, the nation's most highly funded theatre and its designated 'national theatre.'"[13] The initial success of the play in 2007 should have led to numerous future productions, Irish and international tours, publication of the script, and its inclusion in course syllabi around the world as one of the defining works of the Celtic Tiger period. Instead, as Adigun notes, "It has turned out to be the biggest reason for the near extinction of Arambe," due largely to the legal and interpersonal fallout that came on the heels of the production. In the decade since the controversy, there have, of course, been other minority ethnic and migrant artists creating Irish theater productions;[14] but no other migrant-led company has achieved comparable success to Arambe before its fall from grace. Minority-ethnic and migrant-led productions in Ireland have become increasingly consigned to the community arts sector, rather than the national theater. "The challenge now," Adigun claims, "is to focus on the future and ensure that African immigrant actors who want to play the part of Christy Mahon, Pegeen Mike, or, indeed, Public or Private Gar are afforded the same opportunities as their Irish counterparts to tread the mainstream Irish boards, rather than being labeled mere 'community theatre artists.'" It is a formidable challenge. We hope that the publication of Adigun and Doyle's *The Playboy of the Western World—A New Version* will help ensure, in some small way, that it is not an insurmountable one.

13. McIvor, *Migration and Performance in Contemporary Ireland*, 68.

14. See McIvor, *Migration and Performance in Contemporary Ireland*, chaps. 3–8.

The Playboy of the Western World—A New Version (2007). Giles Terera (Christopher). © Ros Kavanagh

The Playboy of the Western World—A New Version (2007). Angeline Ball (Widow Quin) and Eileen Walsh (Pegeen). © Ros Kavanagh

The Playboy of the Western World—A New Version (2007). Angeline Ball (Widow Quin), Phelim Drew (Philly), and Joe Hanley (Jimmy). © Ros Kavanagh

The Playboy of the Western World—A New Version (2007). Olu Jacobs (Malomo), Kate Brennan (Sarah), Aoife Duffin (Susan), Charlene Gleeson (Honor), Phelim Drew (Philly) and Joe Hanley (Jimmy). © Ros Kavanagh

The Playboy of the Western World—A New Version

Bisi Adigun and Roddy Doyle

First produced by the Abbey Theatre, Dublin, from September 29, 2007, with the following company:

CAST

PEGEEN:	Eileen Walsh
SEAN:	Laurence Kinlan
MICHAEL:	Liam Carney
PHILLY:	Phelim Drew
JIMMY:	Joe Hanley
CHRISTOPHER:	Giles Terera
WIDOW QUIN:	Angeline Ball
SUSAN:	Aoife Duffin
SARAH:	Kate Brennan
HONOR:	Charlene Gleeson
MALOMO:	Olu Jacobs

PRODUCTION TEAM

Director:	Jimmy Fay
Set Design:	Anthony Lamble
Lighting Design:	Sinéad Wallace
Costume Design:	Catherine Fay
Sound Design:	Vincent Doherty and Ivan Birthistle

15

Fight Director:	Paul Burke
Company Stage Manager:	Anne Layde
Assistant Stage Managers:	Orla Burke and Triona Humphries
Voice Director:	Andrea Ainsworth
Casting Director:	Holly Ní Chiardha
Hair and Makeup:	Val Sherlock
Photography:	Ros Kavanagh
Graphic Design:	Red Dog

CHARACTERS

PEGEEN:	Young Dublin woman, early twenties
SEAN:	Young Dublin man, early twenties
MICHAEL:	Pegeen's dad, publican and gangster, fifties
PHILLY:	Michael's henchman, thirties
JIMMY:	Michael's henchman, late forties
CHRISTOPHER:	Young Nigerian man, early twenties
WIDOW QUIN:	Dublin woman, late thirties
MALOMO:	Christopher's father, fifties
SUSAN, SARAH, HONOR:	Young Dublin girls, late teens

Act 1

A modern, suburban pub, on the west side of Dublin. There is evidence of an invented form of Irishness: Guinness signs, photos of Michael Flatley, Roy Keane, and Mary Robinson.[1] There is a CCTV screen above and behind the bar counter upstage-centre. On the wall behind the counter are high shelves with bottles and a line of optics. Also behind the counter, a wall-mounted phone. Between the shelves and worktop, there is a wall-length mirror.

To the right is the main door to the outside world. Beside this door, upstage, a large window. To the left, a toilet door. Upstage, left, is another door: the exit to WIDOW QUIN's apartment. Behind the counter is a door and stairs to the living quarters. To the left, downstage from the toilet door, a large, artificial fire—gas, with a real bale of turf beside it.[2] There are seats, tables, and, at the counter, a couple of stools, screwed down. And, beside the fire, a long padded seat/bench, with a low table in front of it.

It is late, after closing time. Occasional outside noises: distant sirens, and a nearby dog, barking and howling. A radio is on, low: late-night music. There is a remote control for the radio on the counter.

1. Guinness is an iconic Irish beer, brewed in Dublin since 1759. Michael Flatley (b. 1958) is an Irish dancer, choreographer, and musician, most famous for his Irish dance shows *Riverdance* (1994), *Lord of the Dance* (1996), *Feet of Flames* (1998), and *Celtic Tiger Live* (2005). Roy Keane (b. 1971) was a professional soccer player (or professional football player outside of the United States) for eighteen years, winning nineteen major trophies, as a midfielder mainly for Manchester United in England and Celtic Football Club in Scotland. He also served as assistant manager for the Republic of Ireland's national football team from 2013 to 2018. The second part of Keane's autobiography, *The Second Half* (2014), was ghostwritten by Roddy Doyle. Mary Robinson (b. 1944) was Ireland's first female president (1990–97), who also served as the United Nations High Commissioner for Human Rights from 1997 to 2002.
2. Turf is also known as sod, or grass.

PEGEEN, an attractive woman in her early twenties, is alone onstage. She sits at a table, browsing a wedding magazine: Irish Bride. *Her mobile phone, a flip model, is also on the table. Also, a pack of cigarettes and lighter.*

PEGEEN (*reading*): "You have full breasts, a bit of a tummy, round hips and behind." No way. "You have a bust, hips and a defined waist." That's more like it. " . . . a V-neck often draws the eyes down to the areas you are trying to deflect." Not my problem. Oh, I like this one. "Mermaid shape." Lovely. (*Turns new page.*) Tiaras; Jesus. "Nancy Full"—no. "Selena; Queen of the Park"—big, silver; fuck the lot of you.

As PEGEEN reads, SEAN KEOGH, also in his early twenties, enters. He is dressed casually, in white shirt and black jacket. He can also be seen, just before entering, on the CCTV screen.

SEAN: Where's your da?
PEGEEN (*without looking at him*): He's on his way.
SEAN: His Beemer's outside.[3]
PEGEEN: Yep.

She continues to read, hiding the magazine cover.

SEAN: What are you reading?
PEGEEN: None of your business.
SEAN: Weddings?
PEGEEN: Football.

She stands up and puts the magazine behind the counter.

---

3. *Beemer* refers to an automobile or motorcycle made by Bayerische Motoren Werke AG, more commonly known as BMW.

SEAN: So, he's not here, no?

PEGEEN: No.

SEAN: Not upstairs, no?

PEGEEN: No.

SEAN: So, you're on your own, yeah?

PEGEEN: Apparently.

SEAN: I was just passing and I saw the Beemer and I thought he'd be here, so—

PEGEEN (*interrupting*): He's gone to someone's funeral.

SEAN: Whose funeral?

PEGEEN: Someone who died.

SEAN: Okay; yeah. But he shouldn't have left you on your own.

PEGEEN: Nothing new there. I'm grand.

SEAN: But it's mad out there tonight.

PEGEEN: Yeah, yeah; what's new?

SEAN: No, listen.

SEAN changes the radio channel, using the remote control, to a phone-in programme. He turns up the volume.

SEAN: Coming here—yeah?—I was listening to this in the car.

RADIO WITNESS 1: There were two of them, an'anyway.

PRESENTER: And you're saying they were dead, Darren?

WITNESS 1: Definitely. You could tell by the way their heads were.

WITNESS 2: Sorry; Fabian?

PRESENTER: Go ahead, Brian.

WITNESS 2: The car was riddled with bullet holes, like. But it was still moving when I was going past it.

PRESENTER: Incredible. On the M50?[4]

4. The M50 is the busiest motorway (similar to an American highway) in Ireland, which circles suburbs of Dublin.

WITNESS 1: Near the Red Cow.[5]

WITNESS 2: It freaked me out, Fabian.

PRESENTER: I'm sure it did. Two more gangland killings? Your thoughts . . .

SEAN *turns down the volume.*

PEGEEN: That's mad.

SEAN: I'll tell yeh, Pegeen, things are getting dangerous. Where's your da?

PEGEEN (*a bit less sure*): I told you. At a funeral.

SEAN: He shouldn't have left you here on your own, anyway. Not with that business between him and The Rattler.

PEGEEN: That's nothing to do with you; lay off.

SEAN: Look, all I'm saying is—

PEGEEN: I can take care of myself.

SEAN: There's no respect, Pegeen. The Rattler and the Viper and that—the old rules are gone. You know your man, Lucky McKenna, from Daffodil?

PEGEEN: With the squint in his eye?

SEAN: He got it fixed for his birthday. Well, anyway, they cut the legs off his husky.

PEGEEN (*disgusted*): Ah.

SEAN: And they put the legs through his letter box. And for what? A couple of euro.

PEGEEN: That's terrible, that is.

SEAN: Yeah; mad. And that new Polish priest—Father . . . you know. They mugged him the other day.

PEGEEN: I heard that, alright. There's no Polish priests in here though.

SEAN: Hang on, but. Did you hear about the guy, off his head on the crack? He broke into someone's house and made them—you know—ride each other. In front of him, like.

5. The Red Cow Moran Hotel is located in South Dublin.

PEGEEN: Did he film it?
SEAN: I don't know. It was on Joe Duffy.[6]

A siren, nearer than usual; the dog howls.

SEAN: And the immigrants, Pegeen. Some of them are head
cases. The ritual killings and that.
PEGEEN: Ah, that's just mumbo-jumbo stuff.
SEAN: It's true. It is. Only Jesus can save us. You shouldn't be
alone at this time of night.
PEGEEN: I told you, I can take care of myself. I'm well used to
being on my own.

SEAN now attempts to hold PEGEEN. She shrugs him off.

SEAN: It'll be fine after we're married.
PEGEEN: You're pretty sure of yourself, Sean Keogh. I never
said I'd marry you.
SEAN: You did.
PEGEEN: I said I might.
SEAN: We're engaged. You've the ring, look it.
PEGEEN: Ah, that's only for show. It means nothing.
SEAN: But your da and my ma have been talking—

*Offstage, a nearby siren, then another, and howling dog. She moves
to the door, to lock it.*

PEGEEN: I'd better lock up.
SEAN: Hang on. Just let me out first.
PEGEEN: I thought you were staying.
SEAN: I have to get home. My ma will be worried.

6. Joe Duffy (b. 1956) is an Irish broadcaster on Raidió Teilifís Éireann (RTÊ),
Ireland's national radio station, based in Dublin.

PEGEEN: Your ma? Worried? That's a laugh. (*Steps back from door.*) Off you go.

SEAN: Thanks.

Sirens fade. SEAN half opens the door.

PEGEEN: Mammy's more important than your future wife.

SEAN: Then we are getting married?

PEGEEN: Bye-bye.

He hesitates, then exits. This can be seen on CCTV.

PEGEEN: Chicken.

SEAN reenters.

SEAN: I'm not.

PEGEEN: Go on.

SEAN: I'm not. I want to stay.

PEGEEN: So, stay.

SEAN: Ah, look it, Pegeen. My ma and your da. They want us to get married, right? For the families and that. And they've been negotiating and that. Well, my ma says that I'm a better catch than you are—

PEGEEN: What?

SEAN: I'm not saying she's right now. But she says the negotiations are at a delicate stage and I'm not—you know—to *be* with you, until the deal is done.

PEGEEN: How are you a better catch? Is she fuckin' blind?

SEAN: I know what you mean.

PEGEEN: Is she blind?

SEAN: I know what you mean; I know what you mean. But it's not about us. I know. You're gorgeous, and I'm . . . ordi nary. But your da wants this marriage more than my ma does. *She* says.

PEGEEN: Why?
SEAN: We're bringing more to the table.

PEGEEN is deflated somewhat; she recognises the brutal truth.

SEAN: So, she says I'm to keep myself—
PEGEEN: Pure?
SEAN: Aloof.
PEGEEN: Aloof?
SEAN: That's what she says.

PEGEEN stands away; she opens the door.

PEGEEN: Goodbye.

SEAN hesitates.

PEGEEN: Off you go.
SEAN: But—
PEGEEN: You're supposed to be keeping aloof. So, fuck off.
SEAN: It'll be grand, Pegeen. She says—
PEGEEN (*walking away from the door*): Fuck her.

She takes her cigarettes from the counter. She takes one from the pack, and gets her lighter. SEAN hesitates, wanting to say more; then starts to exit. Outside noise; an urgent bark.

SEAN: What's that?
PEGEEN (*sarcastic; angry*): It's an aloof.

She runs across and pushes him out the door. SEAN resists. Off-stage, more barking. We hear MICHAEL FLAHERTY. We see him, the top of his head, on the CCTV.

MICHAEL (*off*): Shut up, the fuck.
SEAN: It's your da.

Enter MICHAEL FLAHERTY, PEGEEN'S father, a seemingly jovial, but dangerous, man, about fifty.

MICHAEL: The lovebirds. Sean—the hard man.

MICHAEL is followed by PHILLY CULLEN and JIMMY FARRELL. All three men wear black leather jackets. They're drunk, but still at work. PEGEEN goes behind the counter.

SEAN: Howyeh, Mister Flaherty. What was the dog barking for?

MICHAEL: Jaysis, Sean, what do all dogs bark for? How's your mammy?

SEAN: She's grand, Mister Flaherty.

MICHAEL (*putting his arm around Sean's shoulders*): You know Sean here, lads. Gracie Keogh's lad.

PHILLY and JIMMY acknowledge SEAN. PHILLY prepares three lines of cocaine. Without interrupting dialogue, PHILLY, JIMMY, and MICHAEL snort a line each.

PHILLY: Good man, Sean.

JIMMY: Of course, we know Sean.

PHILLY: Pegeen's chap.

MICHAEL (*with relish*): Fiancé.

PEGEEN: He's just going. (*To SEAN*) You can go now.

MICHAEL: You're not going, Sean. You're only after getting here. (*To PEGEEN, still holding SEAN*) Sean's going to look after you while me and the lads go out. Aren't you, Sean?

PEGEEN: It's midnight, Da. Where are you going now?

MICHAEL (*to SEAN*): You missed a great fuckin' funeral.

PEGEEN: Da? Where are you going?

MICHAEL: Back to the funeral.

PEGEEN (*sarcastic*): Is he not buried?

JIMMY: We just want to make sure he stays buried.

PHILLY: God be good to him.

SEAN: I can't stay, Mister Flaherty.

PEGEEN (*baby-like; quietly*): Mama.

MICHAEL: Of course you can stay, Sean. Just for tonight, till I
    get us a new lad to do the security.

SEAN: I can't, Mr. Flaherty.

MICHAEL: You can keep Pegeen company. No customers. Just
    the two of you for a few hours.

SEAN: I have to get home.

MICHAEL: This is your home.

PEGEEN: I'll be fine on my own.

MICHAEL (*to SEAN*): My little girl, Sean. We can't leave her
    alone.

SEAN: I have to go.

PEGEEN: Let him go, Da.

PHILLY: He can't leave Pegeen.

JIMMY: I'd stay here meself, if I was—

*MICHAEL, still holding SEAN with one arm, thumps JIMMY on
the chest, without looking at him.*

MICHAEL: No, you fuckin' wouldn't. (*To SEAN, less humor-
    ously*) You'll stay, Sean.

PEGEEN: Drop it, Da.

MICHAEL (*turning to PEGEEN*): He'll stay. (*To SEAN*) Sit
    down.

*SEAN hesitates, then begins to sit on a stool. His mobile phone
buzzes: a text. He takes it out and reads. He stands up, moves towards the door.*

SEAN: It's my ma.

MICHAEL (*standing in front of him*): Text her back. She'll
    understand.

SEAN: No, she won't.

MICHAEL: She was young herself once.

SEAN: No, she wasn't.

MICHAEL: Oh, yes, she was. Sit down.

SEAN: Don't stop me, Mr. Flaherty. Let me out.

SEAN moves to get past MICHAEL. MICHAEL shoves him.

MICHAEL: Sit fuckin' down.

SEAN: For the love of Jesus, Mr. Flaherty.

PEGEEN: Let him go. I'll be grand; I don't need him.

MICHAEL puts his arm around SEAN and takes him aside.

MICHAEL: Pegeen, Sean.

SEAN's phone buzzes again. Before SEAN takes it from his pocket—

MICHAEL: Leave it, leave it. Look it, Sean. Pegeen. You like her, yeah?

SEAN: Oh, yeah.

MICHAEL: You love her, maybe. Yeah?

SEAN: Yeah. As Jesus Christ is my witness.

MICHAEL (*after examining SEAN*): Grand. So, the question is: how do you show that love?

SEAN: Like—

MICHAEL: By running away? By leaving the poor girl on her own?

SEAN: No.

MICHAEL: So?

SEAN: My mother—

MICHAEL: Sean, Sean. Your mammy's a great woman. A great woman. But Pegeen there. She's your new mammy. Are you with me?

SEAN: Eh—

MICHAEL: You're at a crossroads, Sean. Happens to us all. You're leaving one life and one woman behind. Yeah?

SEAN: Yeah.

MICHAEL: And you're starting a new life. A new adventure with a different woman. Can't be both, Sean. It's one or the other. It's like a car. You get a new one, there's no point holding on to the old one. You can't drive both. Are you with me?

SEAN: Yeah.

MICHAEL: Good man. So, you understand.

SEAN: . . . Yeah.

MICHAEL: Great. (*To PHILLY and JIMMY*) Yis right, lads?

MICHAEL starts to leave, the lads with him. SEAN dashes to the door, to get there first. MICHAEL grabs SEAN's shoulders.

MICHAEL: For fuck sake.

SEAN: Let me go, let me go. You tried to fool me. My mother said you would. Let me go!

SEAN wriggles out of the jacket, leaving MICHAEL holding the empty jacket. SEAN exits. MICHAEL holds up the jacket.

MICHAEL: Well, there's the coat of a God-fearing man. For fuck sake. That's a decent lad I've got you, Pegeen. I'll tell you one thing. You'll never have to worry about that fella.

PEGEEN: Shut up.

MICHAEL: He wouldn't know what to do with a Russian lap dancer.

PEGEEN: Just, shut up! What right have you to be making fun of him?

She catches JIMMY and PHILLY nudging each other, enjoying her attack on MICHAEL.

PEGEEN: And fuck off, you two. Brokeback Mountain.[7]

It takes a second for JIMMY and PHILLY to "get" the reference, but then they move apart.

MICHAEL (*including the lads*): You'd never guess that poor drip was a son of Gracie Keogh's.

PEGEEN: Shut up. He's alright; he's just a bit shy. And you know what you've done?

MICHAEL: What?

PEGEEN: Sean said that his mother told him he's a better catch than me. Because they're bringing more to the table. And you've just proved her right. I love you, Da, but you're a fuckin' muppet.

MICHAEL: It'll be grand. I'll talk to Gracie.

PHILLY: No better man.

PEGEEN shuts PHILLY up with a glare. She turns to MICHAEL—

PEGEEN: And you're going out, wherever. And I'm stuck here on my own. Again. Sean's not coming back.

Enter SEAN—his head; hesitant.

SEAN: Mr. Flaherty?

MICHAEL (*after looking at PEGEEN somewhat triumphantly*): Sean? Good man.

SEAN: There's a fella.

MICHAEL: What fella?

SEAN (*looking behind, offstage*): He's coming this way.

---

7. *Brokeback Mountain* (2005), directed by Ang Lee, starred Heath Ledger and Jake Gyllenhaal as two cowboys who develop a fraught sexual and emotional relationship with one another while living in the American West from 1963 to 1983. The movie has been heralded as a major step forward for film representation of the LGBTQ+ community.

SEAN steps into the room. He leaves the door ajar. The men, suddenly alert and sober, and PEGEEN wait, expecting the entrance of someone formidable. PHILLY quickly wets a finger and lifts cocaine dust off the counter. They look at the CCTV screen. They see someone; he wears a hat—they/we can't make out facial features. The door opens slowly and squeaks.

Enter CHRISTOPHER, a black man, in his early twenties. He is tired and frightened, in the suit he was wearing when he ran from home. He carries a small case.

CHRISTOPHER (*timidly*): The blessing of the Lord onto this place.

MICHAEL: Yeah; howyeh.

CHRISTOPHER (*to PEGEEN*): Please, how much is a small bottle of Guinness?

PEGEEN: We're closed.

MICHAEL: Ah, give the man a drink.

PEGEEN (*going behind the counter*): We've no bottles. (*Lifting two glasses*) A glass, or a pint. It's 2.80, or 3.98.

CHRISTOPHER: The small one, please. And a bottle of Coke?

PEGEEN (*showing him a small bottle*): Three euro. D'you want it?

CHRISTOPHER: No.

PEGEEN pours the Guinness. They all watch CHRISTOPHER for some time as he counts his money, mostly unfamiliar coins.

MICHAEL: Where're you from, son?

CHRISTOPHER: Africa, sir.

MICHAEL: Big place. What part?

CHRISTOPHER: The West.

MICHAEL: Nigeria?

CHRISTOPHER (*surprised, suspicious*): Yes.

MICHAEL: There's a surprise. (*To the others*) He's from Nigeria, lads.

PEGEEN: Here's your drink. 2.80.

CHRISTOPHER: Thank you.

He moves to the counter. He holds out his hand, still trying to sort out the money. PEGEEN leans across the counter, and takes the right amount from his palm. She doesn't look at him.

PEGEEN: Now, you're grand.

CHRISTOPHER: Thank you very much.

CHRISTOPHER picks up his drink. He tastes the beer and is pleasantly surprised that it is not as bitter as Lagos-brewed Guinness.[8] *He takes off his hat. His hair is noticeably short.*

PHILLY: Hey, Peg. I'll have one of them while you're there.

JIMMY: Good man; me too.

PEGEEN: We're closed.

PHILLY: You're just after serving the African. Discrimination there, Pegeen.

PEGEEN: So, go to the fuckin' Equality Tribunal.

MICHAEL: Go on, Peggie. We'll all have one.

PEGEEN (*to PHILLY*): You're paying.

PHILLY: No problem.

PEGEEN pours three more pints. She takes the cap off an alcopop, for herself.[9]

8. Lagos is Nigeria's most populous city (15.3 million as of 2023), and the second most populated city in Africa.

9. An alcopop (or spirit cooler, wine cooler, or malternative) is a common term in Ireland and the United Kingdom for a sweet, sometimes fruit-flavored alcoholic drink with a relatively low alcohol content.

MICHAEL: Grand. (*To CHRISTOPHER*) You just got here, yeah?

CHRISTOPHER: Yes. . . . This evening. (*Taking a piece of paper from a pocket*) Sorry for bothering you, sir, but please. Do you know where this place is? "45 Rosegarden Court, Dublin 17."

MICHAEL: Show us? (*Takes reading glasses from breast pocket, puts them on, and reads*) 45 Rosegarden Court. Rosegarden . . . Rosegarden. Why do you want it?

CHRISTOPHER has his pint to his mouth, about to drink. He hesitates.

MICHAEL: No, no. Fire away.

CHRISTOPHER: Thank you, sir.

He drinks.

MICHAEL: Would you go a bag of crisps with that?[10] (*Responding to CHRISTOPHER's nonplussed expression*) Show the man, Peggie.

PEGEEN holds up a bag of crisps. During the talk below, the men get their pints. PEGEEN, wordlessly, gives SEAN a bottle of Heineken. He, wordlessly, thanks her.

CHRISTOPHER: Oh, no, thank you.

MICHAEL: Cheese and onion, no?

CHRISTOPHER: No. Thank you.

MICHAEL: So. Rosegarden Court. Lads?

PHILLY: I know the place but I don't think there's a Court. There's a Drive, there's a Terrace, there's a Lawn.

SEAN: A Grove.

---

10. Crisps are the Irish equivalent of potato chips, sold in a variety of flavors.

PHILLY: That's right. No Court, but.

SEAN: No.

MICHAEL: No Court. You're out of luck, son.

JIMMY: The Widow Quin lived in Rosegarden Terrace. Before she moved upstairs.

MICHAEL: Gotcha. (*To CHRISTOPHER*) Have you tried Number 45 all-the-others? The Drive, the Terrace, and what have you?

CHRISTOPHER: Yes.

MICHAEL: And no joy?

CHRISTOPHER: No.

MICHAEL: And where does that leave you?

CHRISTOPHER: I do not know.

MICHAEL gives back the piece of paper. CHRISTOPHER returns the paper to his pocket.

MICHAEL: Let's see about this. You were counting on staying there, weren't you?

CHRISTOPHER: Yes.

MICHAEL: Someone you know?

CHRISTOPHER: A far cousin.

MICHAEL: A far cousin. Doesn't sound promising. Know anyone else?

CHRISTOPHER: Not really.

MICHAEL: Ah. No other addresses, no? Or phone numbers.

CHRISTOPHER: No, sir.

MICHAEL: Not good. You're on your own. So. What's the story?

CHRISTOPHER: How do you mean, sir?

MICHAEL: You're not here on your holliers.

JIMMY: Your holidays.[11]

CHRISTOPHER: Oh, no. No.

---

11. *Holliers* or *holidays* are synonyms for *vacation*.

MICHAEL: So, you're some sort of a refugee or asylum seeker, yeah?

SEAN: Mr. Flaherty?

MICHAEL: Yeah?

SEAN: He can't be a refugee. He just arrived, like.

MICHAEL: What?

SEAN: He has to go through the asylum process first, like. And if he is granted, then he can—

MICHAEL: Good man, Sean. (*To CHRISTOPHER*): So. You're an asylum seeker. Am I technically correct there, Sean?

SEAN: Yeah.

MICHAEL: Great. That's established, so. You're an asylum seeker.

CHRISTOPHER: You may say so, sir.

MICHAEL: I may say so, sir? Are you messing with me, son?

CHRISTOPHER: No, sir.

JIMMY: I think he is, Michael.

PEGEEN: Leave him alone.

MICHAEL: Look it, son. Stop acting the bollix.[12] Just tell us.

CHRISTOPHER: I am here to seek refuge, in Ireland. . . . My life isn't safe at home.

MICHAEL: Is it not?

CHRISTOPHER: No. Not anymore.

SEAN: Is it a war?

CHRISTOPHER: No. Nigeria is relatively peaceful at the moment.

PHILLY: It's a tribal thing, maybe?

CHRISTOPHER: No.

JIMMY: Someone's daughter.

CHRISTOPHER: Certainly not, sir.

PHILLY: Religious strife?

---

12. *Bollix* (or *bollocks*) is vulgar Irish and English slang, meaning "nonsense" or "rubbish."

SEAN: Persecution.

CHRISTOPHER: Not at all. God protects His people.

MICHAEL: He fuckin' does alright. I know what it is. The what-d'you-ma-call-it. The genital mutilation.

PEGEEN: He's a man, for fuck sake.

MICHAEL: Yeah? And?

PEGEEN: They only mutilate women.

MICHAEL: Oh, is that right? Did no one ever get a kick in the balls in Nigeria?

PEGEEN: Maybe it's famine.

MICHAEL: Sure, he wouldn't have the crisps.

SEAN: He's an economic migrant, so he is.

CHRISTOPHER: No.

MICHAEL takes CHRISTOPHER aside and whispers.

MICHAEL: It isn't the oul' AIDS, is it?

CHRISTOPHER: Not at all. Nothing like that, sir.

MICHAEL: Grand; that's good.

PHILLY: I know. A coup.[13]

JIMMY: Fuckin' pigeons?

PHILLY: You know. A coup d'état.

SEAN: Like 1916.[14]

---

13. A coup d'état, or coup, is a sudden change in government, often illegally and forcefully.

14. The year 1916 has immediate, nationalistic meaning in Ireland. In 1916 Ireland was still under control of the United Kingdom. On Monday, April 24, 1916, Thomas Clarke, Seán Mac Diarmada, Patrick Pearse, Thomas MacDonagh, Joseph Plunkett, and James Connolly launched an insurrection against the UK government's rule over Ireland. Approximately 1,800 Irish rebels took over multiple sites around Dublin, including the General Post Office (GPO), where the insurrection established their headquarters. Pearse famously proclaimed the Irish Republic from the steps of the GPO, and declared the insurgents a provisional government; however, British forces gained control over the insurgency by May 1. Fifteen leaders of the Easter Rising were shot to death by firing squad; some members had their

CHRISTOPHER: No. The political situation has been stable at home for a while now.

MICHAEL: Then what is it?

PEGEEN: He did something.

MICHAEL: That's it.

JIMMY: He didn't pay his television licence.[15]

All laugh, except CHRISTOPHER, who doesn't get it.

PEGEEN: He did something wrong. He's running from the law.

Silence, for a few beats.

MICHAEL: Is that true?

CHRISTOPHER nods.

MICHAEL: The law is chasing you.

CHRISTOPHER nods again.

MICHAEL: Good man. Embezzlement.

JIMMY: Fraud.

PHILLY: 4-1-9.

PEGEEN: What's that?

---

death sentences commuted, including Éamon de Valera and Constance Markievicz. Initially, the insurgency did not have much public support, but after the swift execution of its leaders, public opinion swung strongly in favor of the rising. The Easter Rising of 1916 was a major step toward Irish independence, culminating in the formal establishment of the Republic of Ireland in 1949.

15. Owning a television in Ireland requires an annual TV license. In 2021 the annual fee for a TV license was roughly €160. Not paying for a TV license can result in a steep fine of up to €1,000 (or €2,000 for subsequent offences).

PHILLY: It's brilliant. They send you an email, right? That they've got millions to hide. They offer you 30 percent of the money or so, if you send them your bank account details. They sit back and wait. And, believe it or not, some muppets *do* send them their bank account details. And they clean them out.

MICHAEL: And that's you, son.

CHRISTOPHER: No, sir.

MICHAEL: No?

CHRISTOPHER: I would never wish to defraud anybody.

PHILLY: I heard somewhere that fraud was a subject in Nigerian schools.

CHRISTOPHER: That is not correct; that is not true.

MICHAEL: Ah, well. Was it larceny, so?

CHRISTOPHER: Larceny, sir?

MICHAEL: Robbing, theft—

CHRISTOPHER: No—

PHILLY: Armed robbery, like.

CHRISTOPHER: Armed robbery? I am a son of a successful businessman, I'll have you know—God rest his soul.

PHILLY: If it's not robbing, it must be something big.

MICHAEL: Are you "involved"?

CHRISTOPHER: Involved?

MICHAEL: A terrorist, a freedom fighter. One of the lads.

CHRISTOPHER: I am not a terrorist.

PHILLY: What about a freedom fighter?

CHRISTOPHER: No.

JIMMY: Are you a Muslim?

CHRISTOPHER: I am a Christian.

SEAN: He's a brother in Christ.

MICHAEL: He's a brother in Christ but he's still running from the fuckin' law.

PHILLY: Did you marry two women?

CHRISTOPHER: I am yet to marry, but polygamy is perfectly legitimate in my country.

MICHAEL: Go 'way.

PEGEEN: He's done nothing.

CHRISTOPHER: If you say so.

JIMMY: It's something dirty.

PHILLY: Rape.

CHRISTOPHER: No! Definitely not.

JIMMY: Kids.

CHRISTOPHER (*snapping his fingers over his head*): God forbid, bad thing!

MICHAEL: So, what is it then?

CHRISTOPHER: Somebody died . . .

PEGEEN: He did nothing.

CHRISTOPHER: You are not speaking the truth.

PEGEEN: Not speaking the truth? You're just a mouth. You're a sponger, milking the system. You did nothing at all.

CHRISTOPHER: I killed . . .

PEGEEN: Go on. Who?

CHRISTOPHER: I killed my poor dad.

PEGEEN (*amazed*): Your dad?

CHRISTOPHER: Yes.

MICHAEL: The successful businessman.

CHRISTOPHER nods. A beat.

PHILLY: Now, there's a daring fella.

JIMMY (*somewhat sarcastically*): God rest his soul; yeah?

PEGEEN: You killed your da?

CHRISTOPHER: With the help of God, I certainly did. May his soul rest in eternal peace.

SEAN: Amen. You killed him, but?

CHRISTOPHER: Yes, I did.

MICHAEL: That's a hanging crime, mister.

CHRISTOPHER: But not in Ireland, sir.

MICHAEL: Fair enough. But, come here. What in the name of God made you do something like that?

CHRISTOPHER: He was too high-handed. I couldn't take it anymore.

PEGEEN: And you shot him?

CHRISTOPHER (*shaking his head*): I used no weapon. I have no licence, and I am a law-abiding man.

MICHAEL: Was it a knife or something? Did you stab the poor man?

CHRISTOPHER (scandalised): Do you take me for a slaughter-boy?

JIMMY: So, did you strangle him, or what?

CHRISTOPHER: I knocked him down with a pestle.

PHILLY: A pistol?

PEGEEN: You said you didn't shoot him.

CHRISTOPHER: Yes. I didn't shoot him. I hit him on the head with a pestle.

MICHAEL: What the fuck is a pestle?

CHRISTOPHER: Oh. It is a kitchen utensil. It's used for pounding yams.

PHILLY: Pounding?

JIMMY: Yams?

CHRISTOPHER (*demonstrates as he explains*): Let me explain to you. A yam is like your potatoes here. But much bigger. You boil it, then pound it—like this—in a mortar, with a pestle. And it becomes pounded yam.

JIMMY: Is it nice; is it?

CHRISTOPHER: Delicious. Especially with vegetable or melon soup.

MICHAEL: Never mind the fuckin' soup. This pestle yoke. It's a bit like a baseball bat, is it?

CHRISTOPHER: Yes, but much bigger.

SEAN: It must have killed him, did it?

MICHAEL: Of course it fuckin' killed him.

PHILLY: You heard the man. He told you.

SEAN: I mean—*really* killed him. Broke his head.

JIMMY: Absolutely.

MICHAEL (*to CHRISTOPHER*): Go on. What happened?

MICHAEL *makes a sign to* PEGEEN *to give* CHRISTOPHER *a fresh drink. She fills a glass.*

CHRISTOPHER: I raised the pestle and it fell on the ridge of his skull. He went down at my feet . . . like an empty sack. Dead.
MICHAEL: What did you do then? Did you bury him?

As CHRISTOPHER *speaks below,* PEGEEN *takes his empty glass from his hand and replaces it with a full glass. He's not sure whether it has to be paid for.*

MICHAEL: You're grand; you're grand. It's on me.
CHRISTOPHER: Thank you, sir.
MICHAEL: Ah, no bother. So, did you bury him or what?
CHRISTOPHER (*considering*): Yes. I buried him. It was the middle of the night. In our backyard.
MICHAEL: How long ago; when?
CHRISTOPHER: It will be two weeks . . . tomorrow.
PEGEEN: . . . Thirteen days.
CHRISTOPHER: That is correct.
MICHAEL: What about the Guards?
CHRISTOPHER: The Guards?
SEAN: The law.
MICHAEL: The police. Are they after you?
CHRISTOPHER: It's hard for me to say. I've been moving from place to place since I escaped.
MICHAEL: He might still be buried.
CHRISTOPHER: That is possible. He was a prominent businessman, though.
PEGEEN: What about your ma?
CHRISTOPHER: She died. Ten years ago.
PEGEEN: You're an orphan then.
CHRISTOPHER: Yes.

MICHAEL: Hang on, bud. You made yourself a fuckin' orphan. Don't mind me. I'm only messing with you. So, tell us. This happened over in Nigeria; yeah?

CHRISTOPHER: Yes; that is correct.

MICHAEL: So, how did you get here? How did you manage that?

CHRISTOPHER: I took a night bus, to Sokoto, near the border with Niger—two days. From there, I got a ride on a jeep that drove for two more days, in the desert. We came to the border, just before the foot of a mountain. The driver told us to climb this mountain, and, behind it, we would find Niger. I walked, day and night; it took *four* days to get to the top. It was Niger alright, but it took another three days to descend the mountain. I got to Niamey—the capital—where I got a flight to London (*takes a drink, swallows*). Then I flew to Belfast. And then I came to Dublin on the train.[16]

MICHAEL: Good man.

CHRISTOPHER *sits, slumped somewhat, on a stool; drinks from his glass. SEAN goes to the door—he hesitates. While the following happens . . .*

PHILLY: Come here, pal. Why didn't you just fly straight from Lagos?

CHRISTOPHER: It would be too risky. I was afraid his body would be discovered.

PEGEEN: Da. Come here. This fella could do the security.

MICHAEL: I'm way ahead of you, love. (*Quietly, to JIMMY and PHILLY, and PEGEEN*) We could use this guy.

JIMMY: You're right.

MICHAEL: No contacts. No one knows he's here.

PHILLY: And he'd be up for anything. He's after killing his da.

---

16 Sokoto is located in the far northwest corner of Nigeria. Niger is a country in West Africa. Belfast is the capital of Northern Ireland (which is part of the United Kingdom). Dublin is the capital of the Republic of Ireland (where this play is set).

JIMMY: He's a hard-looking unit.

MICHAEL: Grand.

PHILLY: What if he's a plant, but?

MICHAEL: Good point.

PEGEEN: No. He's the real thing.

MICHAEL: D'you reckon, yeah?

PEGEEN: There's no way he's a cop.

MICHAEL: Grand, but we'll keep an eye on him. Here goes.
(*Turning to CHRISTOPHER*) Could you use a job, son?
And somewhere to stay. A few quid; we'll look after you.[17]

SEAN: What?

CHRISTOPHER (*slowly delighted*): A job, sir? And somewhere to
stay? Would I be safe here?

MICHAEL: You make it fuckin' safe. That's your job. Looking
after the place—and Pegeen.

CHRISTOPHER: I mean, what about the police?

MICHAEL (*to CHRISTOPHER*): Don't worry about it.

SEAN: Mister Flaherty?

MICHAEL: We look after the Guards here. You just do your job.

CHRISTOPHER: Security?

MICHAEL: You know, yourself. Let the right people in, keep the
wrong ones out. Look after the place when it's shut.

SEAN: Mister Flaherty?!

MICHAEL: What do you say? And you can do a few messages
for us as well. The odd package, just. It'll be grand; we'll
keep you busy.

JIMMY and PHILLY nod.

MICHAEL: So?

SEAN: Mister Flaherty?

MICHAEL: What?

17. *Quid* is slang for *euro* (the currency in the Republic of Ireland).

SEAN: You can't have him in here.

MICHAEL Why not?

SEAN: He's a murderer. He's a fugitive, like.

PEGEEN: Who asked you?!

SEAN (*to MICHAEL*): But Pegeen . . . he killed his da. You can't—

PEGEEN: Just shut the fuck up.

MICHAEL: You're grand, Sean. Go home to your mammy

SEAN: But, Mr.—

MICHAEL (*escorting SEAN to door*): Good man. Tell her I'll phone her tomorrow. I might even drop in for a coffee, tell her. Good luck now.

Exit SEAN. The door is closed. We see him on the CCTV screen, looking into the camera. He moves, and we then see him at the window; then gone.

MICHAEL (*to CHRISTOPHER*): So, that's it. The job's yours; yeah?

CHRISTOPHER: This is great. I truly appreciate your kindness, sir.

MICHAEL: Ah, no sweat. You'll be great; the head on you. And you'll be company for Pegeen. (*Quietly*) But keep the hands in the pockets, son, yeah? You with me?

CHRISTOPHER (*realising*): . . . Oh, of course! I would never—

MICHAEL: Good man. (*Moving towards the door, to PHILLY and JIMMY*) Yis right, lads? (*Quietly*) That'll show Gracie Keogh and poor Sean who's the better catch. He'll be climbing down the chimney for her. (*To CHRISTOPHER*) Good luck now. You know your duties. What's your name, by the way?

CHRISTOPHER: Malomo, Christopher Malomo.

MICHAEL: Christopher?

CHRISTOPHER: Yes.

MICHAEL: Good man. Good luck, so. (*Searching his pockets*) Where are me keys?

PEGEEN: Da, you're not driving.

MICHAEL (*throwing the keys to PHILLY*): No, I'm not driving. (*To CHRISTOPHER*) By the way—your passport.

CHRISTOPHER: My passport, sir?

MICHAEL: Give it to Pegeen.

CHRISTOPHER: To Pegeen?

MICHAEL: Good man. (*To the men*) Right, lads; we're gone. (*To CHRISTOPHER and PEGEEN*) Look after yourselves.

CHRISTOPHER: Thank you, Mister Flaherty.

MICHAEL: None of the misters. It's Michael.

The men exit, leaving PEGEEN and CHRISTOPHER alone.

PEGEEN: The door.

CHRISTOPHER hesitates, then realises that this is the first act of his new duties. He goes across, and puts the door on the latch. PE-GEEN watches him as she lowers the window blind. He draws the top bolt, and hesitates.

PEGEEN: The bottom.

CHRISTOPHER: Oh.

He bends down and draws the bottom bolt. He checks to make sure the door is locked.

CHRISTOPHER (*satisfied*): Done.

PEGEEN: So . . . I'm having a cup of tea. Yourself?

CHRISTOPHER: Tea?

PEGEEN: Tea.

CHRISTOPHER: Thank you.

PEGEEN goes behind the counter.

PEGEEN: Sit down. Stick on the fire, if you want.

She fills the kettle. CHRISTOPHER yawns and sits. PEGEEN's mobile rings: Akon's "Lonely."[18] She answers it. CHRISTOPHER examines the fire and the turf beside it. He gives up. He looks across at PEGEEN, indicating that he would like to take his shoes off. She nods, as she speaks on the mobile.

PEGEEN: Yeah? . . . I'm fine . . . No. I'm fine. Look.

She lifts the blind. SEAN is outside on his mobile.

PEGEEN: See?

SEAN says "Yes" into the phone. He looks from PEGEEN to CHRISTOPHER, who is taking his shoes and socks off. PEGEEN drops the blind.

PEGEEN (*into the mobile*): Stop fussing, Sean, and go home.
    Seeyeh. (*Turning off the mobile, to CHRISTOPHER*) You
    must be wrecked, are you?

She turns on the fire; a switch at the side. CHRISTOPHER watches this. The pub phone, on the wall behind the counter, rings.

CHRISTOPHER: Yes. Absolutely. I have never walked so much in
    my life . . .
PEGEEN (*re: phone*): Ignore it.

Phone stops. PEGEEN watches him rub his feet.

CHRISTOPHER: At least 150 kilometers, over the mountain.[19]
PEGEEN: Jesus. They don't look too bad. Your feet.
CHRISTOPHER: They hurt.

---

18. Akon Thiam (b. 1973) is a Senegalese American singer from New Jersey.
"Lonely" is his second single from his debut album, *Trouble* (2004).
    19. 150 kilometers is a little over 93 miles.

He holds up one of his feet, feeling his blisters, and looking at them with compassion. He carefully puts his foot back on the ground.

PEGEEN: You've nice hands.

CHRISTOPHER: Really?

PEGEEN: Yeah. They look like you've never done any hard work in your life.

CHRISTOPHER: That is true, actually.

PEGEEN: You're not a prince, are you?

CHRISTOPHER: No.

PEGEEN: Are you not?

CHRISTOPHER: No. Why?

PEGEEN: This African fella I met in a club once, he said he was a prince.

CHRISTOPHER: That could be.

PEGEEN moves back to the counter to make the tea. During the conversation she fills the cups, adds the teabags etc.

PEGEEN: He was full of shite. Good looking, though. Lovely colour on him. D'you take sugar?

CHRISTOPHER: Two cubes, thanks.

PEGEEN holds up a sugar bag.

CHRISTOPHER: Oh. One spoon will do; thank you.

CHRISTOPHER stands and walks a bit, as if testing his feet.

CHRISTOPHER: Did he tell you where he was from?

PEGEEN: Who?

CHRISTOPHER: Your prince.

PEGEEN: He didn't have to. He was African.

CHRISTOPHER: From what country?

PEGEEN (*almost dismissive*): I don't know.

CHRISTOPHER: He might have been an American.

PEGEEN: No. The Yanks are full of themselves. So was he, but in a different kind of way. Not like you. You're nicer.

CHRISTOPHER: Thank you. Nicer?

PEGEEN: Yeah. You didn't come out with the prince stuff, the usual crap.

CHRISTOPHER: Well—

PEGEEN: You're good-looking too.

CHRISTOPHER: Me?

PEGEEN: Yeah. Did you never hear that from the young ones where you come from?

CHRISTOPHER: Young ones?

PEGEEN: Girls; women.

CHRISTOPHER: No. Not really. They find it a bit hard to give compliments, I suppose. Where I'm from.

PEGEEN: Here, too. They haven't a clue.

She hands him his cup and a small stainless steel jug of milk. He pours hesitantly; he is not familiar with fresh milk, or the volume he wants.

CHRISTOPHER: Thank you.

PEGEEN You're welcome.

PEGEEN lights a cigarette. As she lights, she offers him the packet.

CHRISTOPHER: No, thank you.

PEGEEN: Don't smoke?

CHRISTOPHER: No.

PEGEEN: Suit yourself. So. What do you do, an'anyway?

CHRISTOPHER: How do you mean?

PEGEEN: Work, like?

CHRISTOPHER: Oh. I look after my dad's business.

PEGEEN: "Looked," you mean.

CHRISTOPHER: Yes. I "looked" after his business.

PEGEEN: What was it?

CHRISTOPHER: Cocoa. He exported cocoa.

PEGEEN: That sounds a bit boring; is it?

CHRISTOPHER: No. Not really. He was a politician in the First Republic.[20]

PEGEEN: Yeah?

CHRISTOPHER: Yes. There was an election in Nigeria in 1979— after a long period of military dictatorship. And my dad, like most politicians who were elected then, did extremely well for himself. (*Sensing that he is losing PEGEEN'S interest*) Anyway, he quit politics and set up his business.

PEGEEN: Cocoa.

CHRISTOPHER: Yes. And a couple of other businesses as well.

PEGEEN: And are you in charge of them, too?

CHRISTOPHER: Something like that. That was how it was supposed to be . . . After my first degree, my father made me do an MBA—

PEGEEN: What's that?

CHRISTOPHER: Masters in Business Admin.

PEGEEN: Jesus.

CHRISTOPHER: And upon graduating—

PEGEEN: All you Africans have graduated, haven't yis? You've all been to college.

CHRISTOPHER: Well, in Nigeria, especially where I come from, you don't have a choice, actually.

PEGEEN: Choice?

CHRISTOPHER: Most parents will do their utmost to ensure that you go to university, to get a degree.

PEGEEN: You have a degree, so.

CHRISTOPHER: Two, actually. The first is in economics. And the second was in—

PEGEEN: I know. Killing your da. . . . What's wrong?

20. The First Republic of Nigeria lasted from 1963 to 1966.

CHRISTOPHER: I almost forgot about that . . . I know I should feel bad. I should feel remorse. But I don't. And that makes me feel bad.

PEGEEN: For killing your da?

CHRISTOPHER: I mean, for not feeling bad about killing him. Is there something wrong with me?

PEGEEN (*shrugs*): Depends.

CHRISTOPHER: On what?

PEGEEN: Was he looking for it?

CHRISTOPHER: He was a very selfish, insensitive man.

PEGEEN: So you killed him.

CHRISTOPHER: No.

PEGEEN: So, why did you?

CHRISTOPHER: Why? I don't know, really.

PEGEEN: You don't know? You have to have a reason for killing your da. I have; I've a fuckin' list.

Silence, a beat.

CHRISTOPHER: You are the first person I'll be telling my story to—

PEGEEN: Yeah, right. You've said that to every young one you've met on your way here.

CHRISTOPHER: No, I have not. Didn't I just tell you? Aren't you listening? I've told no one. I've met no one like you.

PEGEEN: Wow.

CHRISTOPHER: Yes.

PEGEEN: You're full of it, aren't you?

CHRISTOPHER: I'm serious. I'm serious.

PEGEEN: You are, aren't you?

CHRISTOPHER: Believe me.

PEGEEN (*doubtful, but impressed*): Maybe I do.

CHRISTOPHER: Please. Do you mind if I ask you a question?

PEGEEN: What?

CHRISTOPHER: Are you spoken for?

PEGEEN: What?

CHRISTOPHER (*indicating her hands*): The rings. Are you perhaps engaged?

PEGEEN: You were telling me about killing your da.

CHRISTOPHER: Are you engaged or not?

PEGEEN (*insistent*): Your da.

CHRISTOPHER: You tell me first, then I will tell you.

PEGEEN: No.

CHRISTOPHER: Then I will not tell you—

PEGEEN: No; I just told you. I'm not engaged.

Her phone rings and eventually stops.

CHRISTOPHER: So. You are single.

PEGEEN: Yep.

CHRISTOPHER: Great. We have something in common.

PEGEEN: I didn't kill my da. I'd be afraid to . . . You must have been in some state to have hit him with that pestle yoke.

CHRISTOPHER: I was not aware of my fury until after I had struck him. But then—

PEGEEN: But to look at you, you'd think butter wouldn't melt in your mouth.

CHRISTOPHER: Up to the day I killed him, there was not one single soul who knew the kind of person I was. There I was, minding my own business, a quiet poor guy who nobody really noticed.

PEGEEN: Except the girls.

CHRISTOPHER: Not even the girls. That is the gospel truth. Nobody respected me. Not even my dad's workers.

PEGEEN: You said you were in charge. You should have been living like a prince.

CHRISTOPHER: Like a prince? Driving the length and breadth of the country—and it is vast, mind you. Sweating and slaving, from dawn till dusk, 24-7. (*Chuckles*) Like a prince, indeed. I was meant to be the managing director but, in his eyes, I was always his boy. And that was the way he treated me. Like a child.

PEGEEN: And you killed him.

CHRISTOPHER: Yes. No. I mean, I did not kill him simply because of the way he treated me. I had grown used to that.

PEGEEN: So, why the fuck did you kill him?

CHRISTOPHER is cold. PEGEEN takes a hoodie from a hook, and hands it to him. He takes off his jacket and puts on the hoodie. They both sit.

CHRISTOPHER: I am not his only child. I have brothers and sisters and stepbrothers and sisters in many countries of the world. America, Canada, Australia, Saudi Arabia. And why? Because none of them could stand him. It started with the death of my mother, I think. His temper, and drinking. And violence. He was incarcerated several times, for assaulting men and policemen. He had no regard for the law or anyone. Even his wives had to leave. He had two other wives, you see.

PEGEEN: Two?

CHRISTOPHER: Yes. My mother was the first.

PEGEEN: How did she die?

CHRISTOPHER: She was involved in a motor accident. Her driver died instantly, but she lingered on for three days. Until she gave up the ghost.

PEGEEN: I'm sorry.

CHRISTOPHER: It was a long time ago. And yours?

PEGEEN: Cancer.

CHRISTOPHER: Gracious God. May the souls of the departed rest in peace.

PEGEEN: . . . Yeah. So, there was only the two of yis—you and your da?

CHRISTOPHER: Yes.

PEGEEN: Why did you stay?

CHRISTOPHER: I thought he would change. But things went from bad to worse. I had no peace except, of course, when he was out of town. And that was my life until that day, when I shattered his skull with the pestle. And here I am.

PEGEEN: Well, you'll have a bit of peace here, an'anyway. No one will trouble you—Christopher?

He nods.

PEGEEN: It's about time a sound fella like you had a bit of good luck.

CHRISTOPHER: It *is* about time. I am a sound fellow—as you said—Pegeen. Ambitious, hardworking, and determined—

Loud banging on the side door, upstage-right.

CHRISTOPHER: Oh, Merciful God! Who's that?! (*Whispering*) It can't be the police, can it?

Knocking again.

PEGEEN: Who's that?

VOICE (*outside*): Me.

PEGEEN: The Widow Quin. What does she fuckin' want?

She rushes behind the counter. CHRISTOPHER stands.

PEGEEN: You sit down. I'll handle this.

She exits through the door behind the counter and reenters very quickly with a duvet covered with an old Barbie cover and a pillow. She flings the pillow onto a seat. She throws the duvet to CHRISTOPHER.

PEGEEN: Get under this. And, whatever happens, don't say a word.

CHRISTOPHER (*nervously*): Who is it?

PEGEEN: Another fuckin' murderer. The place is full of them tonight.

Knocking again. CHRISTOPHER sits in a chair and covers himself.

PEGEEN: What d'you want? We're closed.

WIDOW QUIN: I know! Just let me in!

PEGEEN (*unlocking and opening the door*): Leave our fuckin' door alone! What d'you want at this hour of night?

Enter the WIDOW QUIN. She is in her late thirties, elegantly dressed, in black, with a touch of the oul' bling.

WIDOW QUIN: I was talking to your daddy at the funeral—

PEGEEN: Another fuckin' funeral.

WIDOW QUIN: Well, I have the suit.

PEGEEN: Looking for a new husband already, are you?

WIDOW QUIN: Now, now. Anyway, he told me about your man. And he asked me to have a look in at you on my way home—

PEGEEN: Alone.

WIDOW QUIN: Alone—just to make sure that you're alright. (*Quietly*) You never know with these black fellas. They can be a bit wild, you know.

PEGEEN: Look for yourself, if he's wild. He's knackered, look, and on his way to bed.

WIDOW QUIN: Alone.

PEGEEN: Yeah! So, off you go. You've seen him, so you're grand.

WIDOW QUIN: I don't know, Pegeen. A little one like you, and engaged at that. On your own with this fella. Where'll he sleep, anyway?

WIDOW QUIN walks past PEGEEN.

PEGEEN: Hey!

WIDOW QUIN (*to CHRISTOPHER, tapping him on shoulder*): How are you, sweetheart?

CHRISTOPHER (*shyly*): Very well, ma, thank you.

WIDOW QUIN: Well, aren't you a little polite smiling fella? You must have been pushed to the wall to have done what you did.

PEGEEN: Da told you?

WIDOW QUIN: He did.

PEGEEN: The eejit.[21]

WIDOW QUIN: Ah, now. (*To CHRISTOPHER*) You must have been really worked up, were you?

CHRISTOPHER: You may say so, ma.

WIDOW QUIN: Less of the "ma," please. (*To CHRISTOPHER*) Look at you there, in your hoodie. I can see you playing with your PlayStation. Or doing your slam-dunking—isn't that what yis call it? But killing your da? I can't see that at all.

PEGEEN: That's funny, because I have no problem seeing you killing your husband. He did it all alright, don't worry. But he was provoked. So, go on—out. He's tired, look. He's going to sleep.

WIDOW QUIN: Well, I've a spare room for him. I was going to suggest it. (*Turning to CHRISTOPHER*) We've a bit in common. There's a fella from one of the Sunday papers wants to write my story. A buke.[22] I can introduce you to him.

CHRISTOPHER (*innocently*): Ma, did you kill your father too?

PEGEEN: She did not. She poisoned Mr. Quin—her husband, like.

WIDOW QUIN (*smoothly sarcastic*): I killed him with kindness.

PEGEEN: It was a sneaky kind of murder.

---

21. *Eejit* is slang for *idiot*.
22. Pronunciation for "book."

WIDOW QUIN: He was a sneaky kind of man. He slept with his fuckin' eyes open. And anyway—(*turning again to CHRISTOPHER*) Wouldn't you be better off with a woman who's lived a bit than some skinny young one who'd go skidding after any man who'd wink at her?

PEGEEN: And you wouldn't even wait for them to wink. You slut. You were all over my da in here the other night. And here you are again, panting.

WIDOW QUIN (*laughing derisively*): Me, is it? Listen here. From one slut to another one. You use what you've got to get what you want. (*Looking PEGEEN up and down*) Mind you, you have to have something in the first place. (*Turning to CHRISTOPHER*) Amn't I right, sweetheart? (*Pulling his arm*) Get your shoes on and let's go. It's only around the back.

PEGEEN (*seizing his other arm*): He's working here and my da wants him to stay here.

WIDOW QUIN: It'd be mad for him to work *and* sleep here. The poor lad. (*To Christopher*) So, come on. Wait till you see my lovely little apartment.

PEGEEN: He's staying here.

WIDOW QUIN (*to CHRISTOPHER*): You can have your room for nothing till you're on your feet.

PEGEEN (*viciously*): He'll never be on his feet with you around. He's better off in a pub than a fuckin' brothel.

WIDOW QUIN: Do you hear her, sweetheart? D'you hear the way she'll be talking to you inside a week?

PEGEEN: Don't listen to her. Tell her to go back to her customers. There's a queue of them outside.

WIDOW QUIN: Don't worry, love; I'm going. But he'll come with me.

PEGEEN (*shaking him*): Are you fuckin' dumb, Christopher?

CHRISTOPHER (*timidly, to WIDOW QUIN*): Ma, I do appreciate your magnanimity. But I've been offered a job here and a place to stay. And I'd rather stay here.

PEGEEN: You heard him. So, will you fuck off now, ma?

WIDOW QUIN (*ignoring PEGEEN; straight to CHRISTO-PHER*): It must be great to be twenty . . . I'll go. But listen here, sweetheart. Be careful of that one. She might have your eyes but, I'm telling you now, she's engaged to be married to Sean. Sean Keogh.

Exit the WIDOW QUIN. PEGEEN locks the door.

CHRISTOPHER: Is it true?
PEGEEN: It's a pack of lies.
CHRISTOPHER: So why did she say—
PEGEEN: Don't listen to her. She's evil, she is.
CHRISTOPHER: Does that mean you're not getting married?
PEGEEN: No, I'm not! I wouldn't marry that fella if the fuckin' pope brought him in by the bollix.
CHRISTOPHER: Thank God for His little mercies.

PEGEEN pulls a table away from the long seat against the wall, beside the fire. She picks up the duvet, etc.

PEGEEN: You can sleep here, look it. It'll be warm. You lie there now. It's been a long fuckin' day for you.

CHRISTOPHER takes duvet and sits. He studies the duvet cover.

PEGEEN: Don't mind it. It's an old one I used to have. I was mad into Barbie.
CHRISTOPHER: It is very nice.
PEGEEN (*mimicking him*): You may say so. (*Her own voice*) I'll leave you to it. (*Remembering*) Oh yeah, your passport.

He picks up his hat, takes his passport from a pocket inside it. He hands it to PEGEEN.

PEGEEN: Grand. You can have it back whenever you want it. Sleep tight.
CHRISTOPHER: Thank you.

She starts to exit, behind the counter.

CHRISTOPHER: Pegeen. Only God can reward you for your kindness.
PEGEEN: Yeah, right.

She turns off the light as she exits. Still, particular light—perhaps from the gas fire—on CHRISTOPHER.

CHRISTOPHER: This is unbelievable! It is true what they say about Irish people. Their friendliness and generosity of heart. Here I am, with two fine women fighting over me. You know what? I'm beginning to think, wasn't I a foolish man not to have killed my father years ago?

Lights.

Act 2

Scene, as before. Brilliant morning light. The pub phone is ringing. CHRISTOPHER sits up. He has bright yellow eyeshades over his face. He is suddenly awake, and disorientated. Phone still rings. He lifts the shades to his forehead. He finds the phone on the wall behind the counter. As he reaches for it, it stops ringing.

He is alone, in the clothes he lay down in the night before, with matching eyeshades and oversocks. He takes a bunch of chewing sticks from his case. He selects one and starts cleaning his teeth with it.[23] He looks around and examines more closely the photo portraits on the walls.

CHRISTOPHER (*looking at Mary Robinson*): Pegeen does not look like her mum, God rest her soul. (*Re: Michael Flatley*) This might be her uncle. (*Looking again at Mary Robinson, and back at Flatley*) Missis Flaherty's brother, perhaps. (*Re: Roy Keane*) Roy Keane! What is he doing here? He can't be related to her, can he? This is interesting.

He sings softly, and briefly, a song: "Mo so ri re o" by Paul "Play" Dairo.[24]

Mo so ri re o (Fortune has smiled on me)
Eleda mi mo dupe o (My Creator, I give you thanks)

He stops in front of a fire safety notice on the wall beside/behind counter and reads.

---

23. Chewing sticks, or chew sticks, are twigs or roots of plants that are chewed until one end is frayed, which can then be used to brush against teeth.

24. Paul Babatunde Dairo (ak.a Paul "Play") is a Nigerian R&B artist, singer/songwriter, and music producer. He is the son of the legendary Nigerian Afrojuju musician, I. K. Dairo (1930–96), who, along with other Nigerian music giants, ruled the Nigerian airwaves in the 1960s and 70s. Paul "Play" produced a remix of his father's song "Mo So Rire" in 1999 and became a household name.

CHRISTOPHER: "In case of fire, stay calm." Stay calm? We'll see. "Always check the fire extinguisher." Very good; where is it?

He finds the extinguisher under the counter. He tests it.

CHRISTOPHER (*impressed*): It works! That's what is good about this part of the world. There is information. And things work. They don't call them First World for nothing. (*Looking up at the* CCTV) You can see outside without being outside. (*Picking up wall phone, putting it to ear*) Constant dialing tone. I think I'm going to like it here.

Wall phone rings. He picks it up, hesitates, then speaks.

CHRISTOPHER: Hello? . . . Yes, I am awake; of course . . . The Cash and Carry? I see . . . I see; it was you. I tried to, but it stopped ringing . . . Yes. See you soon. Goodbye.

As he talks on the phone, he sights himself in the mirror behind the counter. He removes the eyeshades from his forehead and puts them on the counter. He replaces the phone, and starts humming a few lines of the "Mo so ri re o" song. He turns to the sink, under the counter, turns on the tap and rinses his chewing stick. He sees and picks up Pegeen's compact mirror and examines his teeth.

CHRISTOPHER: "Hello." Clean teeth are healthy teeth. Nothing like a good chewing stick.

He hums again, as he bends down and wets his face. He finds a cloth and dries his face. He recites a half-remembered rhyme—

CHRISTOPHER: Looking pretty, no pimples, but two dimples . . .

He goes to his case and takes out a bottle of Calvin Klein scent. He quickly sprays it on his chest and behind his ears. He takes his hair brush and a tub of wax, Sportin' Waves, from the case. He applies the wax to his hair. As he rubs in the wax, he has another look at Roy Keane.

CHRISTOPHER: Her cousin.

He continues, to the counter. He puts down the wax and picks up the mirror. He brushes his hair.

CHRISTOPHER: I always knew it—there was something wrong with that mirror back home. It was cursed. Well, from now onwards, a good-looking man I shall be.

As he speaks, he removes the hoodie and climbs onto the counter. He squats on the counter, leans sideways, so he can see himself in the wall-length mirror. He lifts his shirt and examines his body.

CHRISTOPHER: I mean, look at that. None of that nonsense back home, where you must be fat to prove your affluence. Men in their thirties, with big tummy. Pretending they are loaded. But I'm here, and I don't have to be that way. Henceforth, it's forward ever, backward never. (*Picking up the compact mirror and brush*) I will be—

He hears noise from outside.

CHRISTOPHER: That must be Pegeen.

He looks at the door and at the CCTV screen. He sees the girls. One of them knocks.

CHRISTOPHER: Girls! God help me—

He grabs the hoodie and slides off the counter and hides behind it, out of view. The main door is pushed open and SUSAN BRADY looks in.

SUSAN: There's no one in.

HONOR BLAKE pushes her in and follows her with SARAH TANSEY. These are local girls, in their late teens. They step further into the room. SARAH has a SuperValu bag; she drops it beside the door.

SUSAN (*calls out*): Pegeen!
SARAH: Maybe they're out.
HONOR: Maybe they're upstairs.

They laugh.

SARAH (*to HONOR*): Dirty bitch.
SUSAN: Sean Keogh was having us on. There's no African fella here.
HONOR (*pointing*): There's a duvet; look it.
SARAH (*joking*): Are they under it?

They approach the duvet.

HONOR: They're not up to much if they are. (*Pulling back duvet*) Gone! It'd be a fuckin' disaster if he's gone already. Imagine. A fella who's after killing his da.
SUSAN: God, yeah. (*Seeing CHRISTOPHER's shoes under the table*) Hang on, but. They're his shoes; I bet they are.
SARAH: There should be blood on them.
SUSAN: Why should there be?

SARAH goes down on her knees, examining the shoes, not touching them yet.

SARAH: Did you never see in the films how murdered men bleed and drip?

HONOR: He'd have washed them. You couldn't get through all that airport security with blood on your shoes.

SUSAN (*agreeing*): Yeah.

SARAH (*picking up one of the shoes, looking at it*): No blood.

HONOR: Told you.

SARAH (*smelling the shoe*): No.

SUSAN: Nice shoes, though.

HONOR: They're a bit wrecked.

SUSAN: What size are they?

SARAH: Why?

SUSAN: You can tell a lot about a fella by the size of his shoes.

SARAH: It's a nine, I'd say.

HONOR: Wow!

They laugh. SARAH drops the shoe to the floor, slips off her own, and puts CHRISTOPHER's shoe on.

SARAH: I'll tell you one thing. He's done a lot of walking.

She walks, like a model, to the window, and back, as if on a catwalk.

HONOR (*commentary*): And now, ladies and gentlemen, we have Sarah Tansey. And Sarah is modeling the shoe that all the murderers will be wearing this season. Steel-capped, pointed-toe pumps, from Manolo. It's the killer style. One good kick will kill your da.

During the above, SUSAN finds the eyeshades on the counter and puts them on, over her eyes. SARAH stops at the window.

SARAH (*looking out*): No sign of them coming back yet.

SUSAN: Shhh!

HONOR: What?

SUSAN: You can hear brilliant with these things on.

SARAH: Are they his?

HONOR: They must be. They come with the plane.

SARAH: But his shoes, look. They're in fuckin' bits.

HONOR: For fuck sake, Sarah. He didn't walk all the way from
Africa.

SUSAN: Yeah, the ocean and that.

*She lifts the shades off her eyes for a beat and places them back over
her eyes.*

SUSAN: It's true. You can hear better if you can't see.

HONOR (*giving SUSAN "the finger"*): That's brilliant. What
can you hear?

SUSAN: Traffic.

HONOR: Fuckin' great.

SUSAN: Shut up a minute. I can hear your ma farting. She's
bending down to get the rashers out of the fridge.

HONOR: Nice one. But there's none there, so she's wasting her
time.

SUSAN: And I can hear—shhh! Shhh! I can hear something.
(*Moving away from the counter and lifting the shades from
her eyes*) A rat or a fuckin' mouse, or something.

SARAH: Yeuh! Hate that. Where?

SUSAN: Back there.

HONOR: We can get the fuckin' health inspectors in on them.
Where is it?

SUSAN: Behind there.

HONOR looks over the counter, and exclaims.

HONOR: Fuckin' Jesus, me heart!

SUSAN: Can you see it?

SARAH: Oh God, is it big?

HONOR: It's him!
SARAH: The rat?
HONOR: The fella.
SARAH: Oh, Jesus.

SARAH removes and kicks CHRISTOPHER's shoe across the room. CHRISTOPHER stands up. He looks caught, a bit sheepish. The girls look at him; he looks at the girls, for a beat or two.

SARAH: Is Pegeen here?
HONOR (*to the girls*): She's behind the fuckin' counter.

They try not to laugh. CHRISTOPHER, perplexed, doesn't answer. SARAH assumes that he doesn't understand.

SARAH (*slower*): Is—Pegeen—here—mister?
CHRISTOPHER: No. She is gone to the Cash and Carry.
SUSAN (*to the girls*): She's not here.
SARAH: Come here; are you the fella that killed his da?
CHRISTOPHER: I am, God help me.
SUSAN: It's him.
SARAH: I'm scarlet.
SUSAN (*getting the SuperValu bag*): We brought you some stuff.
SUSAN: Presents, like.
HONOR: Me first.

Each girl takes an item from the bag. CHRISTOPHER comes out from behind the counter. He is still holding the hairbrush as he accepts each gift. HONOR holds out something wrapped in tinfoil.

HONOR: Welcome to Ireland, by the way . . . It's a rasher sandwich. I thought you might be a bit hungry.
CHRISTOPHER: Thank you . . .
HONOR: Honor.
CHRISTOPHER: Honor?

HONOR: Yeah.

SARAH (*holding out a bag, a bit impatiently*): It's only a couple of boiled eggs. But they're free range. Me da keeps the chickens out the back. He's a culchee.[25] Sarah.

CHRISTOPHER: Thank you very much.

SARAH: Sarah.

CHRISTOPHER: Sarah.

SUSAN: Susan.

CHRISTOPHER: Susan.

HONOR: It's short for slapper.[26]

SUSAN: Fuck off, you. (*To CHRISTOPHER*): Don't listen to her. (*Holding out a ready-packed roasted chicken*) It's a roasted chicken. Me brother works in the Spar.[27] It's a bit damaged, but it's grand.

HONOR: It's still warm; feel it.

CHRISTOPHER (*feeling the chicken*): It is warm indeed, and quite a . . . handful. Thank you very much . . .

HONOR: Slapper.

SUSAN: Fuck off. Susan.

CHRISTOPHER: Susan.

SUSAN (*re: the brush*): Is that the knife?

CHRISTOPHER: What?

SUSAN: That.

CHRISTOPHER: Oh. This? It is my hairbrush.

HONOR: A hairbrush? You've no fuckin' hair, but.

CHRISTOPHER: I do, as a matter of fact. (*Lowering his head and rubbing his hair from back to front*) See? Waves.

HONOR: Here; let's feel it.

CHRISTOPHER: Certainly.

---

25. *Culchee* or *culchie* is a mainly pejorative term describing someone from rural Ireland

26. *Slapper* is slang for a prostitute.

27. Spar is a grocery store chain in Ireland.

CHRISTOPHER, *increasingly pleased, keeps his head lowered, inviting the girls to touch it.*

> SUSAN: Me first.
> HONOR: Fuck off.
> SARAH: Jesus.

One at a time, they touch his hair.

> HONOR: It feels weird.
> SUSAN: It feels lovely.
> SARAH: Kind of spiky-silky, like.
> HONOR: Here; I like the smell of it as well.
> SARAH: Yeah.
> CHRISTOPHER (*lifting his head*): That's my perfume, actually.
> SARAH: Perfume?
> SUSAN: What perfume? Men's perfume?
> CHRISTOPHER: Calvin Klein.
> HONOR: Jesus; men that kill their das sure are a vain lot.
> CHRISTOPHER (*slightly embarrassed*): Well, I thank you very
>   much for your hospitality, and your gifts.
> HONOR: No problem.
> CHRISTOPHER: May God reward you abundantly and shower
>   you with his blessings.
> SUSAN: Doesn't he talk lovely?

Enter the WIDOW QUIN. She is dressed casually, but glamorously, on her way to the gym.

> WIDOW QUIN (*giving a slight wave to CHRISTOPHER*):
>   What're you girls doing here?
> SUSAN: Mrs. Quin, that man killed his da.
> WIDOW QUIN: I know he did; I'm well ahead of yis. (*To
>   CHRISTOPHER*): Your muscles must be locked in on you,
>   Christopher; hanging around airports and that. I'm off to

the gym. I'll put your name down and you can have a work-
out. How's that sound?

SARAH: Which one are you in, Mrs. Quin?

WIDOW QUIN: Fitness City. Are you fasting or fed, young fella?

CHRISTOPHER: Fasting, if you please.

WIDOW QUIN: Can't have that. (*Holding up the tinfoil*) What's
this one?

HONOR: Rasher sandwich.

WIDOW QUIN: White bread, I suppose?

HONOR: What?

WIDOW QUIN: Never mind. (*To CHRISTOPHER*): Come
here to me. (*Grabbing a chair, and holding out the sandwich*) Sit there now and get that into you. Where is she, by
the way?

SARAH: Cash and Carry.

WIDOW QUIN: Grand. You can tell us your story while you're
having your rashers.

CHRISTOPHER (*sitting*): It's a long story; you would be bored
listening to it.

WIDOW QUIN: Don't be letting on you're shy now, a fine,
gamey, treacherous fella like you.

SUSAN: Jesus, will you listen to her.

CHRISTOPHER *starts eating.*

WIDOW QUIN: You don't have any religious objections to rashers, do you? Bacon, like.

CHRISTOPHER (*shaking his head*): No. Not at all. I am an
omnivore.

WIDOW QUIN: Grand. So, was it in your house you cracked his
skull?

CHRISTOPHER (*shy but flattered*): It wasn't. It was outside, in
our compound.

SARAH: What's a—

WIDOW QUIN: Shhh.

CHRISTOPHER: The backyard. It was early in the evening. The sun had just gone down behind the mountains. And there he was, on his chair with a bottle of Star, listening to BBC Radio World Service.[28]

WIDOW QUIN: And you asked him for money.

CHRISTOPHER: I certainly did not. What happened was: he gave me a plot of land for my twenty-first birthday.

WIDOW QUIN: Ah, lovely.

CHRISTOPHER: But I didn't need a plot of land. I'd prefer to travel and broaden my horizons, you see. So I told him I would sell the land and travel with the proceeds. "You squinting idiot," he said. "You are going nowhere." He wanted me to stay, get married, and raise a family.

HONOR: You're engaged, so.

CHRISTOPHER: I don't even have a girlfriend. His intention was to set me up with a daughter of one of his business associates.

WIDOW QUIN: Oh, oh. What was *she* like?

CHRISTOPHER: You need to see this lady. She's older than me, for a start. Much older. And obese. I mean, she is bi-iiig. She can't be less than two hundred kg.[29]

WIDOW QUIN: How big is that?

SUSAN: Fuckin' huge.

CHRISTOPHER: And, to add insult to injury, this is a woman of noted misbehavior. I mean, with many men. Old or young, tall or short. She doesn't mind.

HONOR: A slut.

CHRISTOPHER: Precisely. "It has been arranged and that's it," he said.

28. Star Beer is made in Nigeria by Nigerian Breweries.
29. Two hundred kilograms is over 440 pounds.

WIDOW QUIN takes the legs off the roasted chicken and hands one to CHRISTOPHER. The girls help themselves to chicken.

WIDOW QUIN: So you hit him then.

CHRISTOPHER (*getting almost excited*): No, I did not. "I will not marry her," I said. "This is a woman with a fiery tongue. She hauls back the dead with her curses."

WIDOW QUIN (*teasingly*): That one sounds lovely.

SARAH: Did you kill him then?

CHRISTOPHER: "You should be glad that any woman has agreed to marry you," he says. "I shall not marry this woman, even if you pay me," I say. "I am your father," he says. "And you must do as I say. Or else the ground will be taller than you." "The ground will not be taller than me," I say. "I will not allow this." "Who are you to tell me what you allow and what you won't allow?" he says. "If I hear one more word from you, I will scatter this bottle on your head." "You will not, if I can help it," I say.

HONOR: And you were dead right.

CHRISTOPHER: With that, the sun dipped into the horizon and his shadow loomed large as he stood up. "God have mercy on your soul," he says, lifting the bottle. "Or on your own," I say, standing my ground.

SUSAN: He tells it lovely.

CHRISTOPHER (*flattered, lifting the chicken leg*): He swung the bottle, and I leapt—to my three o'clock. From the corner of my eye, I saw the pestle, leaning against the wall.

SARAH: What's a pestle?

WIDOW QUIN: Shhh.

CHRISTOPHER: I grabbed it. I turned, with my back to my twelve o'clock. He swung at me again. I dodged it (*raising the chicken leg, two-handed, over his head and bringing it down*) and hit him right on the ridge of his skull. His medulla oblongata shattered—into smithereens.[30] In slow motion, he fell. Without a twitch.

HONOR: Jesus, wha'.

SUSAN: He's like you, Mrs. Quin.

WIDOW QUIN: Just a bit.

SARAH (*to CHRISTOPHER*): She was in the *Star*; what she did.[31]

WIDOW QUIN: We're birds of a feather.

HONOR: Murderers, like.

WIDOW QUIN: It was self-defence. Isn't that right, Christy?

CHRISTOPHER: You are right, ma.

The girls nudge each other, at the mention of "ma."

SARAH: You're like heroes, the two of yis.

HONOR: Like Bonnie and Clyde.[32]

SARAH: Ah, yeah. (*Quoting the byline*) "They're young, they're in love, and they kill people."

SARAH links CHRISTOPHER and WIDOW QUIN's hands. They are initially reluctant, then play along.

SARAH: See? Yis are natural together.

WIDOW QUIN: Ah, stop messing, Sarah.

HONOR: Made for each other.

SARAH: Come here. A drink for the gangsters.

---

30. The medulla oblongata is located at the base of the brain, where the brain stem connects to the spinal cord.

31. The *Star* is a tabloid newspaper.

32. Bonnie (Bonnie Elizabeth Parker, 1910–34) and Clyde (Clyde Chestnut Barrow, 1909–34) were an American criminal couple known for their gang, the Barrow Gang, and multiple armed bank robberies during the Great Depression. They likely murdered at least nine police officers and four civilians before being killed by police officers in Louisiana in 1934.

SUSAN grabs two bottles from behind the counter—bright-colored alcopops. She hands one each to CHRISTOPHER and WIDOW QUIN. She gets three more bottles and hands them around.

SARAH: There now; perfect.

HONOR gets ready to photograph them with her mobile phone.

SUSAN: Hang on.

SUSAN takes two cigarettes from a pack and puts them into the WIDOW QUIN and CHRISTOPHER's mouths.

CHRISTOPHER: I don't smoke.
SUSAN (*cheerfully*): Shut up—I'm only messing. (*Removing the cigarette*) There.

SUSAN lights the cigarette, as SARAH raises her bottle.

SARAH: To the two of yis, the walking killers.
HONOR: Hear, hear.
SARAH: And all the others like you; the hitmen, the heroin dealers, coke dealers; crooked cops and politicians, and publicans and lawyers; celebs and DJs, and the whole fuckin' lot of them.
WIDOW QUIN: Good girl. You left out no one.

They drink. PEGEEN enters, carrying goods from the Cash and Carry, some long sticks of French bread, and a tabloid newspaper. She stands aghast. There's a lit cigarette in her mouth. The girls spring away from CHRISTOPHER. The WIDOW lets go of his hand, but stays close beside him.

PEGEEN: We're shut.

She puts the goods on the counter. CHRISTOPHER goes to help, but she shoulders him aside.

HONOR: I need change for the cigarette machine.
PEGEEN: We're shut, I said. (*To SUSAN*) There's a smoking ban.
SUSAN: You're smoking.
PEGEEN: It's my fuckin' pub. Get out. The lot of you.

The girls start to leave, but linger at the door.

PEGEEN (*to WIDOW QUIN*): You too. Out.
WIDOW QUIN: Are you barring me, Pegeen?
PEGEEN: No. Come back at eleven. With your money. (*Looking her up and down*) But no tracksuits.
WIDOW QUIN: You're in your moods this morning, Pegeen. I'll leave you to it. (*Walking to the door*) See you later, Christy, mind yourself.
GIRLS: Bye! Seeyeh! Later!
PEGEEN (*making for the door*): Get out!

WIDOW QUIN and the girls exit. After a few beats—

PEGEEN: "Christy"?
CHRISTOPHER: Yes. It is short for "Christopher."
PEGEEN: I fuckin' know that. (*Picking up a bottle*) You're paying for these. Out of the wages you haven't fuckin' earned yet. . . . Christy.

CHRISTOPHER gathers the bottles and food, eager to please and get rid of the evidence.

PEGEEN: Eleven. Say it.
CHRISTOPHER: Pardon me?

PEGEEN: Eleven. Opening time. No one—fuckin' no one gets in before—?

CHRISTOPHER: Eleven o'clock.

PEGEEN (*pointing at him*): Your job.

CHRISTOPHER: Yes.

PEGEEN: Get rid of all this shit and clean the counter. Fuckin' chicken fat on customers' elbows. The dry-cleaning bills; do you want them as well?

CHRISTOPHER: No.

PEGEEN: Yeah, well. . . . Clean it up. And your own stuff, over there. Take it back there.

CHRISTOPHER *folds the duvet, etc. PEGEEN goes behind the counter to put away the Cash and Carry goods. She finds her mirror with the hair wax. She holds them up.*

PEGEEN: What's this?

CHRISTOPHER: Oh, my hair cream. (*Approaching her, showing his head*) It makes it wavy. See?

PEGEEN: Do I give a fuck?

CHRISTOPHER: I was just trying to look presentable. For the customers.

PEGEEN: Customers? A few sluts and a certain widow.

CHRISTOPHER: No, no; believe me—

PEGEEN: Yeah, maybe.

PEGEEN *picks up the French bread. As she does so, CHRISTO-PHER grabs one. It slides from the bag.*

CHRISTOPHER: You know what this reminds me of? (*Holding the bread aloft*) The pestle. The one I used to kill my father.

PEGEEN: Yeah, yeah. You've told that story six fuckin' times since you got here.

CHRISTOPHER (*reproachfully*): What is your problem? Is familiarity breeding contempt here?

PEGEEN: What?

CHRISTOPHER: Forget it.

PEGEEN: Suit yourself. (*A pause, then, sternly*) Just be fuckin' careful, okay?

CHRISTOPHER: What do you mean?

PEGEEN: Be careful who you talk to around here.

CHRISTOPHER: Why?

PEGEEN: Jesus, are you thick? (*Softening*) Look it, those young ones—those girls. They're not interested in you, not really. They think you're nice and that, but it's the celebrity thing they're after. They all tried for Eurovision, and they were shite.[33] But you'll do instead. They're waiting for the Guards to come in and take you. They want to get into the story. They want to cry at the airport when they're sending you back. And the Widow—she's a has-been. She wants to get in there as well. It's a while since she's been on the front page. She's dangerous.

CHRISTOPHER: Oh. I see . . .

PEGEEN: So, you'd better stop your blabbing. Look it, the hard-chaws around here, the fellas with the guns—do you know what they want, what they're really after?

CHRISTOPHER: What?

PEGEEN: They want some journalist to give them a nickname. The General, the Monk, the fuckin' Viper. That's success around here. And the Rattler. That's fame. And that's what those girls want. Some of yours.

CHRISTOPHER: My what?

PEGEEN: Your fame. Your nickname. But you don't want to be famous, sure you don't?

CHRISTOPHER (*understanding*): No.

---

33. The Eurovision Song Contest, or Eurovision, is an international songwriting competition that has been organized annually since 1956 by the European Broadcasting Union. Ireland has won the Eurovision Song Contest seven times, most recently in 1996.

PEGEEN: Because that'll get you sent back.

CHRISTOPHER: I see.

PEGEEN: Good. (*Picking up the paper*) Have a look at this.

CHRISTOPHER: Is it news of my murder?

PEGEEN (*sardonically*): No, not your murder. Another one. See? (*Reads*) "Murderer Killed in Mountjoy."[34] I went to school with both of them. The murderer and the fella that killed him. (*Pointing*) And see her? Putting the flowers in front of the prison gate? His girlfriend; his partner. I sat beside her in home economics.

CHRISTOPHER: Do you think they will tell? The girls who were here.

PEGEEN: Who knows? Maybe.

CHRISTOPHER: But what would they gain from my downfall?

PEGEEN: Ah, it's only human. Other people's bad luck. "I seen it; I was there." Like an accident—on the road, like. You have to look at it, don't you? Everybody does. That's what causes the traffic jam. Not the accident, the people—us—slowing down to watch it. And you can hear about it on the radio at the same time; you can text in. "I seen it; I was there."

CHRISTOPHER (*quietly*): God save me.

PEGEEN: Are the jails nice in Nigeria, Christopher?

CHRISTOPHER: You've made your point. (*Finding his shoes, putting them on*) If I am not safe here, then it would be best if I continue my wandering. Like Cain. "Cursed be thou by the earth which has opened its mouth and drunk the blood of thy brother."[35]

PEGEEN (*beginning to play with him*): Jesus, did you kill your brother as well?

CHRISTOPHER (*looking up as he ties his shoes*): You can laugh? This is amusement for you? (*Showing her a shoe, holding*

---

34. Mountjoy is a prison in Dublin.

35. "Cursed be thou by the earth which has opened its mouth and drunk the blood of thy brother" is from Genesis 4:11.

it up) Look. I have walked hundreds of kilometers. See? I thought it was over, but now I must start again. (*Puts his foot in the shoe; it's obviously uncomfortable*).

PEGEEN: Where are you going?

CHRISTOPHER (*packing as he talks*): I pray it never happens to you. Looking over your shoulder all the time. Only desperate strangers as your companions—a lonely and terrible experience. Crossing the desert, for days, burnt, scorched, dehydrated, and famished. Guarding your neck and your wallet. *Agony* is the word. You cannot believe how I felt when I finally got on the plane. I slept throughout. And to this city, where everybody stares at me but, truly, I do not exist. I have become simply a feeling. Sheer and utter loneliness.

PEGEEN: You're a strange man, Christopher Malomo.

CHRISTOPHER: How could I be anything else when I'm so alone?

PEGEEN: Well, I'm not strange and I'm alone. Except for my father—wherever *he* fuckin' is.

CHRISTOPHER: You? Alone?

PEGEEN (*sardonically*): Hard to imagine, isn't it?

CHRISTOPHER: Indeed. How on earth could a lovely, pretty—sensationally beautiful—girl like you be alone when all men should be queuing up to hear the sweetness of your voice—

PEGEEN: There's no way a flattering fella like you could ever be lonely.

CHRISTOPHER: Flattering? Is that me?

PEGEEN: You're only letting on to be lonely, yeh chancer; the way you're getting around me now.

CHRISTOPHER: Honest to God, Pegeen, I was lonely all the time. I was born lonely—as the moon of dawn.

PEGEEN: I don't get it, Christopher. It can't be as bad as you're making it. A young fella like you, with enough guts to destroy your da.

CHRISTOPHER: I don't get it myself. But that's life, and I'm used to it. Anyway, I'll leave this place before your hospitality turns to hostility.

CHRISTOPHER *goes to the door.*

PEGEEN: Christopher.

He stops and turns.

PEGEEN: You're the security man in this place, and I won't have you going on the mitch when you should be getting ready for work.[36]

She goes behind the counter and takes out walkie-talkie headsets, tangled.

PEGEEN: Put that bag down, and we'll see if these yokes work.

Her mobile rings. She looks at it and switches it off. She unhooks the land phone.

CHRISTOPHER: I don't understand. I thought you said—
PEGEEN: You'll be fine if you keep your head low. I'm after doing a google—this morning, like. "Nigeria and Malomo." And there wasn't a word about your murder. They haven't found the body. So, you're grand. You're safe.
CHRISTOPHER: Is it true? I can stay. Excellent! And work for you!
PEGEEN: It's only a fuckin' job. You just stay clear of those sluts and you'll be grand. D'you hear me?
CHRISTOPHER: Do I hear you? Your voice is all that fill my ears.
PEGEEN: Jesus.

---

36. "Going on the mitch" is slang for ditching school, or skipping a commitment without a valid excuse.

CHRISTOPHER: And your eyes, the windows to your soul. They are so beautiful. They are mesmerising.

PEGEEN: Ah, fuck off out of that.

They each put on a headset. She turns them on.

CHRISTOPHER (*continues, into headset*): And even more beautiful when you frown.

PEGEEN (*loving every word, into headset*): Fuck off; over. It's no wonder you had those young ones around your little finger. Well, I'll tell yeh; your irresistible African charm doesn't work on me. Over.

Enter SEAN KEOGH.

SEAN: Pegeen! Your da's in the A&E![37]

PEGEEN: What happened?!

SEAN: He got hit by a car. I tried to phone you.

PEGEEN: Fuck. Was it deliberate, was it?

SEAN: I don't know.

PEGEEN: Where?

SEAN: My ma said, near the corner of—

PEGEEN: Where's my fuckin' da!

SEAN: Oh, yeah—Blanchardstown.[38] The A&E.

PEGEEN grabs her keys from the counter and runs to the door.

CHRISTOPHER: I'll go with you.

PEGEEN: No, you look after the place.

She exits.

---

37. A&E stands for Accident and Emergency—in other words, the hospital.
38. Blanchardstown is a large suburb northwest of Dublin.

CHRISTOPHER (*to SEAN*): Should I go with her?

Enter WIDOW QUIN. She closes the main door. She carries a suitbag.

WIDOW QUIN: She'll be well able to find her daddy by herself. And Sean here has a few things he wants to get off his chest.

SEAN takes a brown envelope from his pocket and holds it out to CHRISTOPHER.

SEAN: Here.
CHRISTOPHER: What's that?
SEAN: Open it.

CHRISTOPHER opens envelope and looks into it.

SEAN: A one-way ticket to Belfast and five hundred pounds.
CHRISTOPHER: Belfast?
WIDOW QUIN: You'll fit right in up there, young fella.
CHRISTOPHER (*counts the money in the envelope*): Five hundred pounds, sterling.

SEAN anxiously removes a good suit, with shirt and tie from the suitbag, and places it on a table, so the trouser legs hang.

SEAN: And this, look it. (*Takes out very comfortable, elegant shoes*) And these. They're all yours.
CHRISTOPHER: What is happening here?
SEAN: Listen, I know the system. I've helped some members of my church with their papers. You need to go to Belfast. London being your point of entry, like. And Belfast is part of the UK, kind of. I know some people up there. And they can speed up your asylum application, especially since you're a brother in Christ.

CHRISTOPHER (*with a new arrogance*): Excuse my igno-
rance, but if I may ask: what have I done to deserve this
magnanimity?

SEAN (*looking to the WIDOW QUIN for help*): There's no
point in lying to you. I'm no good at it, brother; it's against
my principles. So, the truth is—I'm marrying Pegeen and I
can't have a fella like you under her roof.

CHRISTOPHER: Marrying Pegeen? You? I see. So you are using
bribery? To banish me?

SEAN: Don't take it badly, brother. It's for the best. It's cheaper
up there. And there'll be better work for you than this. I can
let you have more money—

WIDOW QUIN (*coming over*): He's right, sweetheart. You'll be
better off up there, and not have that poor girl being distracted by you. Sean thinks she wouldn't suit you, though
it's obvious she has her eye on you.

CHRISTOPHER beams with delight.

SEAN (*in terrified earnest*): She wouldn't suit you. With her
temper, you'd be strangling each other inside a week. (*Making the movement of strangling himself*) It's only the like of
me that'd suit her. Quiet, like; laid-back. I wouldn't raise a
finger, even if she tore the skin off me.

WIDOW QUIN (*putting the tie around CHRISTOPHER's neck*):
Look it; try the suit on, an'anyway. It'll look gorgeous on
you. (*Picking up the shoes*) God, they're soft; and your poor
feet—they'll fall asleep in these things. (*Pushing him to the
inner door, behind the counter*) Try the clobber on, and
you can give your answer when you've had a good look at
yourself.

CHRISTOPHER (*delighted with the clothes*): Alright then. I'd like
her to see me in this suit.

He goes into the inner room and shuts the door.

SEAN: Did you hear that? He wants her to see him. He's not going to leave, Mrs. Quin. There's a devil in him; he'll take Pegeen. For definite, he will.

WIDOW QUIN: It's true all girls are fond of courage and hate the likes of you.

SEAN (*walking around in desperation*): Oh, Mrs. Quin, what'll I do? I'd inform on him, but he'd burst out of Mountjoy and come after me. Only my da's already dead, I'd kill him and become a hero, like your man. And I can't kill me mother. (*Coming over to her*) Oh, Mrs. Quin, think of something!

WIDOW QUIN: Plan B, Sean.

SEAN: Great. (*When she doesn't respond*) I'll double the amount I promised you.

WIDOW QUIN: Six hundred? That won't get me far. It's not even the mortgage on me little apartment.

SEAN: I'll pay your mortgage.

WIDOW QUIN: Forever?

SEAN: Two months . . . three. Six months.

WIDOW QUIN: Lovely.

SEAN: What is it?

WIDOW QUIN: Excuse me?

SEAN: Plan B.

WIDOW QUIN: I'll take care of him, Shawn. The oul' Sharon Stone.[39]

SEAN: You?! Are you serious?

WIDOW QUIN: Perfectly serious. He's high as a kite in there. He'd follow any woman. I'll take him away, to a little love nest.

SEAN: The Red Cow.

WIDOW QUIN: A bit further than that, Shawn. Galway, maybe.[40] A nice hotel. A glass of sherry when you sign in. A bit of style.

SEAN: I'll pay for it.

---

39. Sharon Stone (b. 1958) is an American actress and producer, known for her role as Catherine Trammell in the erotic thriller *Basic Instinct* (1992).

40. Galway is a harbor city on Ireland's west coast.

WIDOW QUIN: That's right.

SEAN: And some money for spending—

WIDOW QUIN: Yeah, yeah; he's coming back in.

SEAN: I'll look after you.

WIDOW: Shhh . . . grand.

CHRISTOPHER enters, in the new clothes, also wearing the walkie-talkie. WIDOW QUIN goes to him, admiringly.

WIDOW QUIN: Oh, look. If you could see yourself now, sweetheart, you'd be too full of yourself to talk to us at all. God, I'm beginning to think, it's an awful shame to send you off to Belfast.

CHRISTOPHER: I'm not going. I'm prepared to confront whatever fate throws at me in this place.

WIDOW QUIN makes a sign to SEAN to leave.

SEAN: Well, I've to go to . . . a meeting. God bless you, brother. You can keep the suit.

He exits.

WIDOW QUIN: Well, you look mighty dapper, Christy, love.

CHRISTOPHER: Thanks. I'm going to look for Pegeen. Where is the hospital, please?

WIDOW QUIN: You'll have time and plenty to be with Pegeen. Sit down here, till I tell you. The two of us would make great company for each other.

CHRISTOPHER: I have no shortage of company, ma; everyone is bringing me provision and clothing. (*Swaggering to the door*) They so much admire a gallant man who, with one blow, smashed his father's skull to smithereens. (*Into walkie-talkie*) "On my way, Pegeen; over." (*Opens door, then staggers back*) Holy Jesus! The son of God!

WIDOW QUIN (*going over*): What's wrong?
CHRISTOPHER: It's the walking spirit of my murdered father!
WIDOW QUIN (*looking out*): Getting out of the taxi?
CHRISTOPHER (*wildly*): Gracious God! He mustn't see me!

CHRISTOPHER *dashes here and there, and hides behind the counter. The door is pushed open, and* MALOMO *(fifties) walks in. He wears a traditional attire; agbada (flowing gown), complete with cap. There is a pair of reading glasses around his neck. He carries a small business case and holds a diary. He also has a walking stick. He speaks with an educated Nigerian accent.*

WIDOW QUIN (*in great amusement*): Good morning, mister. Can I help you at all?

MALOMO *opens the diary and puts on his reading glasses.*

MALOMO: Do you know where this is? (*reads*) "45 Rosegarden Court, Dublin 17."
WIDOW QUIN (*joining in*): "Dublin 17." You don't say hello where you come from, no?
MALOMO: I beg your pardon?
WIDOW QUIN: Good morning.
MALOMO: Good morning to you, too. I was asking if you knew this address.
WIDOW QUIN (*takes the diary, brings it closer to her eyes*): Sorry, love; it doesn't exist. There's no such place as Rosegarden Court.
MALOMO: That is rather preposterous.

He takes a photograph from the case. He shows it to the WIDOW.

MALOMO: Have you, by any chance, come across this young man?

WIDOW QUIN: Let's see. Who is he?

MALOMO: He is my boy.

WIDOW QUIN: Ah, look. You must be proud of him.

MALOMO: That one? He is nothing to be proud of. He is a good-for-nothing, murderous bastard. I found this address in his room. Have you seen him?

WIDOW QUIN: Ah, sure, we have all sorts of Africans around here now. It's hard to know who's who. (*Looks at photo*) No, I don't think so.

MALOMO: That is somewhat disappointing. However, I do appreciate your help.

WIDOW QUIN: Ah, you're grand.

MALOMO prepares to leave; he picks up the case.

WIDOW QUIN: If you don't mind me asking. Why d'you want him, an'anyway?

MALOMO: Why? (*Puts down case*) To kill him, of course. (*Takes off cap to reveal his bandaged head*) See? Look at that. His handiwork. It was God that saved me. (*Lifts his arm to his head, explaining*) But for the wall behind me, my gray matter would have been food for dogs.

WIDOW QUIN: Gray matter?

MALOMO: My brain.

He inclines his head slightly. The WIDOW takes his head in both hands and examines it with extreme delight.

WIDOW QUIN: That was some whack. And who was it hit you? A robber or something?

MALOMO: Weren't you listening to me? It was my son. Not a robber or anybody else. My own begotten son.

She lets go of his head and wipes her hands on her tracksuit.

WIDOW QUIN: You should let the air into that scalp; it'll heal up faster . . . You must have pushed him right to the wall, to have made him leave a gash like that in his da.

MALOMO: Is that me?

WIDOW QUIN: Yeah, and isn't it a shame when the old lads torment the young?

MALOMO (*raging*): Torment him? Torment who? Me, with the patience of a martyred saint? I did everything a good father would do, to bring up his child. (*Tapping his head*) And how has he expressed his gratitude?

WIDOW QUIN: He looks like a nice enough chap in the photo.

MALOMO: Nice? Him? He is stupid. He is an imbecile and a liar. And lazy! He snores while his peers are hard at it, earning their living.

WIDOW QUIN: Not working at all, no?

MALOMO: Useless, no good—to himself or anyone. If he is not eating or sleeping, he is in front of the mirror, looking at his own reflection.

WIDOW QUIN goes behind the counter, pretending to get a glass of water. She looks down, at CHRISTOPHER, as she speaks.

WIDOW QUIN: Admiring himself.

MALOMO: Admiring himself?

WIDOW QUIN: Doing himself up for the girls.

MALOMO: What girls? Girls! (*Chuckles mirthlessly*) If he saw a girl coming his way, he would run and hide himself in the nearest tall grasses. And you would see his sheep's eyes poking out from between the blades, and his two ears sticking up through a gap, like a rabbit. The only girl he ever had a chance with was my friend's daughter . . . Comfort; yes, that's her name—and *I* arranged it. Girls, indeed.

WIDOW QUIN: He fell into bad company—the drink.

MALOMO: If he has ever tasted any alcohol drink—not in my sight. Not even a glass of Dubonnet.[41] And bad company?! He hasn't got any friend. None that I've seen. I am a member of Rotary International, Mrs. —?[42]

WIDOW QUIN: Quin.

MALOMO: Mrs. Queen?

WIDOW QUIN: Yes. Q.U.I.N.

MALOMO: Mrs. Quin. I am Chief Clement Malomo. And, as I said, I am a Rotarian.

WIDOW QUIN: Well done.

MALOMO: But, believe it or not, he refused to become a Rotaractor. He doesn't understand social network. The cornerstone of prosperity.

WIDOW QUIN: Oh, he wouldn't be a chip off the block, so.

MALOMO: Most certainly not.

WIDOW QUIN: Here, give us a look at that pic again—the photo.

MALOMO shows her the photograph.

MALOMO: A small low fellow, fair-complexioned.

WIDOW QUIN: Fair?

MALOMO: Yes, a shade lighter than me.

WIDOW QUIN: D'you know what? I think I have seen him.

MALOMO: Really? Where? The ugly squinting bastard.

WIDOW QUIN (*agreeing*): Jesus, stop, and a ringer for you.

MALOMO: When did you see him, where?

WIDOW QUIN: Right here, last night. I'd swear it was him. (*Pointing*) He was sitting there, and he was talking to a fella about going to Belfast.

---

41. Dubonnet is a sweet blend of fortified wine, herbs, and spices.

42. Rotary International is a nonreligious, nonpolitical service organization, founded in 1905 in Chicago, that promotes goodwill, peace, and humanitarian causes around the world.

MALOMO: Belfast?

WIDOW QUIN: Yeah, up the north. This morning, like. On the train. So he said, an'anyway.

MALOMO: Where would one get the Belfast train, Mrs. Quin?

WIDOW QUIN: It'd be Connolly. They do all the nordie trains.

MALOMO: Connolly Station?[43]

WIDOW QUIN: That's right. You'll make it if there's a taxi going past.

MALOMO (*picks up case, goes to the door*): Thank you for your help, good woman.

He exits.

WIDOW QUIN (*goes to door; shouts after him*): Give him a good hiding, when you catch up with him. Just make sure the law isn't looking at you. Mountjoy's already full of chiefs.

She closes the door and looks at CHRISTOPHER, who is peeking over the counter. She bursts into a laugh.

WIDOW QUIN: Well, you're the walking son of Chief Clement Malomo. Get out of that, Geronimo.[44] And that's the poor man whose skull you scattered all over the place.

CHRISTOPHER (*coming out from behind counter*): Oh God, what will I do—what is Pegeen going to say to me now?

WIDOW QUIN: She'll knock the head off you, so she will, and send you packing. Poor girl. Taking you for a playboy, and you, only a little schemer making up the story that you destroyed your da.

43. Connolly Station is the busiest railway station in Dublin.
44. Geronimo (Mescalero-Chiricahua; 1829–1909) was a prominent Native American leader and medicine man from the Bedonkohe band of the Apache people.

CHRISTOPHER (*nearly speechless with rage*): The old bastard. Pretending he was dead, and now—following me here— coming in here and changing my story—I mean, he is supposed to be dead! Eaten by termites, or devoured by the vultures!

WIDOW QUIN: That's no way for a man to talk about his father.

CHRISTOPHER: My father? Listen to this. The next time I see him, may he have only one tooth left, and it should be aching. May he be left with only one eye to see devils wherever he looks. And may he be blessed with an old wooden leg, on which he will limp into his scalding grave. That is my prayer for my father. (*Looking out*) Look at him, getting into the taxi; the fool. Oh Lord, let them crash and—

WIDOW QUIN: What's wrong? You're not crying, are you?

CHRISTOPHER: I saw the love in her eyes, this morning—captivating—shining straight back at mine. I could hear her voice; she told me I would have peace and happiness here. Now she will change, and be throwing hard words at me, like an old madam giving out to her driver.

WIDOW QUIN: There's poetry for a girl you'd see scratching her arse behind the counter while she's serving slops to the unfortunate punters.

CHRISTOPHER: It is in the high heavens she should be serving slops. She's . . . What will I do now? I mean, I've been a hero for less than a day, for Christ's sake!

Distant noise, perhaps screeching brakes.

WIDOW QUIN: We'll get away before she finds out.

CHRISTOPHER: How do you mean?

WIDOW QUIN: We can go—somewhere. Anywhere.

CHRISTOPHER (*suspiciously*): We?

WIDOW QUIN: The two of us. It'll make you even more interesting.

CHRISTOPHER: I don't understand.

WIDOW QUIN: Don't be thick, Christy. We're alike, the pair of us. You're the talk of the town. And they'll be talking even more about you, if you run away with me.

She's distracted by the noise outside, which is now nearer. She looks up at the CCTV screen. She looks out the window.

CHRISTOPHER: Is Pegeen there? What's happening?

WIDOW QUIN: There's something up. We can go out the back.

CHRISTOPHER: No.

WIDOW QUIN: Come on; we'll have a ball. (*Takes a step to front door*) Or I'll have to tell Pegeen about your da.

CHRISTOPHER: No, no, no, you can't do that.

He drops to his knees. More commotion outside.

CHRISTOPHER: Please. Don't tell, in the name of God.

WIDOW QUIN (*almost embarrassed*): For fuck sake; will you get up.

CHRISTOPHER: I'm begging you, don't tell her. May God grant you all your heart's desires—

WIDOW QUIN: Someone's coming. Will you get up.

CHRISTOPHER: May He shower you with His blessings and make your better become best—

WIDOW QUIN: Get up!

CHRISTOPHER: Promise me you won't tell. I cannot lose Pegeen.

WIDOW QUIN: I'm not talking to you; get up.

CHRISTOPHER stands.

WIDOW QUIN: You'll have to do something for me. (*Looks at him for a beat*) Money.

CHRISTOPHER: Money?

WIDOW QUIN: I owe her father money. A lot of money. If I keep this to myself, will you help him to forget about it when—*if* things work out between you and Pegeen?

CHRISTOPHER (*delighted*): Thank you; thank you very much— that's no problem.

WIDOW QUIN: Believe me, sweetheart; it *is* a problem. Pegeen's da's a tough customer.

CHRISTOPHER: I promise you, I'll do whatever I can.

WIDOW QUIN: . . . Alright. Pegeen won't know the story. Not from me, an'anyway.

CHRISTOPHER: God bless you, Mrs. Quin; God bless you. . . . But wait a minute.

WIDOW QUIN: What now?

CHRISTOPHER: What if somebody else has seen him, coming in or going out? They'll tell Pegeen.

More commotion.

WIDOW QUIN: Then do what I did. Brazen it out. Stick to your story.

CHRISTOPHER: But you actually did kill your husband.

WIDOW QUIN: I didn't . . . But that's my story. I'm the notorious Widow Quin. Without that, I'm nobody.

CHRISTOPHER: You didn't kill him?

WIDOW QUIN: Nope.

CHRISTOPHER (*with an upward inflection*): I see . . . So, who . . . ?

WIDOW QUIN: Pegeen's da and his pals.

The door bursts open. PEGEEN rushes/falls in, holding MICHAEL. One of his legs is in a cast. More commotion outside, very close.

PEGEEN: Lock the door!

CHRISTOPHER (*trying to assist PEGEEN*): What is happening?

PEGEEN: The door! They're coming. Just lock the fuckin' door!

CHRISTOPHER goes to the door. He starts to shut/lock it. Someone outside pushes heavily against it. We see some figures on the CCTV screen. CHRISTOPHER can't lock the door; he keeps pushing.

PEGEEN: Christopher!

Lights.

Act 3

Scene, as before. A half hour later. JIMMY comes in, drunk.

JIMMY: An empty pub; for fuck sake. Must be the fuckin' smoking ban. (*Calls out*) Knock, knock! Knock, knock! (*Crosses to the inner door*) Anyone in?! Pegeen! Michael! . . . Grand . . .

He starts to pour two pints. PHILLY enters, also drunk.

PHILLY: What's the story?

JIMMY: There's no one here. They might be gone to have Michael's leg checked—up to the clinic or something.

PHILLY: Where's the African fella, but? What's his name?

JIMMY: I'd forgotten about him.

PHILLY: Security me hole. Fuckin' waster.

JIMMY: I'd be careful with the slagging, Philly.[45] That fella killed his own da.

PHILLY: I'm not his fuckin' da. He's not here an'anyway.

JIMMY: Here we go.

JIMMY puts pints on counter, adds a dash of Red Bull to each glass. They lean on the counter, one on each side.

PHILLY: Maybe the law caught up with him. Interpol or something.[46]

JIMMY: Wouldn't be surprised. That fella couldn't go ten words without bragging about the way he killed his da, with . . . the yam yoke.

PHILLY: A man can't be convicted by informing on himself.

45. *Slagging* is an informal Irish term for an insulting and critical comment.

46. Interpol is a common abbreviation for the International Criminal Police Organization, which facilitates international police cooperation and crime control.

JIMMY: What about your man up in Donegal? The fella in the cottage. He fuckin' grassed on himself.[47] And they shot the fuckin' head off him.

PHILLY: That was the Provos.[48] This is different. There has to be evidence.

JIMMY: There's the body—the da.

PHILLY: He'll be rotten by now—the heat over there an' all.

MALOMO passes window slowly.

JIMMY: No, listen. Supposing there's a fella over there digging—fuckin'—the yams, righ'? And supposing he flings up, say, the teeth, and bits of bone—

PHILLY: And his mobile phone.

JIMMY: Fuck off. The body, basically. In bits.

PHILLY: It'd make a brilliant film.

JIMMY: What?

PHILLY: No, listen. They're digging out the body. And it's ancient—it looks it, brown and that. Like those fuckers they found in the bog down the country, with the prehistoric hair gel and that. Remember?

MALOMO comes in, this time dressed in buba and soro (top and trousers) without the flowing agbada.

JIMMY: Yeah.

MALOMO: Excuse me.

PHILLY: What?

---

47. *Grassed* is an informal Irish term meaning "informing the police of criminal activity or plans."

48. The Provos is a common, informal term for the Provisional Irish Republican Army (IRA), an Irish republican paramilitary group, whose goal was to end British rule in Northern Ireland. The United States and the United Kingdom have declared the Provos a terrorist organization; in the Republic of Ireland, the organization remains illegal. The Provos have been on official cease-fire since 1997.

MALOMO: I am looking for the woman of the house.

PHILLY: She's not here.

JIMMY: Her da got the smack of a car.

PHILLY: She'll be back in a bit.

MALOMO: Oh. Thank you. I'll wait.

PHILLY: No problem. (*To JIMMY*) So, there's the old body. And they're digging and they're thinking, this is a great historical, archaeological, fuckin' discovery—and his fuckin' phone goes off.

JIMMY: And wha'?

PHILLY: So, the archi—the fuckin' archaeologists have to get out of the fuckin' hole cos it's a fuckin' crime scene now. So, they call in—

JIMMY: Vodafone.[49]

PHILLY: Fuck off a minute. They call in the state pathologist.

JIMMY: Dr. Marie Cassidy.[50]

PHILLY: Yeah.

JIMMY: Helen Mirren.[51]

PHILLY: Past it.

JIMMY: Angelina Jolie.[52]

PHILLY: Yeah, okay. Or your fuckin' woman—the legs—Julia Roberts; she'd be good.[53] And she has to piece the skull together, for forensic, like.

JIMMY: Tricky fuckin' job. Is she up to it—Julia?

PHILLY: What?

JIMMY: Piecing the skull together. Would you have a flashback?

PHILLY: What?

---

49. Vodafone is a leading telecommunications company in Europe and Africa.

50. Dr. Marie Cassidy (b. 1951) is a professor of forensic medicine at the Royal College of Surgeons of Ireland and Trinity College Dublin. From 2004 to 2018, she was the first female state pathologist of Ireland.

51. Dame Helen Mirren (b. 1945) is an English actress.

52. Angelina Jolie (b. 1975) is an American actress, filmmaker, and humanitarian.

53. Julia Roberts (b. 1967) is an American actress.

JIMMY: Like in that one, *CSI*.[54] You'd see what happened—the backstory. How the poor cunt got his skull smashed in the first place.

PHILLY: Hang on, whose fuckin' film is this?

MALOMO: Gentlemen. Apologies for interrupting your conversation.

PHILLY: What?

MALOMO: Did I hear you say someone's skull was smashed?

PHILLY: Yeah.

JIMMY: What about it?

MALOMO: This is an unprecedented coincidence.

JIMMY: What?

MALOMO (*removes cap*): Look at that.

PHILLY: Fuckin' hell. That's a lovely job.

JIMMY: You didn't get that done in an Irish hospital; that's for fuckin' sure.

PHILLY: What happened to you?

MALOMO: My son did it. Would you believe that?

JIMMY: Jaysis, that's mad.

PHILLY (*suspiciously*): How did that happen?

MALOMO: It is a tragic story really, and rather long. I doubt if you'd have time to listen.

JIMMY: Fair enough.

PHILLY: No, hang on. Will you have a drink?

Enter the WIDOW QUIN. She stands aghast, behind MALOMO.

PHILLY (*to JIMMY*): Give him a drink.

JIMMY: What?

MALOMO: A drink would be nice. A glass of Merlot, perhaps.

JIMMY (*after a quick glance at bottles*): No.

---

54. *CSI* is short for *Crime Scene Investigation*, an American crime drama television series.

WIDOW QUIN (*to MALOMO*): You're back. You didn't get far, did you?

MALOMO: Oh, there you are.

WIDOW QUIN: I thought you'd be well on your way by now.

MALOMO: I did buy a ticket. But the young man who checked it—an African, actually—assured me that nobody resembling my son had boarded the train. I checked it, myself, and the only black person on board was a woman with her two young children. So, I returned here, in the hope of finding him in this vicinity.

WIDOW QUIN: Sit down there, you poor man; you must be exhausted. It's muggy enough weather to be charging across the city. And then back again into the bargain.

MALOMO sits. WIDOW QUIN goes behind the counter.

WIDOW QUIN (*to PHILLY and JIMMY, quietly*): That poor man's off his rocker.

She opens, and pours, a small bottle of red wine. She hands MALOMO the glass.

WIDOW QUIN: There now. Let that seep through you.

MALOMO: Thank you very much.

WIDOW QUIN: Ah, no problem. (*To the men, quietly*) He was in earlier, and his head had been split by something that fell off a scaffold. Then he heard about Christy—the new security fella—and he started saying it was his son, that cracked his skull, you know. Ah, God love him.

PHILLY: Has he seen him yet, Chri—?

WIDOW QUIN: Shhh. No, he hasn't, and don't mention him, for fuck sake, or you'll be up in the box telling the court about the killing you witnessed. (*She goes to MALOMO.*) How's the poor head now, sweetheart?

MALOMO: It seems to be getting better, thank you.

WIDOW QUIN: Ah, grand. And how are you feeling?

MALOMO: A bit tired, I must admit . . . It is rather upsetting, actually. I mean, can you imagine? I believe I did my best, given the circumstances. I nurtured him, virtually from birth. His mother—my wife—died when he was very young, you see. But I made sure he wasn't in lack of anything. Best of schools—opportunities—and everything that should have opened doors for him. I protected him. . . . Perhaps I was a bit high-handed, at times. But I didn't want to spare the rod and spoil him. That was how I was brought up, under harsher conditions, of course. God knows, I did my best. And, after all that, what? He tried to murder me—my son. It is hard to believe, isn't it? But *kokoro to njefo inu efo lo ngbe.* The bug that feeds on the spinach lives *in* the spinach. Isn't it?

PHILLY (*to JIMMY*): He's not raving. (*To MALOMO*) Here, your son—what's he like?

WIDOW QUIN (*interrupting*): Is he the type of lad who could take on three hard men and send them running?

MALOMO: Didn't you hear what I said?! He is a coward, and lazy. Take on three men?! Three men indeed!

Commotion—excitement—outside.

MALOMO (*holding his hands to his head*): What in the name of God is that racket about?

WIDOW QUIN: They must have released them.

JIMMY: Who?

WIDOW QUIN: The Guards.

PHILLY: Released who?

WIDOW QUIN: The young lad and Pegeen and Michael. I was going to tell yis.

JIMMY: What young lad?

WIDOW QUIN: The security fella.

PHILLY: What about him?

WIDOW QUIN: You missed it.

JIMMY: What?

WIDOW QUIN: The fight. Outside. He decked the Rattler.

JIMMY and PHILLY (*disbelief*): What?!

Enter HONOR, SARAH, and SUSAN.

SUSAN: They're coming back.

PHILLY: Who's that?

SARAH: Pegeen and her da; they'll be here soon.

HONOR: The Guards didn't hold them for long.

JIMMY: What?

SARAH: You should have seen it, Jesus.

JIMMY: What?

SARAH: The fight.

PHILLY: Fuck this—hang on. What's the story?

HONOR takes out her mobile phone. They gather around her, as she plays footage of the fight.

HONOR: There was a fight. Here, look it.

SARAH: Look at this bit.

SUSAN: It's amazing.

SARAH: His foot.

SUSAN: Bang.

MALOMO: This is strange.

HONOR: No, watch.

JIMMY: That's—

PHILLY: It's the fuckin'—

HONOR: He's brilliant.

MALOMO: I would swear . . . this man fighting is Chris. But—it can't be.

WIDOW QUIN: Not at all.

HONOR (*re: the phone film*): I've run out.

SARAH: I got more, look it.

HONOR: Oh, I love this bit.

SARAH: Look.

SUSAN: Right . . . in the . . . bollix.

JIMMY: The Rattler's bollix. I don't believe this.

HONOR: Well, it happened. We seen it.

MALOMO: Who is this man? I must see.

He starts to move towards the window. WIDOW QUIN grabs his arm.

WIDOW QUIN: Wait and see this, look.

SARAH: It's over; that's it.

PHILLY (*nodding at phone*): What fuckin' happened?

HONOR: The Rattler, like, came after Mr. Flaherty and—

WIDOW QUIN: Hang on. Back a bit. (*Particularly to PHILLY and JIMMY*) You were there earlier, when the car swiped Michael, yeah?

JIMMY: Yeah, we brought him to the A&E.

WIDOW QUIN: And yis fucked off. (*To MALOMO*) Pardon— and yis left him there—

JIMMY: He was grand—

WIDOW QUIN: And yis left him and got back to your grieving. Meanwhile, the Rattler and his boys came after him, right into the hospital.

HONOR: At the exact same time that—

WIDOW QUIN: Shut up a minute, love—at the same time Pegeen arrived.

MALOMO (*to HONOR*): May I, perhaps, see that footage on your handset again, please?

WIDOW QUIN (*to MALOMO*): No; you'll like this bit.

HONOR continues to show the footage to MALOMO.

WIDOW QUIN (*continuing*): So, Pegeen got him out, out the back way. How she did it, I don't know; she's a great girl. She got him into her little car and back here. But they were

right behind her. All sorts of skidding and braking. She got
poor Michael out of the car—

SARAH: Yeah, yeah; we saw this.

SUSAN: We were at the fuckin' bus stop.

HONOR: She kind of dragged him—

SARAH: In here.

SUSAN: We thought it was the law after them. They drove up
on the path and all.

MALOMO: It is him.

SARAH: But it wasn't.

HONOR: It was the Rattler and them.

SUSAN: And they ran up to the door (*pointing*)—that one.
There were three of them, like.

HONOR: And they were pushing—

MALOMO: It is my son.

SARAH: And they were at the door; they were pushing it, like—

MALOMO: It's him.

SUSAN: And it opened—

SARAH: And they were just baling in—

HONOR: And it happened.

SUSAN: He burst out—

JIMMY: Who did?

SUSAN: Christy.

HONOR: And he just knew who to go for—

*The girls start to reenact. SUSAN is the Rattler; HONOR mock
headbutts her.*

SARAH: I was still going for my mobile.

SUSAN: The Rattler—he staggered but he didn't fall.

HONOR: Then Christy smacked the second one—right in the
face.

SARAH: And he kicked the last one, the Rattler's cousin; he was
falling back before I saw it.

SUSAN: And the Rattler came at him again, and I think he had a gun—

HONOR: He did, in his jacket.

SUSAN: He was getting it out—

HONOR: But Christy grabbed his arm—

SARAH: But the other fella was coming at him—

SUSAN: The Rattler pulled his arm back from Christy—

SARAH: For the gun, like.

HONOR: And you could tell, he thought he had him—

SUSAN: But Christy—

SARAH: Christy's foot came up and he got the first fella—

HONOR: In the chest, like—

SUSAN: And—

HONOR: No, listen. Before the foot came down, I swear, his other foot went up and—

SUSAN: He got the Rattler right in the—

HONOR and SUSAN: Bollix.

MALOMO: No. It can't be my son.

Noise from outside: a car.

WIDOW QUIN: Then the Guards came, but they were too late, of course. The gun was gone and it was all over.

HONOR: And they took them all down to the station.

SARAH: They're back, listen.

SUSAN: Deadly.

The girls exit. JIMMY and PHILLY move to the window. MALOMO also moves to the window, and the WIDOW still holds his arm.

WIDOW QUIN: Mind yourself, sweetheart.

JIMMY (*looking out*): There they are now.

MALOMO (*looking out*): It is Chris—my son! By the stars of heaven!

PHILLY: Your man?

WIDOW QUIN: No, love—

MALOMO makes for the door. The WIDOW QUIN deftly trips him; he falls against the wall. She helps him up, but won't let him move on.

WIDOW QUIN: You're exhausted; poor man.

PHILLY: Let him out.

WIDOW QUIN: Stay quiet, will you. (*To MALOMO*) It's not your son. (*To PHILLY*) Give us a hand here, or there'll be murder. And we'll have the law back on us.

JIMMY: Here.

JIMMY holds/restrains MALOMO with the WIDOW.

MALOMO: Please, let me out! Wait till I get my hands on him!

WIDOW QUIN (*shaking him*): Listen here! It's not your son! You saw, yourself—the fight in him. That fella outside is doing a line with the girl in here—the owner's daughter. And all the girls—they're daft about him.

She and JIMMY let go of MALOMO.

MALOMO: They are daft about who?! Him?! Christopher? This is unbelievable. Daft! The females in this place are daft, indeed.

WIDOW QUIN: Calm down; hold on. He's a different fella, I'm telling you. It's the knock on your head. You need a rest, a little lie-down.

MALOMO (*pointing at window, insistent*): I saw my son!

WIDOW QUIN: But you said it yourself. He's a coward, and hopeless with young ones.

MALOMO: Could my eyes be deceiving me? This is all rather confusing. The voice is definitely Jacob's but the skin is

Esau's . . . Perhaps I should rest a while. (*Going to door*) I must locate a taxi.

WIDOW QUIN: Look it; you're exhausted. I've a spare bed; you can lie down for a while.

MALOMO: You are right; I am exhausted.

WIDOW QUIN: Sure, that's why your imagination's all over the place. Lie down for a bit and you'll be grand.

MALOMO: Mrs. Quin. Thank you for your kind consideration.

WIDOW QUIN: Ah, no bother. We're out this way. It's only up a bit of a stairs.

She leads MALOMO to the back door.

PHILLY (*to the WIDOW QUIN, quietly*): You're up to something, aren't you? (*She doesn't answer*) Aren't you?

WIDOW QUIN (*viciously*): Fuck off, you.

She exits, after MALOMO.

JIMMY: What's the story?

PHILLY: I'm not certain. But I'll tell you one thing; we haven't seen the end of this.

We hear a burst of voices, and see figures on the CCTV. Enter CHRISTOPHER, PEGEEN, SUSAN, SARAH, and HONOR. The girls photograph each other with CHRISTOPHER. PEGEEN enjoys this. The girls sing.

GIRLS: "One Git Malomo—there's only one Git Malomo." Etc.

PEGEEN (*cheerfully*): Fuckin' eejits.

HONOR: God, he's massive.

SARAH: He should be in a group.

SUSAN: Can you sing, Christy?

CHRISTOPHER: My voice has been complimented a number of times, actually.

HONOR: Great. You stand there—there. And we'll be behind
you, like this.

SARAH: Nice one.

PHILLY: Where's Michael?

PEGEEN: I dropped him off at Mrs. Keogh's. He had to talk to
her.

PHILLY: Is he alright?

PEGEEN: He's grand; he'll be grand.

*HONOR organises the girls; they are ranked, very close to
CHRISTOPHER.*

HONOR: What'll we sing, but? (*To CHRISTOPHER*) Were you
not scared shitless when the Rattler went for his gun?

SUSAN: "I Believe I Can Fly."[55]

CHRISTOPHER (*to HONOR*): Not really. Actually, you know
what it reminded me of? The feeling I had as my dad lifted
the bottle shortly before I struck him that deadly blow.

PHILLY: Ah, yeah. Tell us again.

SUSAN & SARAH (*singing*): "I believe I can fly . . . I believe I can
touch the sky . . ." etc.

*HONOR joins in. She leans into CHRISTOPHER. PEGEEN has
had enough.*

PEGEEN: Out. Come on. We've work to do. Come on.

HONOR: We'll have a drink.

PEGEEN: Over twenty-ones. You'll need ID. Out.

*As they leave, they continue to sing to CHRISTOPHER. HONOR
blows him a kiss. They exit.*

---

55. "I Believe I Can Fly" is a song by R. Kelly (b. 1967), from the soundtrack
of the film *Space Jam* (1996).

PEGEEN (*to the men*): You, too. Come on. Out.

PHILLY: We're over twenty-one.

PEGEEN: Go on. Go home and sleep it off.

JIMMY: Fair enough; I'm a bit knackered.

PHILLY: Okay, right. But we'll be back in a bit.

PEGEEN: I can't wait.

PHILLY: One thing, but. (*To CHRISTOPHER*) Just how dead was your da?

PEGEEN: Out!

The men exit.

CHRISTOPHER: What did he mean?

PEGEEN: Don't mind him; he's only jealous. (*Proudly*) There's no stopping you, Christopher Malomo. You have them eating out of your hand. They all love you.

CHRISTOPHER: Yep, they may all love me. But it is only one woman I love.

PEGEEN: Who's that?

CHRISTOPHER: Can't you guess? I have to tell you?

PEGEEN: Yeah. You'll have to tell me.

CHRISTOPHER: It is you.

PEGEEN: Just as well for yourself.

CHRISTOPHER: Will you marry me?

PEGEEN: For fuck sake, Christopher!

CHRISTOPHER: What is wrong?

PEGEEN: I only met you last night.

CHRISTOPHER: You have heard about love at first sight, haven't you?

PEGEEN: Yeah, but—

CHRISTOPHER: But what? You don't want to be with me?

PEGEEN: No, I do. I do.

CHRISTOPHER: So—

PEGEEN: But—

CHRISTOPHER: But what?

PEGEEN: You'll be going back to Nigeria and your other life, when the heat is off and the body's rotten.

CHRISTOPHER: What life? What other life? I'm not going back. And nothing on earth will make me go back. This is my life now, here—with you. Pegeen, we shall walk hand in hand along the River Liffey and . . . and Blanchardstown Shopping Centre. We are near the sea, yes?

PEGEEN: Yeah, not too far.

CHRISTOPHER: We can walk by the sea and watch the sun go down.

PEGEEN: Sorry, Christopher, wrong coast.

CHRISTOPHER: Wrong coast?

PEGEEN: This is the east.

CHRISTOPHER: Oh. Even better, we can watch it come up. We can stay up all night and wait for it.

PEGEEN: And what'll we do while we're waiting?

CHRISTOPHER: I will close your eyelids, one at a time, so you can feel my two hands stretched around you. (*Touching each place with a finger*) I will plant a kiss on your forehead, each eyelid, the tip of your nose, each earlobe, each cheek, your chin, and then, finally, and very gently, your puckered lips.

PEGEEN (*eyes stayed closed*): My wha'?

CHRISTOPHER (*keeping his finger tip on her lips*): And I will continue to kiss you, until I feel pity for God the Creator who sits alone on His heavenly throne.

PEGEEN (*opening her eyes*): I like the sound of that.

CHRISTOPHER: Listen . . . We tenderly kiss. I whisper sweet something into your wetted mouth. As the tresses of your hair mingle with the flowers of the earth.

PEGEEN (*warmly*): And what is it I have, Christopher, that'd make a match for someone like you, with all your guts and eloquence?

CHRISTOPHER: I have never been this way before, never—

PEGEEN: Yeah, go on.

CHRISTOPHER: With you beside me, anything is possible.

PEGEEN: We'll be able to rule these streets. The whole of Dublin.

CHRISTOPHER: The whole of Ireland.

PEGEEN: And no fucker will stop us; we'll take care of them— the lot of them. (*A beat*) But maybe we're only talking . . . I don't think this place will be big enough for you—this country, like. America, maybe.

CHRISTOPHER: You could be right. But, even then, you can come with me.

PEGEEN: I don't know, Christopher—

CHRISTOPHER: Okay, let's cross that bridge when we get there. (*Holding her*) I am here now and that is all that matters.

PEGEEN: I'm finding it hard to believe this.

CHRISTOPHER: Well, it is rather unbelievable. But it is real. When I set out that day, I didn't realize that every step I took was leading me to this moment.

PEGEEN: And I didn't know you were on your way. Like, I had different plans, kind of. I never thought I'd feel like this, for someone who isn't even Irish.

CHRISTOPHER: There you go. When man plans, God laughs. If I was told a few days ago that I would feel like this about a woman who is not from my country—my tribe, I would have laughed. But here I am.

PEGEEN: Tribe. Jesus . . . Well, the heart's a wonder. My granny used to say that. Now I know what she fuckin' meant.

There's a noise outside: a car horn.

PEGEEN: That's probably my da. We'll tell him—no. We can tell him after he's had a rest.

They separate. MICHAEL enters, on crutches. SEAN is right be-
hind him. MICHAEL goes straight to CHRISTOPHER.

MICHAEL: Fair fucks to you, son. You saved the fuckin' day back
there. I won't forget it, don't worry. You'll be looked after.

CHRISTOPHER: That's alright, Mr. Flaherty. How is your leg,
by the way?

MICHAEL: Fuckin' killing me, but not too bad. I'm alive and
that's the main thing, thanks to you.

CHRISTOPHER: It was nothing.

MICHAEL (*slapping him on the back*): Fuckin' sure. God, you're
the hard man. Too hard for this place. Am I right, Sean?

SEAN doesn't speak, but nods once, anxiously.

MICHAEL: That's right. (*To CHRISTOPHER, re: SEAN*)
That's my future son-in-law and he won't want a chap like
you hanging around the premises. We'll find something else
for you to do. Something a bit more challenging. (*Patting
his arm*) And rewarding.

CHRISTOPHER: Did you say your son-in-law?

MICHAEL: That's right. Finalised this morning; thank Jaysis.
(*To PEGEEN, thumbs up*) It's all arranged with Sean's ma,
love. Great woman.

PEGEEN: What's arranged?

MICHAEL: What? The fuckin' wedding, of course. (*Winking at
CHRISTOPHER*) And in the nick of time.

PEGEEN: You've missed your nick of time, Da. I'm going with
Christopher.

MICHAEL and SEAN: What?!

PEGEEN: I'm going with Christopher.

MICHAEL (*loudly, with horror*): You're fuckin' not—you're not
fuckin' serious. (*Whispering fiercely to PEGEEN*) We'll
never be able to control him. He killed his da! The blood is
still on him.

PEGEEN: D'you really want me married to (*pointing at SEAN*) him, a chinless muppet with no guts or fine words in him at all?

MICHAEL (*still fiercely quiet*): Are you out of your fuckin' mind? Are you trying to destroy us? You're marrying Sean—it's a done deal. We *need* the Keoghs. You fuckin' know that.

PEGEEN: I've changed me mind, Da.

MICHAEL (*gasping, and sinking into a chair*): For fuck sake— me heart. Jesus, Pegeen. Gracie Keogh will kill us—she will. Yeh bitch, yeh. (*Turning his head, up, to SEAN*) Here, you, are you not fuckin' jealous?

SEAN: I wouldn't want to be jealous of a man who committed the crime of parricide.[56]

PEGEEN: See? I can't marry that.

MICHAEL: For fuck sake.

SEAN: Mr. Flaherty, my ma's not going to be happy.

PEGEEN (*to SEAN*): Jesus, I'm glad I didn't get stuck with you.

SEAN: And you'd prefer to be with *him*?! He's nobody, Pegeen. He's black. He's a Nigerian, for the love of God.

PEGEEN: And he's lovely. And look at you. D'you think I'd go with you now? You're like a chicken. You even look like one. One of those small little chickens you get in Tescos— two in the one pack, like.[57]

SEAN: What's happening, Pegeen? Think of your da—the families. You're throwing it all away, the whole thing—your whole future. I can give you whatever you want.

PEGEEN: Oh, you're too good for me, Sean. You should be off with Paris Hilton or some rich bitch like that.[58] She'd be your match. So good luck to you.

---

56. Parricide is killing of one's father.

57. Tesco is a grocery store chain in Ireland and the United Kingdom.

58. Paris Hilton (b. 1981) is an American businesswoman, model, singer, actress, and DJ.

She moves closer to CHRISTOPHER.

SEAN: Won't you listen to me—

He moves toward her.

CHRISTOPHER: One more step from you, sir, and murder will be added to my list of deeds today.

MICHAEL (*standing up*): Murder?! Are you fuckin' mad?! The Guards will be sniffing all over the place, upstairs and all. (*To PEGEEN*) You won't be marrying anyone if they find some of the stuff we have here. Not for a long time, missis. (*To the men*) Go outside or somewhere else if you want to fight and kill each other.

He pushes SEAN toward CHRISTOPHER. SEAN shakes himself free and gets behind MICHAEL. They struggle.

SEAN: Fight him yourself, or all deals are off. I'm phoning me ma.

MICHAEL: Go on; be a fuckin' man.

SEAN: No way am I fighting him. I'd prefer to stay a bachelor than face that savage.

CHRISTOPHER pulls a crutch away from MICHAEL. MICHAEL falls. CHRISTOPHER holds the crutch like a weapon he intends using.

CHRISTOPHER (*to SEAN*): What did you say?!

He follows SEAN as SEAN retreats. MICHAEL, from the floor, holds up the second crutch for SEAN.

MICHAEL: There you go, Sean.

PEGEEN: Da!

PEGEEN takes the crutch from MICHAEL, and slides it across the floor, away from the action. CHRISTOPHER still holds the crutch, ready, but he does not strike.

PEGEEN (*to SEAN*): Get out.
SEAN: I didn't say anything.
PEGEEN: Get out.
SEAN: I didn't mean—
PEGEEN: No. Out.

SEAN exits. CHRISTOPHER lowers the crutch and steps towards MICHAEL. He offers his hand to help him up.

CHRISTOPHER: That man is not suitable for your daughter, Mr. Flaherty. Pegeen and I are going to be together. Give us a chance and you will never regret it.
PEGEEN: There's no going back, da. It's me and Christopher. We'll stay here, or we'll go.

MICHAEL stands up.

MICHAEL: Ah Jesus, I'm in no fit state for making decisions. Look it. (*To CHRISTOPHER*) There's a lot of men would be scared having you under their roofs. But I'd prefer to take that risk and see a load of little grandsons growing up big and bold like you—(*to PEGEEN*)—instead of the weedy little gets you'd have for Sean Keogh. (*To CHRISTOPHER*) You're in, son. But remember, the both of yis, we've lost the Keoghs and there's unfinished business with The Rattler and his pals. We've a lot of hard work ahead of us. There'll be blood; there'll be killing. But you're a lovely couple and you'll go far.
CHRISTOPHER: Thank you.

Hubbub outside. MALOMO rushes in, followed by WIDOW QUIN. He makes a rush at CHRISTOPHER, knocks him down, and begins to kick and hit him with his walking stick, mouthing invective in his mother tongue.

PEGEEN (*trying to pull him back, hitting him*): Stop it! Who the fuck are you?!

MALOMO (*continuing to hit*): His father, God help me! And mind your language, young woman.

PEGEEN stops hitting; she steps back. We see one of the girls looking in the window.

PEGEEN: You're not dead.

MALOMO (*still hitting and kicking*): Thank God for His little mercies; I am alive and kicking. (*To CHRISTOPHER*) You think you could snuff life out of me with the tap of a pestle?

PEGEEN (*glaring at CHRISTOPHER*): It was all lies! Letting on you killed him!

PHILLY, JIMMY, and the girls come in the front door.

CHRISTOPHER (*grabbing MALOMO's stick*): He's not my father. He's a psychiatric patient! (*Pointing to the WIDOW QUIN*) Ask her. She has seen him before.

PHILLY: No, he's not. He's no mentler.

HONOR (*to CHRISTOPHER*): You're only a liar.

CHRISTOPHER (*indicating MALOMO*): He is the liar; lying down, stretched out, pretending he was dead.

MALOMO: Did you check my pulse? He was gone before I hit the ground. Lying down, indeed.

PEGEEN: And we were thinking he was a hard man. And he did nothing to earn it, except tap his da's head with the yoke, and run away in a sweat. (*To CHRISTOPHER*) Get out of here.

CHRISTOPHER (*piteously*): You saw what I did today. Didn't you? Get this mad man off me—Pegeen—please!—do you want him to kick me to death?

PEGEEN: I can't believe you're the same fella I fell for—Jesus—half an hour ago. (*To MALOMO*) Get him out of here—please. The fucker. I can't look at him.

MALOMO (*to CHRISTOPHER*): Rise up now to retribution, and come with me, young man.

JIMMY: There's the fella who thought he was taking over.

SUSAN: Kill him now, mister.

CHRISTOPHER (*getting up*): How did you get here? Why did you come after me? Why don't you leave me alone, for God's sake?

MALOMO: Why don't I leave you alone? Because the evil that men do lives after them. (*Pushing him*) Move.

CHRISTOPHER: What, in the name of Almighty God—

MALOMO: Stop troubling the Lord God, young man. Remember, He is quick to anger.

CHRISTOPHER (*to WIDOW QUIN*): Mrs. Quin—please, do something.

WIDOW QUIN: I've tried my best. You're on your own now, sweetheart.

CHRISTOPHER (*looking around in desperation*): So I have to go back? To that hell of a life? Suffering and smiling. (*Shaking off MALOMO*) For the rest of my life?

SARAH: Ask Pegeen to help you. She might change her mind.

CHRISTOPHER: I will not. The window to her soul is closed, and I am outside of it. She is too good for me now.

PEGEEN (*to MALOMO, afraid she will cry*): Take him out of here, or we'll fuckin' do him.

MALOMO (*grabbing CHRISTOPHER*): You see? You've overstayed your welcome.

He leads/pulls CHRISTOPHER towards the door.

> PEGEEN (*half laughing, through her tears*): That's it. There
> he goes. The fuckin' liar, playing the hero and the hard
> man.
> CHRISTOPHER (*to MALOMO, shaking him off*): Let go of me!
> JIMMY: Here we go.

The girls take out their mobile phones.

> MALOMO (*making a grab at CHRISTOPHER*): Who are you
> talking to, like that? Come here!
> CHRISTOPHER (*more threateningly*): I said, let go of me!
> MALOMO: I shall. When you have learnt your lesson.
> HONOR: This is great.
> PHILLY: My money's on the ol' lad.
> JIMMY: I'll take it off you.
> SUSAN: Go on—hit him—get started.
> CHRISTOPHER (*to the crowd*): Shut up! All of you! This is all
> your fault. Turning me into a hero because of my story. You
> know what? I'm beginning to think it is better to be lonely
> than to be in the company of idiots like you.
> PHILLY: What did he fuckin' say?!

MALOMO takes a step towards CHRISTOPHER.

> CHRISTOPHER: Stay where you are! This time I will do it! Be-
> lieve me.

He grabs one of MICHAEL's crutches.

> MICHAEL: For fuck sake.
> SARAH: He's going mad.
> HONOR: Watch out.

They step back, but continue to film as they talk.

MICHAEL: Christ, you're some clown.
CHRISTOPHER: Who is a clown? Me? Today, I have coined
    words as well as the greatest poets. Andrew Marvell.
    Wordsworth. Keats.[59] And I *decked* your Rattler and his
    cronies. Didn't I—?
MALOMO: Shut your trap and let's go.
CHRISTOPHER: I'm going, but I'll kill you first.

*He runs at MALOMO with the crutch and chases him out the door.
He is followed by ALL, including MICHAEL.*

MICHAEL: Hang on, for fuck sake.

*There is a great noise outside, then a yell, and dead silence for a
beat. CHRISTOPHER comes in, half dazed, and sits. WIDOW
QUIN hurries in.*

WIDOW QUIN: They're turning against you, sweetheart. Come
    on, or they'll fuckin' hang you.
CHRISTOPHER: Now I am certain Pegeen will love and respect
    me, as she did before.
WIDOW QUIN (*impatiently*): Come on to the back door. I won't
    have you on my conscience. Listen—
CHRISTOPHER: No.
WIDOW QUIN: Ah, look it—you'll be no worse off than you
    were last night. And now you'll have *two* murders you can
    tell all the girls about.
CHRISTOPHER: I'm not leaving Pegeen.

59. Andrew Marvell (1621–78) was an English metaphysical poet. William
Wordsworth (1770–1850) was an English Romantic poet. John Butler Keats (1795–
1821) was also an English Romantic poet.

WIDOW QUIN (*more impatiently*): There are young ones like
   her all over the place. Come on—you'll find girls better than
   that one wherever you go.
CHRISTOPHER: It's only Pegeen that my heart beats for. You
   can present me with a long line of the most beautiful girls in
   Ireland—naked! beautiful!—I am not interested.

SARAH runs in.

SARAH: They're going to do him—they're going to bring him
   up the mountains.
WIDOW QUIN (*to CHRISTOPHER*): I told you.

*SARAH starts to remove her pink hooded Britney Spears–style
tracksuit.*[60] *The word "BITCH" is printed across the backside.
SARAH puts on CHRISTOPHER's suit jacket. WIDOW QUIN
dresses CHRISTOPHER in the tracksuit. As they do this—*

SARAH: Put these on him—quickly—and we might be able to
   get him away.
WIDOW QUIN: Good idea. There's not much else we can do.
   Give us a hand.
SARAH: Okay. (*Looking at CCTV*) They're not coming in yet.
   They're scared of him.
WIDOW QUIN: We can get him out the back.
SARAH: The pink looks nice on him.
WIDOW QUIN: Stand up, sweetheart.

CHRISTOPHER stands, still dazed.

CHRISTOPHER: You don't expect me to leave now, do you? After
   I have actually proven myself a hero? God forbid; bad thing.

---

60. Britney Spears (b. 1981) is an American singer, songwriter, and dancer.

WIDOW QUIN puts the pink hood over his head.

> WIDOW QUIN (*quietly, to SARAH*): He's raving a bit; he'll be
> grand. (*The WIDOW QUIN and SARAH take a sleeve each.*)
> Come on now, Christopher, and we'll get you out of here.
> CHRISTOPHER (*suddenly resisting*): I said, I'm not leaving, or
> are you deaf?! You want to abduct me, ehn! You are jealous
> of Pegeen, aren't you?! I know your type. Get out of here!

He snatches up a stool and threatens them with it.

> WIDOW QUIN: Ah here, fuck yeh—enough. We've done our bit.
> (*Sees men on CCTV*) We'll go out the back way. I've had to
> watch one man die. I'm not going to watch another.

*She goes out with SARAH. MICHAEL, SEAN, PHILLY, JIMMY,
and PEGEEN come in. They stay near the door. MICHAEL has
both crutches. SEAN carries a length of rope with a noose. CHRIS-
TOPHER sits on the stool, exhausted, unaware of the others.*

> MICHAEL (*quietly, lifting the crutch*): There isn't much weight in
> these things. Are you sure he's dead?
> PHILLY: There was no pulse left, an'anyway. He's done it right
> this time.
> MICHAEL: Positive?
> PHILLY: Yeah, he's gone.
> MICHAEL (*to JIMMY*): Cover him up for now.

Exit JIMMY.

> MICHAEL: We'll put the body in the boot with this fella—
> bury them both.[61] Look at him: he's away off in his

---

61. The *boot* is an Irish and British term for the trunk of a car.

head somewhere. Come on. (*Steps aside, to SEAN*) Go up behind him and you can get the rope over his head, no bother.

PHILLY: Off you go.

SEAN: Bad idea, Mr. Flaherty. He'll go madder if he sees me.

PEGEEN: I'll do it.

She takes the rope and goes to CHRISTOPHER. The others follow. She drops the noose over CHRISTOPHER's head and shoulders. They tighten it around him, trapping his arms at the elbows.

CHRISTOPHER: What the hell is this?!

SEAN (*triumphantly*): Make your peace with God, Brother. You're going for a drive.

CHRISTOPHER: A drive?

MICHAEL: Sorry about this, son. It's nothing personal. But we can't have a murderer around here, with the evidence out in the fuckin' car park. We'll have the law on top of us in no time. So, make it easy on yourself and come on.

CHRISTOPHER: I'm not moving. (*To PEGEEN*) What do you think now, Pegeen? You witnessed it this time. I did it in the presence of all.

PEGEEN: You want to know what I think? I think you're a fuckin' eejit. Listen to this, Christopher. There's a huge difference—right?—between a big story and a dirty deed. A huge fuckin' difference. (*To the men*) Take him out of here, or we'll be doing serious time for what he's after doing.

PHILLY takes a gun from his belt, behind his back. He points it at CHRISTOPHER's head. PEGEEN lights a cigarette. JIMMY reenters.

PHILLY: Let's go.

CHRISTOPHER (*to PEGEEN*): I can't believe this. You are going to let them execute me?

JIMMY and SEAN pull the rope. CHRISTOPHER resists.

JIMMY: Come on, for fuck sake.
CHRISTOPHER: Pegeen!

PHILLY hits him across the head with the gun. CHRISTOPHER falls.

MICHAEL: It shouldn't have come to this.

JIMMY and SEAN pull CHRISTOPHER across the floor. PHILLY goes to the door to check the coast is clear.

CHRISTOPHER: Let me go! Let me go! Tell them to let me go, Pegeen. Please. I promise—I will depart from here. And go somewhere—anywhere. Far away from you. Please. You'll never see me again.
PEGEEN: Yeah, yeah. And what do we do with the blood and the body, and your big mouth? Get him out of here, hurry up.

CHRISTOPHER manages to free his hands, and grabs a screwed-down high table leg. He curls himself around it.

PHILLY: Let go or I'll take your fuckin' head off.
MICHAEL: Not here. (*To SEAN*) Get the rope around his neck. That'll work.
SEAN: I don't want to go too near him, like.
PEGEEN: For fuck sake.

She gets down on her hunkers, inhales the cigarette, then points it over CHRISTOPHER's leg. She waits till she has his attention.

PEGEEN (*after exhaling*): Let go of the fuckin' table.
CHRISTOPHER: What are you going to do?! Torture me?! (*His voice rising; stronger*) Now I know your kind! I know I'm going to die. But one of you will die first!

SEAN: Hurry up, Pegeen.

CHRISTOPHER (*almost cheerfully, mimicking SEAN*): "Hurry up, Pegeen." (*To SEAN, who crouches near him*) Let me get my hands on you—any of you—and you will soon be with my father—in hell.

SEAN: I've done nothing!

CHRISTOPHER: Exactly! You have done nothing. But I will die as I have lived!

He lets go of the table and grabs SEAN's leg and bites it. The cigarette is knocked from PEGEEN's hand.

SEAN (*shrieking*): Me leg! Me fuckin' leg! He's bitten me! Oh, God, I'll be infected! I'm going to die!

CHRISTOPHER (*delighted with himself, still holding the leg*): Of course! And you will be going straight to hell—to await my arrival. I am sure Satan has not encountered many men like me, who have killed their dad in Nigeria, and in Ireland too.

MALOMO, dazed and blood-soaked, comes in on all fours and looks on, unnoticed.

PHILLY (*to PEGEEN*): Just burn him, for fuck sake.

PEGEEN (*coming over*): Ah, fuck this.

She burns CHRISTOPHER's leg.

CHRISTOPHER (*kicking and screaming*): Ye! Ye! Ese mi o![62]

He lets go of SEAN and they drag him towards the door.

JIMMY (*seeing MALOMO*): Will you look what's come in?

---

62. *Ye! Ye! Ese mi o!* is Yoruba for "Oh my God! God Almighty! My leg!"

They let go of CHRISTOPHER. As he gets up onto his knees, he comes face-to-face with MALOMO.

CHRISTOPHER: Have you come to be killed the third time, or what in God's name is your problem?

MALOMO: Why have they tied you?

CHRISTOPHER: They are going to kill me, because I killed you.

MALOMO: Jungle justice?

CHRISTOPHER: On the ball, Dad.

MICHAEL: No offence, lads. But we couldn't have the Guards sniffing around.

MALOMO: Is that so?

MICHAEL: We've a business to run—merchandise. You know, yourself—and what would happen to my daughter if I was implicated in your row?

MALOMO (*grimly, loosening CHRISTOPHER*): To be honest with you, I don't give a damn about you or your daughter. Right this moment, my son and I will be on our way. And I can assure you that we shall have lots of fun, telling the stories of the villainy of Ireland and the fools that people it. (*To CHRISTOPHER*) Come on, son. Let's go home.

CHRISTOPHER: Home? With you?

MALOMO nods, once.

CHRISTOPHER: Fine. But you lead the way. I will be right behind you. And henceforth, Dad, I am my own boss. No more *boy boy*. (*Indicating with his hand*) Go ahead.

MALOMO: You are not serious, are you? You want me go ahead of you?

CHRISTOPHER: Dad, please, don't let us argue. Just do as I say.

MALOMO walks towards door and looks back over his shoulder at CHRISTOPHER. CHRISTOPHER pick up his suitcase.

CHRISTOPHER: My passport, please.

PEGEEN goes behind counter, finds passport, and brings it to CHRISTOPHER.

CHRISTOPHER: Thank you.
MALOMO: Jesus Christ. (*With a broad smile*) This is fantastic.

MALOMO exits. As CHRISTOPHER speaks, he retrieves his hat and puts the passport into its inside pocket.

CHRISTOPHER: I'll be on my way now. We meet to part and we part to meet. The blessings of God on you all. For, after all's said and done, you have transformed me into a *hard* man. From now and forever more, I am the master of my own destiny. (*Sardonically*) Cheerio.

He puts on his hat and exits.

MICHAEL: We'll have a bit of peace now an'anyway. (*To PEGEEN, concerned*) Alright, love?

PEGEEN doesn't answer. She tries to light a cigarette, but can't get the lighter to work; she is visibly shaken.

MICHAEL: Don't worry. I'll phone Gracie Keogh in the morning.
PEGEEN: Fuck off!

She sobs.

Curtain.

1

Identity, Audience, and Power Dynamics in *The Playboy of the Western World— A New Version,* 2007

Kelly Matthews

In September 2019 I embarked on teaching an Irish literature survey course within the Honors program at my regional public university, Framingham State University (about twenty miles west of Boston). I knew my students would be drawn from a range of academic disciplines, with most concentrating in the sciences and business-related fields; this might be the last literature course they would ever take. I also knew they would represent a range of racial and ethnic backgrounds, as my campus has increasingly become more diverse in the decade I have taught there, to the point that nearly half our current students are people of color. And I knew for certain that nearly all of them had been impacted, as had I, by hate crimes that had rocked our campus the prior year, when officers of our Black Student Union found the N word scrawled across their dorm room doors. The university's tepid response to these incidents was met with impassioned demonstrations, public discussions, and other forms of student and faculty activism in which I had been a vocal participant. In conversations with students protesting racism on our campus, I heard demands for increased diversity in our curriculum and increased discussion of difference within our classrooms. Meanwhile, in the larger conversations that engulfed the United States during the same time period, our president engaged in xenophobic rhetoric that manifested in border walls, Muslim bans, and family separations, dramatic enactments of the anti-immigrant policies that dominated our daily news.

The time seemed ripe to update my Irish literature syllabus. In my teaching, I have long considered Ireland an appropriate focal point for broader discussions of identity, diversity, and globalization, which are not new concepts in Ireland, nor anywhere else. I hope that the more we can connect Irish studies to present questions facing society—in Ireland as well as the United States—the more we can persuade young people of all backgrounds to study Ireland as a lens through which to gain perspective on where they come from and where they are going. My background as a former resident (and naturalized citizen) of Northern Ireland has pointed my teaching of Irish literature, especially in general education offerings like this survey course, toward discussions of social difference and writers' responses to political upheaval and violence. In 2019 I foregrounded these issues by posing a framing question for my entire syllabus: "What is the role of the writer in times of social change?" I outlined three major ideas that would connect to all our readings, from the Ulster Cycle to Jonathan Swift to Seamus Heaney and beyond: identity (of individuals, groups, and writers); audience (who are this writer's readers?); and social engagement (how is a work received, in the writer's own time, and since?).

I had heard of the 2007 *The Playboy of the Western World—A New Version*, co-written by Bisi Adigun and Roddy Doyle, with the "playboy" character Christy Mahon recast as a new immigrant to Dublin from Nigeria. It seemed a perfect text to center questions of social engagement and Irish identity in a contemporary context, and to deepen students' understanding of writers' power to influence public debates. Through academic contacts, Bisi Adigun generously granted permission for my students to purchase copies of the unpublished script as part of our required course readings. As usual, the syllabus proceeded chronologically, so that students would be able to examine the self-referential nature of Irish literature: the trope of the hero, for example, apparent in the Ulster and Red Branch cycles and later celebrated by William Butler Yeats in Celtic Revival poems about Cuchulainn, Oisín, and the Sídhe. Students read *The Playboy of the Western World* by John Millington Synge and watched a recording of a full performance by the Druid Theatre, in which the physicality of Synge's humor takes center stage. The class debated whether Christy Mahon was a hero, or whether Synge was mocking the heroic ideal, and we carried those debates forward as we moved on to discuss some of James Joyce's antiheroic epiphanies in *Dubliners*, followed by readings from more recent decades in Northern Ireland, and, at last, by Adigun and Doyle's ambitious update of Synge's tale, their 2007 adaptation of *The Playboy of the Western World*.

Reading the play in our contemporary American context gave added resonance to its title. In Synge's 1907 script, the western world represents an idealized dream of emigration, a place where new arrivals to the United States "have golden chains and shiny coats" and ride on horseback "with the ladies of the land."[1] Economic migration provides a mass-scale backdrop to Christy Mahon's individual wanderings, grounded by the factual landscape of constant outbound Irish migration in the early twentieth century. When Sean Keogh feels threatened by Christy's flirtation with Pegeen Mike, he offers him "the half of a ticket to the Western States,"[2] and when Widow Quin is interrogated by Christy's father as to whether she has seen his son, she replies, "There's harvest hundreds do be passing these days for the Sligo boat"[3]—a reference to the Sligo Steam Navigation Company, founded by Yeats's grandfather William Pollexfen, which ferried thousands of Irish emigrants to Liverpool for embarkation to North America. When parallel moments arise in Adigun and Doyle's script, Sean Keogh offers a one-way ticket to Belfast to help with Christopher's asylum application, since his first point of entry was

---

1. John Millington Synge, *The Playboy of the Western World: A Comedy in Three Acts* (Boston: John W. Luce, 1911), 61.

2. Synge, *Playboy of the Western World*, 61.

3. Synge, *Playboy of the Western World*, 66.

through London.[4] The contemporary Widow Quin's dissembling line, when asked by Chief Clement Malomo whether she has seen young Christopher, is "Ah, sure, we have all sorts of Africans around here now. It's hard to know who's who."[5] In the early twenty-first century, Ireland's inbound immigration rate was four times that of the United States.[6] The contemporary adaptation of *The Playboy of the Western World*, far from forcing new issues onto an old story, successfully surfaces elements so long ingrained in the original script that they risked becoming invisible to modern audiences.

Visibly, one shock of Adigun and Doyle's adaptation is the innovation of making Christy Mahon—transfigured into Christopher Malomo—Black. In his 2017 address to a Dublin conference on collaborative arts, interculturalism, and human rights, Adigun explained that he had long considered Christy Mahon "a quintessential refugee, asylum seeker, somebody who wants to better his lot. Let me get a Black man to play the role—and the rest is history."[7] My students watched the address and discussed Adigun's emphasis on interculturalism rather than multiculturalism; he argues that the term *interculturalism* better acknowledges power imbalances and ongoing inequities within Ireland's still-evolving racial diversity. We also discussed his perception of Black characters in Irish theater and film when he first arrived in Ireland in 1996: "When Irish theatre was trying to represent the Other, the Black, where I'm concerned, every time I saw a Black person on the stage, I was never proud of what I saw."[8] Such

4. Bisi Adigun and Roddy Doyle, *The Playboy of the Western World—A New Version*, 78.

5. Adigun and Doyle, "Playboy of the Western World."

6. Kerry Capell, "Ireland: A Nation of Immigrants?" *Businessweek*, July 25, 2004.

7. Bisi Adigun, Address, Create IHREC (Irish Human Rights and Equality Commission), Collaborative Arts, Interculturalism and Human Rights Seminar, Dublin, April 6, 2017, https://vimeo.com/216565070.

8. Adigun, Address. Adigun explained that he came to Ireland in 1996 intending only to apply for his visa to reenter the United Kingdom, where he had been living since leaving Nigeria, but instead settled in Dublin for the long term.

a critique echoes Irish nationalists' dismay at seeing stage Irishmen serve as comic relief in British drama a century earlier, spurring Yeats and Lady Gregory's foundation of the Irish Literary Theatre, which evolved into the Abbey Theatre. In their 1897 manifesto, Yeats, Lady Gregory, and their collaborator Edward Martyn promised to "show that Ireland is not the home of buffoonery and of easy sentiment, as it has been represented."[9] *The Playboy of the Western World* was an attempt by Synge to depict Irish peasants' linguistic richness as authentically as possible, as he explained in his preface to the published 1907 script.[10] In adapting *The Playboy of the Western World* with Doyle, Adigun not only recognized the play's significance as "the most important play in the Irish canon,"[11] but challenged audience perceptions of Irishness itself, especially in relation to the Other.

A second shock of Adigun and Doyle's script is the geographic relocation of Pegeen Mike's "country public house or shebeen"[12] on "a wild coast of Mayo"[13] to a "modern, suburban pub, on the west side of Dublin"[14] which is implied, at several points in the action, to be a crime den. In transposing *The Playboy of the Western World—A New Version* to an urban setting, the authors capitalize on tabloid media coverage of Dublin's gangland feuds, fueled by warring drug dealers and competing family cartels. The rise of drug-related crime had skyrocketed with the influx of cash brought by Celtic Tiger prosperity, and in the first decade of the 2000s, the number of drug arrests more than quadrupled, according to Garda statistics. The area of Blanchardstown, where *The Playboy of the Western World—A New Version* is set, became notorious for shootings between rival families, often masterminded by patriarchs with nicknames like

---

9. Augusta Gregory, *Our Irish Theatre: A Chapter of Autobiography* (New York: G. P. Putnam's Sons, 1913), 9.

10. Synge, *Playboy of the Western World*, v.

11. Adigun, Address.

12. Synge, *Playboy of the Western World*, 9.

13. Synge, *Playboy of the Western World*, 7.

14. Adigun and Doyle, *The Playboy of the Western World—A New Version*, 17.

"the Penguin" or "the Monk."[15] Hence, Pegeen's "seemingly jovial, but dangerous" father Michael Flaherty influences every subplot.[16] He presses his daughter toward marriage with Sean Keogh because Sean's mother Gracie is a powerful underworld figure, and he sees Christopher Malomo, newly arrived and on the run from Nigeria, as a "hard-looking unit" who might be counted on to carry out murders or drug deliveries without a trace: "We could use this guy. . . . No contacts. No one knows he's here."[17] Michael's ongoing conflict with a local crime boss, the Rattler, lends a menacing undercurrent that surfaces at the end of act 2, when Christopher holds the door against the Rattler's men as they pursue Michael in an attempt to kill him.

The cult of the "hard man,"[18] which replaces Synge's concept of the playboy, draws upon stereotypes stoked by tabloid sensationalism, echoing strains of journalistic influence in Synge's 1907 script. As T. J. Boynton has discussed, the Mayo villagers who marvel at Christy Mahon's parricide and transform him into a local celebrity make frequent reference to newspapers that describe similarly heinous crimes and gruesome consequences for their culprits.[19] Douglas Hyde had warned Irish men and women to "set our face sternly against penny dreadfuls, shilling shockers" and all forms of "garbage" printed in the "vulgar English weeklies,"[20] but over a century later, headlines about brazen killings and reprisals continue to captivate Irish readers and television viewers alike. The RTÉ drama

15. Conor Lally, "Gangland 2021: A World Veronica Guerin Would Not Recognise," *Irish Times*, June 25, 2021, https://www.irishtimes.com/news/crime-and-law/gangland-2021-a-world-veronica-guerin-would-not-recognise-1.4603561.

16. Adigun and Doyle, *The Playboy of the Western World—A New Version*, 24.

17. Adigun and Doyle, *The Playboy of the Western World—A New Version*, 40.

18. Adigun and Doyle, *The Playboy of the Western World—A New Version*, 24.

19. Boynton, "'The Fearful Crimes of Ireland': Tabloid Journalism and Irish Nationalism in *The Playboy of the Western World*," *Éire-Ireland* 47, nos. 3/4 (Fall/Winter 2012): 230–50.

20. Douglas Hyde, "The Necessity for De-Anglicising Ireland," in *Language, Lore and Lyrics*, ed. Breandán Ó Conaire (Dublin: Irish Academic Press, 1986), 169–70.

Love/Hate, for example, reached record audience numbers in 2012, feeding on public fascination with gangland violence (my students and I watched clips from that series as context).[21] In Adigun and Doyle's *Playboy of the Western World—A New Version*, the Widow Quin draws notoriety from her purported poisoning of her husband, as one of the local girls boasts on her behalf: "She was in the *Star*; what she did."[22] Although Widow Quin later reveals to Christopher that the true killers were "Pegeen's da and his pals,"[23] her tabloid fame has so subsumed her identity that she now embraces her reputation as a wife who committed murder. "I didn't. . . . But that's my story. I'm the notorious Widow Quin. Without that, I'm nobody."[24] Her elevation to stardom deflects attention from the truth of Michael Flaherty's crime. As in Synge's play, however, the characters discover that "there's a huge difference—right?—between a big story and a dirty deed" when Christopher reattempts to murder his father before their eyes.[25]

This preference for media-narrated violence rather than its reality raises the question of audience, not only within the play itself but also within the theater and within Irish society at large. The ubiquity of mobile phones enables characters to take photographs and videos of scenes within the 2007 script even as the audience watches along, as when the play's starstruck local girls photograph Christopher and Widow Quin in a Bonnie and Clyde pose, share video footage of Christopher's offstage fight against the Rattler, and prepare to record Christopher's final fight with his father as Michael Flaherty's underlings bet on the outcome. When Synge's 1907 play debuted at

21. "*Love/Hate* Tops the 2012 Ratings," RTÊ Archives, https://www.rte.ie /archives/exhibitions/681-history-of-rte/709-rte-2010s/482242-love-hate-tops-the -ratings/.

22. Adigun and Doyle, *The Playboy of the Western World—A New Version*, 69.

23. Adigun and Doyle, *The Playboy of the Western World—A New Version*, 89.

24. Adigun and Doyle, *The Playboy of the Western World—A New Version*, 89.

25. Adigun and Doyle, *The Playboy of the Western World—A New Version*, 117.

the Abbey Theatre, it portrayed a rural setting to an urban audience, and many in the crowd protested its characters' earthiness and their veneration of the outlaw Christy Mahon. Transposing the action to a contemporary suburban setting meant that 2007 audiences viewed characters who lived only a few miles from the high-priced seats in which they sat. The play's dialogue follows colloquial speech patterns familiar to any reader of Roddy Doyle: a Northside Dublin dialect that makes Christopher a "chancer"[26] and the Widow Quin a "slut,"[27] with inflections of working-class syntax in every line spoken by the Irish characters. Matt McGuire, among other critics, has explored how Mikhail Bakhtin's concept of heteroglossia and "linguistic hierarchy" applies to class tensions in Doyle's work. "In Doyle's fiction, dialect functions to expose the prejudice inherent in the dominant value system which would seek to label and denigrate the working class," tapping into a power dynamic familiar to Dublin residents and, likely, to most contemporary Abbey audiences.[28]

Doyle had already challenged the boundaries of Irish literature in his earlier novels, stories, and scripts. His debut novels, the Barrytown trilogy—*The Commitments* (1987), *The Snapper* (1990), *The Van* (1991)—traced the multigenerational Rabbitte family largely through dialogue as they emerged from Ireland's economic struggles of the 1980s. As McGuire points out, "Doyle's insistence on a text founded on dialect is a political choice, testifying to the existence of both a people and a culture that the grand narrative of economic progress would ignore, marginalize and ultimately silence."[29] The Irish characters in *The Playboy of the Western World—A New Version* are anything but silent as they gradually come to recognize Christopher Malomo as a fully rounded human being. Pegeen does not

26. Adigun and Doyle, *The Playboy of the Western World—A New Version*, 75.

27. Adigun and Doyle, *The Playboy of the Western World—A New Version*, 54.

28. Matt McGuire, "Dialect(ic) Nationalism?: The Fiction of James Kelman and Roddy Doyle," *Scottish Studies Review* 7, no. 1 (Spring 2006): 84.

29. McGuire, "Dialect(ic) Nationalism?," 85.

understand the abbreviation MBA, but she comments that "All you Africans have graduated, haven't yis? You've all been to college,"[30] marking the difference between her opportunities and his. Doyle had made a commitment to writing stories of such encounters for the multicultural newspaper *Metro Éireann*, founded as a monthly in 2000 by Nigerian journalists Abel Ugba and Chinedu Onyejelem, who had immigrated to Dublin. In a series of eight-hundred-word episodes, Doyle spun fictional tales that centered, as he explained, on a basic premise: "Someone born in Ireland meets someone who has come to live here."[31] My students and I read one of them, "The New Boy," in which a child refugee from an unnamed African country is bullied by his Dublin classmates; it was also adapted into an award-winning short film in 2007.[32] Like the child in that story, Doyle described feeling as if "I went to bed in one country and woke up in a different one"—a sense of displacement familiar to many in a rapidly changing Ireland.[33]

In *The Playboy of the Western World—A New Version*, as in Doyle's short stories, power dynamics and speech patterns highlight the interculturalism inherent in interactions between Irish characters and newly arrived immigrants. Adigun has argued that "Ireland can never be multicultural; Ireland can only be intercultural," explaining that the term *interculturalism* recognizes the power differential between those of a majority culture and those in smaller minority groups.[34] The play's working-class Dublin characters initially perceive the highly educated Christopher Malomo as something of a blank slate, an Other onto whom they can project their own preconceptions and misconceptions about Black men, Nigerians, and

---

30. Adigun and Doyle, *The Playboy of the Western World—A New Version*, 47.

31. Roddy Doyle, *The Deportees* (Toronto: Knopf Canada, 2008), xiii.

32. Steph Green, *New Boy* (Dublin: Zanzibar Films, 2007), https://www.youtube.com/watch?v=FdeioVndUhs.

33. Doyle, *Deportees*, xi.

34. Adigun, Address.

Africans in general. Christopher, whom the stage directions first describe as "tired and frightened"[35]—the same adjectives as in Synge's 1907 script—passively accepts others' statements about him, as when he accepts the label of "asylum seeker" from Michael Flaherty,[36] who then exercises power over Christopher by confiscating his passport.[37] Michael's daughter Pegeen and the other Irish characters gradually remake Christopher in their own image of a "hard man."[38] Pegeen dresses him in a hoodie to replace the suit coat he has been wearing since his departure from home, and she similarly applies new adjectives, which Christopher then uses to describe himself: "I am a sound fellow—as you said—Pegeen. Ambitious, hard-working, and determined"[39]—until the Widow Quin's knock on the pub's fortified door prompts him to cower under a duvet.

Here as in multiple other instances, Adigun and Doyle deploy the language of Synge's 1907 script in clever and destabilizing ways, reinvigorating stage directions and comic lines of dialogue. As in Synge, for example, the 2007 Widow Quin helps herself to Christopher's chicken, his gift from the admiring local girls, while he tells his tale of murder and woe. In Synge, the chicken was "a little laying pullet . . . crushed at the fall of night by the curate's car."[40] In the contemporary script, it is a ready-packed rotisserie meal from Spar, cast off because "it's a bit damaged, but it's grand."[41] Adigun and Doyle subversively add new layers to this scene when they update Synge's toast "to the wonders of the western world"[42] to include "the hitmen, the heroin dealers, coke dealers; crooked cops and politicians, and

---

35. Adigun and Doyle, *The Playboy of the Western World—A New Version*, 29.

36. Adigun and Doyle, *The Playboy of the Western World—A New Version*, 33.

37. Adigun and Doyle, *The Playboy of the Western World—A New Version*, 43.

38. Adigun and Doyle, *The Playboy of the Western World—A New Version*, 111.

39. Adigun and Doyle, *The Playboy of the Western World—A New Version*, 51.

40. Synge, *Playboy of the Western World*, 47.

41. Adigun and Doyle, *The Playboy of the Western World—A New Version*, 64.

42. Synge, *Playboy of the Western World*, 52.

publicans and lawyers, celebs and DJs, and the whole fuckin' lot of them."[43] Christopher Malomo, in turn, suggests an authorial critique on corruption in Nigeria as he explains that his father's wealth stems from service as an elected official in the First Republic, when "my dad, like most politicians who were elected then, did extremely well for himself."[44] And Christopher's description of his journey to Ireland expands descriptively on the plight of the modern migrant, adding vivid contemporary details to the playboy's lonely wanderings: "I pray it never happens to you. Looking over your shoulder all the time. Only desperate strangers as your companions—a lonely and terrible experience. Crossing the desert, for days, burnt, scorched, dehydrated and famished. Guarding your neck and your wallet. Agony is the word. You cannot believe how I felt when I finally got on the plane. I slept throughout. And to this city, where everybody stares at me but, truly, I do not exist. I have become simply a feeling. Sheer and utter loneliness."[45] Christopher's identity as the embodiment of loneliness offers a stark reminder to contemporary audiences not to ignore the plight of refugees arriving on their shores.

Nowhere more skillfully do Adigun and Doyle wield the language of Synge's script than in act 3, when the word *savage* leaps from 1907 into our contemporary context, acquiring racial and postcolonial overtones in the journey. In Synge, the word was an insult to Christy's apparent lack of patrimony: timid Sean Keogh calls him "a lepping savage" who "has descended from the Lord knows where."[46] In the 2007 adaptation, all know exactly the location of Christopher's descent, and when contemporary Sean Keogh declares, "I'd prefer to stay a bachelor than face that savage," Christopher wheels on him, brandishing a crutch like a weapon and demanding "What did you say?!"[47] It is left to Pegeen to demand Sean's depar-

43. Adigun and Doyle, *The Playboy of the Western World—A New Version*, 70.
44. Adigun and Doyle, *The Playboy of the Western World—A New Version*, 47.
45. Adigun and Doyle, *The Playboy of the Western World—A New Version*, 75.
46. Synge, *Playboy of the Western World*, 97.
47. Adigun and Doyle, *The Playboy of the Western World—A New Version*, 109.

ture; she is offended by Sean's use of the word and his racist appeal that "He's nobody, Pegeen. He's black. He's a Nigerian, for the love of God."[48] Yet Christopher's father, Chief Clement Malomo, later provides a civilized foil to the Irish characters' brutality, when they prepare to tie Christopher and drive him outside city limits, "up the mountains"[49] for execution without trial—a plan Malomo characterizes as "jungle justice."[50]

Thus, using linguistic and cultural markers from contemporary Irish society, Adigun and Doyle shift the power dynamics of Synge's original tale when they set the story of the wandering playboy against a backdrop of modern-day migration. In the process, the hapless Christy Mahon is transmuted into the self-possessed Christopher Malomo, "master of my own destiny" as he declares in his final lines, leaving the weeping Pegeen alone onstage.[51] Christopher strides offstage empowered to lead as his father follows, a symbolic shift of generational power for the play's Nigerian characters. Just as Doyle's earlier work made room in Irish literature for working-class characters and their demotic dialogue, so too does *The Playboy of the Western World—A New Version* expand the scope of Irish drama to include the Other. My students saw this, as evidenced in their classroom comments and essays about the play. I hope our shared experience of studying the text gave them insights into the "subsurface tensions" they described within the fabric of Ireland's evolving intercultural society—and their own.[52]

48. Adigun and Doyle, *The Playboy of the Western World—A New Version*, 108.

49. Adigun and Doyle, *The Playboy of the Western World—A New Version*, 115.

50. Adigun and Doyle, *The Playboy of the Western World—A New Version*, 120.

51. Adigun and Doyle, *The Playboy of the Western World—A New Version*, 121.

52. Donald Halsing, "Representing Populations of Change" (undergraduate paper, Framingham State Univ., 2019).

2

The Playboy of the Western World—A New Version in Adaptation Practice and Theory

Matthew Spangler

Adapting an iconic text is never easy. For that matter, adapting any text is a challenge, but in the case of exceptionally well-known ones, the adaptation will always be measured against its source material, and when the source in question is "the *Hamlet* of the Irish dramatic tradition," the bar for success is exceedingly high.[1] Moreover, some people do not like adaptations.[2] They see them as a form of theft or, at best, disfigurement—an act of changing an original that is better left alone. To these critics, adaptations are like the gremlins in the 1984

---

1. Christopher Murray, *Twentieth-Century Irish Drama: Mirror Up to Nation* (Manchester: Manchester Univ. Press, 1997), 80. For Murray, the similarity between *Hamlet* and *The Playboy of the Western World* is in the way in which both plays defy easy interpretation—"The pursuit of any one coherent reading immediately leaves exposed vast areas awaiting further excavation." To this point, Adrian Frazier writes, "publishing on this subject [*Playboy of the Western World*] is nearly a required rite of passage for scholars of Irish literature." See Adrian Frazier, "'Quaint Pastoral Numbskulls': Siobhán McKenna's Playboy Film," in *Playboys of the Western World: Production Histories*, ed. Adrian Frazier (Dublin: Carysfort Press), 59–74.

2. Thomas Kilroy, "Adaptation: A Privileged Conversation with a Dead Author," *Irish Times*, February 13, 2010, https://www.irishtimes.com/culture/stage /adaptation-a-privileged-conversation-with-a-dead-author-1.621741.

movie that spring from a pristine "original," dangerous knock-offs threatening to disrupt things as they are and do irrevocable harm.[3]

These dynamics play out despite the fact that adaptation in theater has a long history going back to the ancient Greeks and that completely pure originality in storytelling is so rare it practically does not exist. John Millington Synge, for example, based *The Playboy of the Western World* on a story he heard on the island of Inishmaan about "a Connaught man who killed his father with the blow of a spade when he was in passion and then fled to this island and threw himself on the mercy of some of the natives" who hid him from the police and eventually smuggled him to the United States.[4] Synge reports "often" hearing the story from an "old man, the oldest on the island [who] is fond of telling me anecdotes—not folk-tales—of things that have happened here in his lifetime."[5] Nicholas Grene notes that the old man in question appears to have repeatedly told the story to visitors on the island, for Arthur Symons recounts hearing the same story told to him on Inishmaan two years before Synge's first visit to the island.[6] But the *Hamlet* of the Irish dramatic tradition is not considered an adaptation, largely because there is not a preexisting written text on which the play is based. Had Synge's Aran Islands storyteller published a collection of stories that included this one about the protected murderer, sometime before *The Playboy of the Western World* premiered at the Abbey Theatre on January 26, 1907, then Synge's play probably would be considered an adaptation, but as far as anyone knows, no such publication exists. In contrast, Bisi Adigun and Roddy Doyle's *Playboy of the Western World—A New Version* is very much considered an adaptation. After all, the subtitle welcomes it.

3. The film *Gremlins* (1984) is itself based on a children's story by Roald Dahl (1943).

4. Synge, *The Aran Islands*, in *The Collected Plays and Poems and "The Aran Islands"* (London: Everyman, 1996), 297.

5. Synge, *Aran Islands*, 297.

6. Nicholas Grene, *The Politics of Irish Drama: Plays in Context from Boucicault to Friel* (Cambridge: Cambridge Univ. Press, 1999), 87.

This distinction between Synge's *Playboy of the Western World* and Adigun and Doyle's *Playboy of the Western World—A New Version*—in which one is an adaptation but the other not—reveals the textual bias, what Dwight Conquergood calls "textocentrism," at the heart of determinations of originality.[7] A subsequent work based on a preexisting oral source is rarely considered an adaptation, whereas subsequent works based on preexisting written sources almost always are. So despite the fact that Synge, Doyle, and Adigun all inherited their stories from other sources, Synge is the author of an "original," while Adigun and Doyle are the authors of a play that will always be measured against another one. Glenn Jellenik refers to this as adaptation's "originality problem."[8] Even as adaptations are their own creative works, often substantially different from their source material, and bearing unique aesthetic characteristics, they are, nonetheless, seen by some as not truly original. "It is much easier," Thomas Leitch writes, "to dismiss adaptation as inevitably blurred mechanical reproductions of original works of art than to grapple with the thorny questions of just what constitutes originality."[9] Adding to adaptation's "originality problem" is a broad dedication among readers, critics, and audiences to the historically specific, Romantic-era notion of individual creative genius that still frames considerations of art today. The result is that writers of adaptations often "occupy a liminal space" and are often "rendered invisible or deemed not-quite-writer."[10]

7. Dwight Conquergood, "Performance Studies: Interventions and Radical Research," *Drama Review* 46, no. 2 (2002): 151.

8. Glenn Jellenik, "Adaptation's Originality Problem: 'Grappling with the Thorny Questions of What Constitutes Originality,'" in *The Routledge Companion to Adaptation*, ed. Dennis Cutchins, Katja Krebs, and Eckart Voigts (London: Routledge, 2018), 182.

9. Thomas Leitch, "Twelve Fallacies in Contemporary Adaptation Theory," *Criticism* 45, no. 2 (2003): 163.

10. Katja Krebs, "Adapting Identities: Performing the Self," in *The Routledge Companion to Adaptation*, ed. Dennis Cutchins, Katja Krebs, and Eckart Voigts (London: Routledge, 2018), 582.

This chapter situates Adigun and Doyle's *The Playboy of the Western World—A New Version* within the canvas of adaptation in the Irish context as well as alongside certain theoretical concerns as they pertain to adaptation studies. My central claim here is that Adigun and Doyle's play may be temporally second, and based on a preexisting source, but it is by no means unoriginal, nor should it be considered a lesser work of art because it is an adaptation. Moreover, I argue that their play engages in an interpretation of Synge's play for the purpose of making a contemporary social critique that Synge's play does not make. In this respect, it illustrates what Linda Hutcheon calls a "transcultural adaptation," one in which the setting, time (historical era), or characters in the source material are re-presented in a way that allow the new work to engage intercultural, political, or critical ideas not present in the source.[11] Such an adaptation provides an opportunity for setting the source material in conversation with contemporary concerns—in this case, the topics of race and immigration to Ireland.

Despite the frequent positioning of adaptation as a "lesser" art, we are, nonetheless, living in an age of ubiquitous adaptation, especially in the theater.[12] As Dennis Cutchins notes, "more than half of the plays on Broadway or the West End at any given moment are adaptations of films, novels, and television shows."[13] One does not have to think hard to come up with recent adaptations on London or New York stages: Simon Stephens's *The Curious Incident of the Dog in the Night-Time*, Nick Stafford's *War Horse*, Dennis Kelly's *Matilda*, Aaron Sorkin's *To Kill a Mockingbird*, Robert Icke and Duncan Macmillan's *1984*, or my own adaptation of *The Kite Runner*, to say nothing about the copious number of adaptations for film and

11. Linda Hutcheon, *A Theory of Adaptation* (New York: Taylor and Francis, 2013), 145.

12. Hutcheon, *Theory of Adaptation*, xxvii.

13. Dennis Cutchins, "Introduction to the Companion," in *The Routledge Companion to Adaptation*, ed. Dennis Cutchins, Katja Krebs, and Eckart Voigts (London: Routledge, 2018), 2.

television. Adaptation is also nothing new. Aeschylus, Sophocles, and Euripides reconfigured preexisting narratives for their plays. William Shakespeare famously mined history. Charles Dickens essentially created one-person shows of his novels that he performed for audiences on tour. More recently, playwrights as distinct as Marina Carr, Eugene O'Neill, and Luis Alfaro have written widely celebrated adaptations of Greek plays. One might say, following Irish playwright Thomas Kilroy, that the "history of European theatre, like that of other performing arts, such as music, both orchestral and operatic, is a history of adaptation."[14]

It is in the Irish context that adaptation really takes off. Owing to the high status of both prose fiction and theater, the Irish stage has seen an incredible number of adaptations in recent years. Consider, for example, Patrick McCabe's stage adaptations of his own novels *The Butcher Boy* (as *Frank Pig Says Hello*, 1992) and *The Dead School* (1998); Edna O'Brien's *The Country Girls* (2011); Roddy Doyle's stage adaptations of *The Snapper* (2018) and *The Commitments* (2013); P. J. O'Connor's adaptation of Patrick Kavanagh's *Tarry Flynn* (1966), followed by Conal Morrison's adaptation of the novel three decades later (1997); Emma Donoghue's adaptation of her novel *Room* (2017); Annie Ryan's *A Girl is a Half-Formed Thing* (2014), from the novel by Eimear McBride; Meadhbh McHugh's *Asking for It* (2018), from the novel by Louise O'Neill; the many adaptations of Flann O'Brien's *At Swim-Two-Birds*, including adaptations by Audrey Welsh (1970), Alex Johnston (1998), and Jocelyn Clarke (2009); J. P. Dunleavy's adaptation of his novel *The Ginger Man* (1959); Marina Carr's adaptations of Greek plays; Thomas Kilroy's adaptation of Chekhov's *The Seagull* (1981); Brian Friel's adaptations of Anton Chekhov; and John Scott's modern dance adaptation of *King Lear* (2014). The works of James Joyce, as is often the case, occupy an outsized space in this conversation. Consider Dermot Bolger's *Ulysses* (2018); Hugh Leonard's *The Dead* (1967); Frank

14. Kilroy, "Adaptation."

McGuinness's *The Dead* (2012); Richard Nelson and Shaun Davey's musical *The Dead* (2000); Paul Muldoon and Jean Hanff Korelitz's audience-immersive *The Dead* (2018); Michael West and Annie Ryan's *Dubliners* (2012); Olwen Fouéré's *riverrun*, an adaptation of *Finnegans Wake* (2013); Declan Gorman's *The Dubliners Dilemma* from James Joyce's letters and short stories (2012); Donal O'Kelly's *Jimmy Joyced!* (2004); the many performances of Joyce's fiction on Bloomsday, including those by Paul O'Hanrahan's Balloonatics and the Diddlem Club; and *The Parable of the Plums*, a street theater and dance adaptation of the "Sirens" episode of *Ulysses* by Philip Mullen, Brian Fleming, Raymond Keane, and Bisi Adigun (2004).[15] As exhaustive as this list is, some readers are probably thinking, "But you missed . . . ," and that's my point: adaptation in the Irish context has an abundant and especially rich history. When Hutcheon writes that "adaption is the norm, not the exception," it would seem she had Irish theater in mind.[16]

Adigun and Doyle started writing *The Playboy of the Western World—A New Version* with the aid of an Irish Arts Council grant in 2006. Setting it in a gangland pub in west Dublin, they made the main character, formerly Christy Mahon, Christopher Malomo, an asylum seeker looking for refuge in Ireland, after he has attempted to kill his father back in Nigeria. Christopher thinks he has a family friend in Dublin who will shelter him, but the address he has scrawled on a piece of paper seems not to exist. The fact that the "persecution" Christopher is trying to escape—for the attempted murder of his overbearing father—would not likely gain him refugee status under existing immigration law is never taken up by the play. But that is not really the point. We are simply meant to understand Christopher as an outsider seeking refuge, much the same way that

---

15. See Matthew Spangler, "Winds of Change: Immigration, Bloomsday, and 'Aeolus' in Dublin Street Theatre," *James Joyce Quarterly* 45, no. 1 (2007): 47–68, on how *The Parable of the Plums* functions as adaptation and social commentary.

16. Hutcheon, *Theory of Adaptation*, 177.

Synge's Christy sought refuge in the County Mayo pub, or the murderer in the Aran Islander's story on Inishmaan.

Perhaps because the notion of a mysterious outsider entering a communal enclave (a stranger walks into a bar) is such an eternal storytelling device, and because *The Playboy of the Western World* mixes three of the most popular themes in theater—sex, violence, and comedy—the play has proven exceedingly popular for adaptation over the years. *The Playboy of the Western World—A New Version* coincided almost to the year with another highly respected adaptation: Pan Pan Theatre's Mandarin-language production at the Beijing Oriental Pioneer Theatre and Project Arts Centre in Dublin in 2006, directed by Gavin Quinn. In the Pan Pan version, which projected English surtitles of Synge's text above the stage, the action of the play was set in a Chinese hairdressers and foot massage parlor that doubled as a brothel. Two decades before saw what remains probably the best-known theatrical adaptation of *The Playboy of the Western World*: Mustapha Matura's *Playboy of the West Indies*, which toured the United Kingdom in 1984 and the United States in 1993 to great acclaim, and was revived by London's Tricycle Theatre and the Nottingham Playhouse in 2004–5.

There are many others. A musical version titled *The Heart's a Wonder* (1958), adapted by sisters Nuala and Mairin O'Farrell (later Maureen Charlton), had probably the most successful run of the several adaptations set to music. It was produced at the Gaiety Theatre in Dublin 1958, followed by the Lyric Theatre in Belfast, and Westminster Theatre in London, with subsequent productions in the United States and Scandinavia, as well as a televised version of the play by the BBC. Another, less successful, musical, *Back Country* (1978), book and lyrics by Broadway director Jacques Levey, placed the action of the story in a rustic bar in western Kansas in the 1890s. The production opened at the Wilbur Theatre in Boston and ran for fifteen days in September 1978. Another musical, *Christy* (1975), book and adaptation by Bernie Spiro, opened at the Bert Wheeler Theatre in New York City in October 1975 and should receive mention if only for the description of the actors' accents in Mel Gussow's

New York Times review, in which he wrote they "waver all the way from Erin to Brooklyn (as in 'is youse the man who killed yer father?')."[17] Yet another and more recent musical version, *Golden Boy of the Blue Ridge* (2009), music and book by Peter Mills and Cara Reichel, sets the action of the play in 1930s Appalachia with a bluegrass score and was presented off-Broadway at 59E59 Theaters in April and May 2009. Perhaps the most notable operatic version is Giselher Klebe's *Ein wahrer Held* (A True Hero), presented at the Zurich Opera House in January 1975. The 1962 Brian Desmond Hurst film, starring Siobhán McKenna, remains the best-known cinematic adaptation of the play, though there are others, including Brad Turner's (director) and Lee Gowan's (screenwriter) film *Paris or Somewhere* (1994), in which a mysterious American shows up in a small town on the Saskatchewan prairie claiming to be a serial killer. Of Synge's other plays that have been adapted perhaps the most notable is Derek Walcott's *The Sea of Dauphin* (1954), an adaptation of *Riders to the Sea* set in a village fishing community in Saint Lucia.

John Harrington writes that there are essentially three distinct eras of interpreting Synge's *Playboy of the Western World*. The first has to do with the play's political edge and capacity to function as social critique, to inspire riots, which the play did, of course, when it was first performed in Dublin in 1907. The second took place around the mid-twentieth century and saw the play become "high art" and praised for its lyricism. And in the third, more recently, starting sometime in the 1980s, the play has become emblematic of an exotic, culturally specific, and, at the same time, sentimental Ireland, as in the smell of turf fires and unexamined poverty.[18] During the early years of the twenty-first century, we might identify a fourth

17. Mel Gussow, "Stage: 'Christy,' Musical." *New York Times*, October 16, 1975, https://www.nytimes.com/1975/10/16/archives/stage-christy-musical.html.

18. See John Harrington, "The Playboy IN the Western World: J. M. Synge's Play in America," in *Playboys of the Western World: Production Histories*, ed. Adrian Frazier (Dublin: Carysfort Press, 2004), 46–58.

era, in which there was much energy surrounding *The Playboy of the Western World* driven by the upcoming centenary (2007) of the first production (1907), and also, as Patrick Lonergan notes, by Garry Hynes and the Druid Theatre's work with Synge's plays over the preceding two decades, including their groundbreaking production of *The Playboy of the Western World* in 1982 and the DruidSynge project of 2004–6 that staged all of Synge's six plays in a single day.[19]

So when Adigun and Doyle's *Playboy of the Western World—A New Version* opened in the newly renovated main-stage auditorium of the Abbey Theatre in October 2007 as part of the Dublin Theatre Festival, it was on the back of a long history of adaptations of the play, and with much fanfare. The cast certainly lived up to the play's billing. Eileen Walsh (Pegeen) was coming off a number of recent successes: her shattering performance as Crispina, a single mother gone mad in *The Magdalene Sisters* (2002); her role in Mark O'Rowe's play *Terminus* (2007), which was produced at the Peacock Theatre earlier that summer (2007); and, before that, her breakthrough performance as Runt in Enda Walsh's *Disco Pigs* (1996) with Cillian Murphy. Echoes of these other roles—unhinged, sexually charged, dangerous—underpinned the subtext of Walsh's Pegeen. Olu Jacobs, cast as Malomo, Christopher's father, is widely regarded as one of the greatest actors of his generation. Jacobs, who hails from Nigeria, brought to the production a level of gravitas and even legitimacy, having acted in dozens of plays and over one hundred films and television programs and being the recipient of many awards, including an Africa Movie Academy Award for Best Actor. Angeline Ball (the Widow Quin) was also known for her film work specifically, having memorably played Imelda Quirke in Alan Parker's *The Commitments* (1991) and recently been seen as Molly Bloom in *Bloom* (2003), for which she received an Irish Film and Television Award for Best Actress. The London actor Giles Terera was cast as Christopher.

---

19. Patrick Lonergan, *Irish Drama and Theatre since 1950* (London: Bloomsbury-Methuen, 2019), 126.

Terera had a respectable stage-acting career in 2007 with credits on the West End and at the Royal Shakespeare Company, National Theatre, and Young Vic, but he would later go on, even more notably, to star as Aaron Burr in the London production of *Hamilton*, for which he won the 2018 Olivier Award for Best Actor in a Musical.[20]

When the production opened on September 29, 2007, it received a rapturous audience response and largely positive critical reviews, though not universally positive.[21] Jimmy Fay's direction amplified

20. Other *Playboy of the Western World—A New Version* cast members included Laurence Kinlan (Sean), Liam Carney (Michael), Phelim Drew (Philly), Joe Hanley (Jimmy), Aoife Duffin (Susan), Kate Brennan (Sarah), Charlene Gleeson (Honor). The cast was somewhat different for the 2009 remount of the play and included Ruth Bradley (Pegeen), Rory Nolan (Sean), Liam Carney (Michael), Joe Hanley (Jimmy), Chuk Iwuji (Christopher), Hilda Fay (Widow Quin), Liz Fitzgibbon (Susan), Kate Brennan (Sarah), Charlene Gleeson (Honor), and the esteemed playwright and actor George Seremba (*Come Good Rain* and other plays), who was born in Uganda but has since lived in Kenya, Canada, and Ireland.

21. RTÊ called it "a hilarious tour-de-force" (Steve Cummins, "*The Playboy of the Western World*," RTÊ, October 8, 2007); the *Guardian*, "an intriguing, freewheeling farce" (Helen Meany, "*The Playboy of the Western World*," *Guardian*, October 6, 2007, https://www.theguardian.com/stage/2007/oct/06/theatre1); and the *Sunday Tribune*, "superb, wickedly entertaining . . . Roddy Doyle and Bisi Adigun have given us a *Playboy* for our times. And in doing so, they have returned it to its comic roots" ("The Big Issues," *Sunday Tribune*, October 7, 2007). The *Sunday Independent* wrote, "The only riot at the opening of the new version of *The Playboy of the Western World* was riotous laughter. Deservedly so." (Emer O'Kelly, "Playboy of the Badlands a Riot," *Sunday Independent*, October 7, 2007, https://www.pressreader.com/ireland/sunday-independent-ireland/20071007/282205121518890). Peter Crawley of the *Irish Times* wrote that the play was a "hugely entertaining, often laugh-out-loud funny and superbly acted piece of theatre. I really think you'd like it. And yet it should be more." See Peter Crawley, "Dublin Theatre Festival Review: *Playboy of the Western World* at the Abbey Theatre," *Irish Times*, October 5, 2007, 16. Karen Fricker, writing for *Variety*, and Susan Conley, writing for *Irish Theatre Magazine*, were both critical of what they saw as the play's inability to more fully examine questions of race, interculturalism, and immigration in Ireland. See Karen Fricker, "*The Playboy of The Western World*," *Variety*, October 9, 2007, https://variety.com/2007/legit/reviews/the-playboy-of-the-western-world-8

the fast-paced and humorous qualities of the play and had an undeniable audience appeal. I saw the production two times in October
2007 and rarely have I witnessed a theater audience more enthusiastic
and positively responsive. The Abbey Theatre seems to have agreed,
for it produced the play again in 2008–9, which was the staging that
prompted the court case (see chapters 4 and 5 in this volume).

Part of the pleasure in watching an adaptation is experiencing
the "oscillation"—points of similarity and difference—between the
new work and the source material.[22] In some sense, the more we are
familiar with the source, the more pleasurable (and disappointing) it
can be to watch an adaptation of it. But what is immediately striking
about the text of Adigun and Doyle's adaptation, in this regard, is
how much it does not depart from its source material. Their adaptation maintains nearly every nuance of the dramatic structure of its
source, from the shape of the plot, to the intention of specific lines,
right down to character entrance and exit points, all of which are
nearly identical to Synge's play. Generally, "fidelity" studies has been
eschewed in contemporary approaches to adaptation as an "academic
backwater" and an out-of-date holdover of text-centric criticism,[23]
but in this case, a recognition of how precisely Adigun and Doyle
sought to replicate Synge's dramatic structure is revealing, largely because the similarities between the two make the differences stand out.

-1200555477/, and Susan Conley, "*The Playboy of the Western World: A New Version* by Bisi Adigun and Roddy Doyle," *Irish Theatre Magazine*, October 5, 2007.

22. Hutcheon, *Theory of Adaptation*, xvii.

23. Frances Babbage, Robert Neumark Jones, and Lauren Williams, "Adapt-
ing Wilde for the Performance Classroom: 'No Small Parts,'" in *Redefining Adap-
tation Studies*, ed. Dennis Cutchins, Laurence Raw, and James M. Welsh (Lanham,
MD: Scarecrow Press, 2010), 2; Suzanne Diamond, "Whose Life *Is* It, Anyway?
Adaptation, Collective Memory, and (Auto)Biographical Processes," in *Redefining
Adaptation Studies*, ed. Dennis Cutchins, Laurence Raw, and James M. Welsh
(Lanham, MD: Scarecrow Press, 2010), 95; Simone Murray, *The Adaptation In-
dustry: The Cultural Economy of Contemporary Literary Adaptation* (London:
Routledge, 2012), 2.

These textual differences—additions and subtractions that Adigun and Doyle made in adapting Synge's source text—might be placed into three broad categories: (1) contemporary cultural references, (2) well-known lines from Synge's play adapted in a way that echo the original, and (3) additions that seek to make something of a social critique in the spirit of a "transcultural adaptation."[24] The first of these accounts for much of the play's humor in performance. References to things like the television show *CSI*, the pop song "I Believe I Can Fly," PlayStation, Barbie dolls, and *Brokeback Mountain*, as Pegeen calls Michael and Philly, her dad's obsequious sidekicks and drinking buddies, keep the audience laughing and in a state of anticipation awaiting the next joke. One such reference that has already passed its time, but was nonetheless humorous in 2007–9, is when Sarah, Susan, and Honor replay mobile phone recordings of Christy's defense of the pub, but the recordings keep running out after ten seconds or so and the girls have to stop and bring up multiple additional recordings to watch the entire fight.

The play contains few spoken references to Christy's race, or his status as an immigrant, which Adigun has said in interviews was intentional.[25] Karen Fricker and Susan Conley, in their reviews of the play in *Variety* and *Irish Theatre Magazine*, respectively, would lament this absence as an example of the play missing an opportunity to engage the topics of immigration and race more fully, especially given the high degree of racism immigrants to Ireland were facing in those years.[26] But what this play does give us is a window into a par-

---

24. Hutcheon, *Theory of Adaptation*.

25. Bisi Adigun, interview by Colin Murphy, "Nigerian *Playboy of the Western World*," *Le Monde Diplomatique*, November 2007, 13.

26. Fricker, "*Playboy of the Western World*"; Conley, "*Playboy of the Western World*." See Bryan Fanning, "Racism, Rules and Rights," in *Immigration and Social Change in the Republic of Ireland*, ed. Bryan Fanning (Manchester: Manchester Univ. Press, 2007), 6–26; Ronit Lentin and Robbie McVeigh, *After Optimism? Ireland, Racism and Globalisation* (Dublin: Metro Éireann Publications, 2006); Ronit Lentin and Robbie McVeigh, eds., *Racism and Anti-Racism in Ireland* (Belfast:

ticular historical moment in Ireland when immigration was, almost overnight, widely discussed in public forums. In one memorable and telling (and also comic) interaction, Michael refers to Christy as a "refugee" and Sean corrects him:

> MICHAEL: So, you're some sort of a refugee or asylum seeker, yeah?
> SEAN: Flaherty?
> MICHAEL: Yeah?
> SEAN: He can't be a refugee. He just arrived, like.
> MICHAEL: What?
> SEAN: He has to go through the asylum process first, like. And if he is granted, then he can—
> MICHAEL: Good man, Sean. (*To CHRISTOPHER*) So. You're an asylum seeker. Am I technically correct there, Sean?

Sean is right. Christy is not a "refugee," because he just arrived in Ireland as an undocumented person, and not via an official resettlement program, so one might consider him an "asylum seeker" with the possibility that he could become a "refugee" sometime in the future—though probably not, as I have already noted, because his cause of persecution would not fit the legal requirements to earn refugee status. The play's joke is in Sean's precise familiarity with the nuance and vocabulary of asylum procedure. The 2007 premiere came on the heels of several years of media coverage about the increasing number of refugees, asylum seekers, and other immigrants coming to Ireland, a "rate of transformation, which was extraordinarily rapid" and came to be perceived as a national "crisis."[27] An unexpectedly large proportion of people living in Ireland during those years, like

---

Beyond the Pale, 2002); and Declan Kiberd, "Strangers in Their Own Country: Multi-Culturalism in Ireland," in *Multi-Culturalism: The View from the Two Irelands*, by Edna Longley and Declan Kiberd (Cork: Cork Univ. Press, 2001), 45–78.

27. Patrick Lonergan, *Theatre and Globalization: Irish Drama in the Celtic Tiger Era* (London: Palgrave Macmillan, 2010), 192; Bryan Fanning, *Migration and the Making of Ireland* (Dublin: Univ. College Dublin Press, 2018), 158.

Sean, would likely have been able to describe the difference between a refugee and an asylum seeker.

Second, specific lines from Synge's play are rewritten in the text of the adaption in ways that echo with the language of the source material—a verbal example of Hutcheon's "oscillation." For example, Synge's play reads, "Well, it's a clean bed and soft with it, and it's great luck and company I've won me in the end of time—two fine women fighting for the likes of me—till I'm thinking this night wasn't I a foolish fellow not to kill my father in the years gone by."[28] In the Adigun and Doyle adaptation, the line is rendered thus: "It is true what they say about Irish people. Their friendliness and generosity of heart. Here I am, with two fine women fighting over me. You know what? I'm beginning to think, wasn't I a foolish man not to have killed my father years ago?" Synge's famous line about "chosen females, standing in their shifts"[29] is rendered thus: "It's only Pegeen that my heart beats for. You can present me with a long line of the most beautiful girls in Ireland—naked! beautiful!—I'm not interested." Synge's "loy," the object Christy uses to hit his father in the head, is changed to a "pestle" in the adaptation, which we are told is a "kitchen utensil, used for pounding yams." Pegeen's final line, "Oh my grief, I've lost him, surely. I've lost the only Playboy of the Western World,"[30] is rendered in the adaptation as "Fuck off!" Whether one likes these adapted lines or not, whether one thinks Synge's play is more poetic and the adaptation crass, or whether the adaptation should be lauded for updating the language and "speaking" to a contemporary audience is somewhat beside the point, because when these lines are spoken onstage, one also hears the echo of Synge's language—in oscillation—an experience for the audience that is essential to the play's theatricality. In other words, the difference between

28. John Millington Synge, *The Playboy of the Western World*, in *The Complete Plays* (New York: Vintage, 1960), 30.

29. Synge, *Playboy of the Western World*, 75.

30. Synge, *Playboy of the Western World*, 80.

what one knows in one's mind and what one hears is part of the intended aesthetic experience of this play.

Lastly, Adigun and Doyle add elements to the story that are beyond Synge's play. I want to focus on one of these additions because its inclusion seeks to make a specific social critique related to questions of immigration and race. A closed-circuit video camera hangs outside above the door of the pub and feeds an image of the alley onto a television screen above the bar. Everyone who approaches the door from the outside is first seen on the television, and everyone who exits is seen walking away down the alley. Oddly, there is little mention of the camera or television in the play's dialogue. This is odd because the camera and television appear many times in the play's stage directions, and the television images feature so prominently in the scenic design, they are impossible for a viewing audience to ignore. Every time an actor enters, the audience sees them on the television above the bar before they open the door and come into the playing space. Every time an actor exits, the audience sees them go. There are many exits and entrances throughout the play, and several dramatic ones, most memorably in act 3 with the physical struggle in the alley between Christopher and his father.

The inclusion of the camera and television screen—and their undeniable contribution to the production's visual rhetoric onstage—begs the question of what we are supposed to make of them. I want to suggest one possible reading here, drawing from Homi Bhabha's notion of "surveillant culture." Bhabha argues that Western nations have created and work to maintain a "surveillant culture of 'security,'" the purpose of which is to answer the questions, "How do we tell the good migrant from the bad migrant? Which cultures are safe? Which unsafe?"[31] One of the material effects of surveillant culture is the refugee application process itself, in which would-be refugees not only have to prove persecution in their home country due to one of five specific and limited conditions—their race, religion,

31. Homi Bhabha, *The Location of Culture* (London: Routledge, 1994), xvii.

nationality, membership in a particular social group, or political opinion—but they must also undergo a series of invasive security and health screenings. The ultimate point of this is to determine who gets refugee status, who is allowed to stay in the host country, who will be detained, and who will be deported. Surveillant culture extends beyond bureaucratic spaces and into almost every aspect of everyday life and subjugates immigrants, people of color, and all marginalized people to a judging and state-sponsored gaze of hegemonic authority and control.

The camera and television images, then, become a metaphor for the ways in which all our lives are circumscribed by surveillance, even more now than when the play was first produced in 2007, but especially for members of minoritarian groups, such as refugees and other kinds of immigrants. The idea of being seen is a widely recognized theme in Synge's play, and is often framed as an act of radical subjectivity on Christy's part, a capacity to craft a new identity through narrative and "construct himself out of his own desire," rather than the desires of others.[32] Adigun and Doyle's adaptation, additionally and by contrast, applies the idea of "being seen" to Western "surveillant culture" and minoritarian identity. The camera above the door of the pub and television screen above the bar function to make foreign bodies visible—foreign to the world of this pub, and in the case of Christopher, foreign also to Ireland—and in so doing, the play seeks to offer a critique, via foregrounded visibility, of pervasive surveillance in the context of immigration and race.

The Playboy of the Western World—A New Version also takes its place alongside similar activities the authors were engaged in at the time. Adigun's production of Jimmy Murphy's *The Kings of the Kilburn High Road* (2007), a play about Irish immigrants in London, featured a cast of Black actors living in Ireland (for more on this production and Adigun's subsequent adaptation of the play as

---

32. Declan Kiberd, *Inventing Ireland: The Literature of the Modern Nation* (London: Jonathan Cape, 1995), 184.

The Paddies of Parnell Street [2013], see chapters 3 and 5 in this volume). Adigun's *Kings of the Kilburn High Road* and *Paddies of Parnell Street* sought to destabilize the idea of Irish immigration as singular and unique, and instead place it in a broader canvas of other global immigrant experiences in a way that begs the consideration of linkages and influences among them. The Irish, in this telling, are as much a host culture to immigrants today as they are an emigrant-sending culture, as traditionally figured. Doyle, too, was working to challenge traditional notions of Irish identity through his short stories about immigrant experiences in Ireland published in the Dublin newspaper *Metro Éireann* and later collected in *The Deportees*. So for both writers, their adaptation of *The Playboy of the Western World* not only reflected a particular moment in Irish history, but it also grew out of their larger program of work at the time dedicated to reimagining the markers of Irish and immigrant identities.

A number of commentators have noted the value of adaptation for destabilizing established hegemonies. John Severn calls this "adaptation's queer agency."[33] Margaret Hamilton describes it as adaptation's capacity for "formative interruption rather than [being] merely a derivative process of reinterpretation and recreation."[34] Or it is adaptation as "a creative and critical act," one that is "frequently, if not inevitably, political," has the capacity to create "hybrid spaces of cultural recycling," and, one might add, spaces of *reordering*, in a way that challenges the old and imagines something new.[35] To this point, Adigun noted in a 2007 interview about *The Playboy of the*

33. John Severn, *"All Shook Up* and the Unannounced Adaptation: Engaging with *Twelfth Night*'s Unstable Identities," *Theatre Journal* 66, no. 4 (2014): 549.

34. Margaret Hamilton, "Hayloft's *Thyestes*: Adapting Seneca for the Australian Stage and Context," *Theatre Journal* 66, no. 4 (2014): 531.

35. Babbage, Neumark Jones, and Williams, "Adapting Wilde for the Performance Classroom," 1; Julie Sanders, *Adaptation and Appropriation* (London: Routledge, 2007), 97; Milan Pribisic, "The Pleasures of 'Theater Film': Stage to Film Adaptation," in *Redefining Adaptation Studies*, ed. Dennis Cutchins, Laurence Raw, and James M. Welsh (Lanham, MD: Scarecrow Press, 2010), 148.

Western World—A New Version, "If there's anything political about the play, it's about shaking up a classic of Irish drama," a point underscored by Brian Singleton, who writes that the play provides an example of "how the Irish canon can be contested in a spirit of social change."[36] As I have sought to argue here, this adaptation may be temporally second to its source material, but it should not be seen as diminutively derivative of that material, and certainly not unoriginal, nor limited in its thematic scope, political commentary, or theatrical power. In fact, this adaptation speaks to topics that are as relevant today—principally, race and immigration—as they were in 2007, and maybe even more so.

36. Adigun, "Nigerian *Playboy of the Western World*," 13; Brian Singleton, *Masculinities and the Contemporary Irish Theatre* (London: Palgrave Macmillan, 2011), 20.

3

The Playboy of the Western World— A New Version, the Celtic Tiger, and the Immigrant-as-Sequel

Sarah L. Townsend

In 2006, one year before Bisi Adigun and Roddy Doyle's adaptation *The Playboy of the Western World—A New Version* premiered at the Abbey Theatre, the Dublin-based Pan Pan Theatre company produced a contemporary adaptation of John Millington Synge's play in Beijing, set in a beauty salon and performed in Mandarin by a Chinese cast. Together, the Pan Pan and Adigun/Doyle adaptations appeared to herald the definitive globalization of Irish theater. On the one hand, the Beijing production attested to the increased circulation of Irish plays and touring companies during the Celtic Tiger era. In selecting Synge's *The Playboy of the Western World* as its chosen source text, the Pan Pan adaptation drew on the proven success of what Patrick Lonergan calls Ireland's "national brand": theater that reads as authentically Irish and yet travels easily within a globalized marketplace, allowing for different interpretations in many disparate locales.[1] On the other hand, by 2007, Ireland was at the tail end of the economic boom, which had transformed the country into a destination for overseas migrants. By casting a Nigerian migrant as the eponymous Playboy, in a production commissioned by Adigun's

1. Patrick Lonergan, *Theatre and Globalization: Irish Drama in the Celtic Tiger Era* (London: Palgrave Macmillan, 2009), 85–97.

theater company, Arambe Productions, and staged at the Abbey during the Dublin Theatre Festival to commemorate the centenary of Synge's premiere, Adigun and Doyle's adaptation reimagined canonical Irish drama and the National Theatre stage as sites for multiracial, multicultural self-reckoning.

Of course, Irish theater had traveled globally long before the 1990s and 2000s. The Abbey Theatre embarked on its first American tour in 1911–12, and it was there that *The Playboy of the Western World* met with resistance that outstripped anything encountered during its initial run in Dublin, including the actors' arrest and trial in Philadelphia on charges of indecency. Both Synge and the Abbey would go on to forge an international reputation on the notoriety of the US tour.[2] Nor were the linguistic and geographic liberties taken by the Pan Pan and Arambe adaptations without precedent. Over the course of the twentieth century, Synge's play had been translated into multiple languages, adapted for a variety of media (including radio, film, and television), produced on stages across the world, and updated to reflect a number of different settings. The best-known adaptation is Trinidadian playwright Mustapha Matura's *The Playboy of the West Indies* (1984), which transposed Synge's play to the mid-twentieth-century Caribbean, and which roughly coincided with the rise of postcolonial Irish studies in the late 1980s and early 1990s. It is Matura's adaptation that punctuates Declan Kiberd's influential reading of *The Playboy of the Western World* as a "blueprint" for Irish and postcolonial self-fashioning in his 1995 study *Inventing Ireland*.[3] While the physical and imaginative distances bridged by the Pan Pan and Arambe adaptations may have been novel, the two productions traversed global pathways long since navigated by Irish artists and critics.[4]

---

2. Christopher Morash, *A History of Irish Theatre, 1601–2000* (Cambridge: Cambridge Univ. Press, 2002), 146–47.

3. Declan Kiberd, *Inventing Ireland: The Literature of the Modern Nation* (Cambridge, MA: Harvard Univ. Press, 1995), 187.

4. The Pan Pan production was unusual insofar as the translation of the playscripts, the casting, and rehearsal all occurred on location in China with Chinese

What distinguished the Abbey production from the Pan Pan production and other previous adaptations of Synge's play was the direction of the global influence. Rather than exporting Irish drama to far-flung locales, Adigun and Doyle's play placed an African "asylum seeker"—a figure who by the 2000s was a familiar feature of both the political landscape and the Irish multicultural imaginary—on the Abbey stage in the iconic role of Christy Mahon, or Christopher Malomo in the adaptation.[5] Embedded in *The Playboy of the Western World—A New Version* are a number of visual elements that offer the potential to hold the proverbial mirror up to contemporary society, elements that ought to have produced unsettling self-reflection in the 2007 audience. For instance, the stage directions in the playscript call for a wall-length mirror behind the bar, which would have presented the predominantly white middle-class Abbey Theatre audience with the sight of their own image as they watched a Black Playboy take the stage (and which, regrettably, was replaced in the Abbey production with several smaller mirrors scattered around the set, which failed to produce the same effect). Similarly, recording devices featured onstage like the closed-circuit television mounted

collaborators (a model Pan Pan had employed in prior projects). The Arambe adaptation more closely mirrored *The Playboy of the West Indies* in that both were written in English for English-speaking audiences by Dublin-based and London-based playwrights, respectively. The London-based Matura's play premiered at the Tricycle Theatre and went on to tour the United Kingdom, while the Arambe production premiered at the Abbey Theatre.

5. As I have noted elsewhere, Christopher cannot actually seek asylum, as both his freedom from persecution and his criminal act of murder in Nigeria would disqualify him per the Irish Refugee Act of 1996. Yet, as Charlotte McIvor suggests, the persistent misidentification of Adigun and Doyle's protagonist as an asylum seeker is indicative of the tendency in Celtic Tiger theater and culture to portray African immigrants as foreign and/or illegal. See Sarah Townsend, "Cosmopolitanism at Home: Ireland's Playboys from Celtic Revival to Celtic Tiger," *Journal of Modern Literature* 34, no. 2 (Winter 2011): 60, and Charlotte McIvor, *Migration and Performance in Contemporary Ireland: Towards a New Interculturalism* (London: Palgrave Macmillan, 2016), 69–72.

above the bar and the mobile phones with which the girls photograph, film, and later watch Christopher generate an atmosphere of surveillance that ought to have prompted 2007 audiences to recognize the racialized gaze that Irish society foists on migrants of color. A promotional trailer for the play even toyed with this idea (whether self-consciously or not) by featuring CCTV footage of a shadowy figure, accompanied by the tagline "Who is the Playboy?" as Charlotte McIvor has noted.[6] Yet, the Abbey production completed a successful seven-week run without generating any of the controversy it seemingly sought to provoke. Ticket sales were strong, and theater critics reserved their criticisms for specific elements of the adaptation, like the dialogue or plot twists, rather than its multiracial premise.

The Abbey's production of *The Playboy of the Western World—A New Version* failed to provoke anything resembling the early twentieth-century theater riots it was staged to commemorate because, I suspect, it painted a largely flattering portrait of Celtic Tiger Ireland. Whereas Synge's play had directed "his dreadful searchlight into our cherished accumulation of social skeletons . . . and revealed to us there truly terrible truths, of our own making, which we dare not face for the present," according to Patrick Kenny in his 1907 *Irish Times* review of *The Playboy of the Western World*, Adigun and Doyle's adaptation confirmed what audiences in 2007 wanted to believe about the stability of an upswing whose days were already numbered.[7] As we shall see, Celtic Tiger–era narratives about Ireland's new arrivals often double as narratives about the Irish themselves. This self-reflective quality is especially apparent in literary and theatrical works that, like *The Playboy of the Western World—A New Version*, celebrate pluralism in order to perform the permanence, even nonchalance, of Irish prosperity. In what follows, I situate Adigun and Doyle's play within a recurring subgenre in Celtic

---

6. Charlotte McIvor, "Staging the 'New Irish': Interculturalism and the Future of Post-Celtic Tiger Irish Theatre," *Modern Drama* 54, no. 3 (Fall 2011): 316.

7. Patrick Kenny, "That Dreadful Play," *Irish Times*, January 30, 1907, in *The Playboy Riots*, ed. James Kilroy (Dublin: Dolmen, 1971), 37–40.

Tiger and post–Celtic Tiger fiction and drama—the multicultural sequel or adaptation—in which immigrants assume the homes, jobs, rituals, and literary and theatrical roles formerly occupied by the native Irish. This tendency to return to familiar narrative territory is more than a gimmick. Rather, the very process of adapting or sequelizing reinforces—and in some cases, challenges—the ideological work of what Gargi Bhattacharyya has referred to as "feel-good" multiculturalism.[8] By tracking the production of a form I call the immigrant-as-sequel through the Celtic Tiger and the subsequent recession, this chapter considers both the congratulatory and critical narratives about Irish society that are unleashed through the act of envisioning the immigrant as a variation on the same.

In electing to adapt Synge's play, Adigun and Doyle appeared to enter into the well-established postcolonial tradition of rewriting canonical literature and drama, whether obliquely or through prequels, sequels, adaptations, and translations that directly engage with European classics. As Bill Ashcroft, Gareth Griffiths, and Helen Tiffin memorably argue in their 1989 study, such revisionist literary texts constitute an anticolonial strategy through which "the empire writes back."[9] Often critical of their source texts, these works interrogate the imperial assumptions and erasures that undergird the Western literary canon, all the while giving voice to the marginalized subjects who have been silenced or misrepresented on the page and stage. According to Helen Gilbert and Joanne Tompkins, it is the specific legacy of colonial education that accounts for the frequency with

---

8. Gargi Bhattacharyya, "Riding Multiculturalism," in *Multicultural States: Rethinking Difference and Identity*, ed. David Bennett (London: Routledge, 1998), 252–66; Paul Gilroy, *Against Race: Imagining Political Culture beyond the Color Line* (Cambridge, MA: Harvard Univ. Press, 2000), 21.

9. Bill Ashcroft, Gareth Griffiths, and Helen Tiffin, *The Empire Writes Back: Theory and Practice in Post-Colonial Literatures* (London: Routledge, 1989). Their phrase is borrowed from Salman Rushdie's 1982 article "The Empire Writes Back with a Vengeance," which itself plays on the title of the Star Wars film *The Empire Strikes Back*.

which postcolonial playwrights, in particular, return to canonical dramatic works in order "to invest them with more local relevance and to divest them of their assumed authority/authenticity."[10] More recent critical assessments have emphasized the degree to which postcolonial rewritings seek less to respond to an assumed Western canon than to renegotiate the very concept of canonicity within the increasingly mobile configurations of global and world literature.[11] On the surface, *The Playboy of the Western World—A New Version* appeared to forward a revisionist agenda insofar as it asked audiences to recognize the modern-day migrants who, like Synge's vaunted hero, arrive to an unfamiliar environment "very tired and frightened" and in search of a safe haven.[12] Nevertheless, by electing to update *The Playboy of the Western World*'s script quite literally, the adaptation departed from postcolonial revisionism in two ways. First, it neglected to question the fraught canonicity of Synge's play, a once-provocative anticolonial work that since has been redeployed as a cornerstone of Ireland's lucrative culture industry, and second, it failed to probe the play's questionable utility as a narrative model for contemporary migrant self-fashioning.

The more appropriate literary analogue to *The Playboy of the Western World—A New Version* is the serialized fiction that Doyle wrote in the early 2000s, later republished in 2007 as a short story collection, *The Deportees and Other Stories*, for the multicultural Irish newspaper *Metro Éireann*, which was founded in 2000 by journalists Abel Ugba and Chinedu Onyejelem. Notably, Doyle's first two stories for the paper took the form of adaptations or sequels: "Guess Who's Coming for the Dinner," which updates the 1967

10. Helen Gilbert and Joanne Tompkins, *Post-Colonial Drama: Theory, Practice, Politics* (London: Routledge, 1996), 16.

11. See Ankhi Mukherjee, *What Is a Classic? Postcolonial Rewriting and Invention of the Canon* (Stanford, CA: Stanford Univ. Press, 2014), 111–43.

12. John Millington Synge, *The Playboy of the Western World*, in *J. M. Synge: Collected Works: Plays*, vol. 4, book 2, ed. Ann Saddlemyer (Gerrards Cross: Colin Smythe, 1982), 67.

Stanley Kramer film *Guess Who's Coming to Dinner*, and "The Deportees," a sequel to Doyle's 1987 novel *The Commitments*, which was adapted into a film in 1991. (Other stories like "Home to Harlem," which borrows its title from Claude McKay's 1928 novel, and "I Understand," which plays very loosely with ideas from Ralph Ellison's 1952 novel *Invisible Man*, more obliquely reference the Harlem Renaissance but cannot be considered adaptations or sequels in their own right.) Together, "Guess Who's Coming for the Dinner" and "The Deportees" provide a framework for understanding the aesthetic and political priorities of *The Playboy of the Western World—A New Version* and the post–Celtic Tiger adaptations and sequels that followed in its wake. Although many scholars have written about Doyle's *Metro Éireann* stories, no one has examined their specific role in shaping a Celtic Tiger and post–Celtic Tiger tradition of multicultural adaptations and sequels. It should also be noted that the idea to adapt *The Playboy of the Western World* originated with Adigun, who later invited Doyle to collaborate with him on the playscript in 2006, and that dramatic adaptation was a key component of Arambe Productions from its inception, a point to which I will return. Nevertheless, *The Playboy of the Western World—A New Version* bears the mark of Doyle's fiction, especially in its framing of immigration as a retreading of familiar territory.

In May 2000 Roddy Doyle published his first story for *Metro Éireann*, which bore the familiar title "Guess Who's Coming for the Dinner." An update of the American film starring Sidney Poitier, the story's action centers on a Dublin father, Larry Linnane, whose daughter Stephanie announces she is bringing a Nigerian refugee named Ben home for dinner. Larry immediately assumes the two are dating, and his anxieties begin to mount. He spends the intervening days worrying about the prospect of having a Black man at his table and, potentially, in his family, but he also worries about saying the wrong thing, causing offense, or coming across as racist. In the end, his concerns are for naught. The "small, handsome, intelligent" guest, an accountant, arrives impeccably dressed and proceeds to upset Larry's bigoted assumptions about African men (like Kramer's film, the story does not contemplate what would ensue were the guest not of the professional class).[13] Larry conquers his prejudice and even grants the couple his blessing just in time to learn that Stephanie and Ben are merely friends. In "Guess Who's Coming for the Dinner," the bar for tolerance proves low and the rewards high. Larry need only meet the minimal criteria of hospitality—which he fails decisively to do at several points in the evening, rescued only by his wife's intervention—in order to reap the social and psychological satisfaction of having welcomed a Black man into his home. Just the simple act of shaking Ben's hand affords him the sense of being "sophisticated—not a bother on him," an experience matched only by driving on the Artane roundabout in north Dublin, which always makes Larry feel "modern, successful, Irish."[14] It is no coincidence that proximity to Celtic Tiger–era diversity elicits in Doyle's patriarch the same sensation as a suburban roadworks project erected in the mid-twentieth century during an earlier wave of Irish modernization, for both operate as outward markers of societal progress. Later in the evening, Larry's ability (purely speculative) to accept Ben as his daughter's lover instills in him a full-blown sense of self-satisfied accomplishment: "He wasn't a racist. There was a black man sitting across from him and he wanted to be his father-in-law. He wasn't sure why, but that didn't matter. Larry was happy with himself."[15] Although the character's about-face seems unrealistically abrupt, Larry is correct in saying that the reasons for it do not matter, at least narratively speaking. He is rescued from further introspection by the convenient revelation that Stephanie and Ben are not, in fact, dating. Unlike its source text, Doyle's story requires its characters not to confront, but merely to imagine confronting, the tensions and obstacles that accompany interracial romance. Its referencing of Kramer's film acts more as a red herring than a narrative and thematic guidepost.

13. Roddy Doyle, *The Deportees and Other Stories* (New York: Viking, 2008), 12.

14. Doyle, *Deportees*, 11, 3.

15. Doyle, *Deportees*, 25.

In "Guess Who's Coming for the Dinner," Doyle establishes a tone and arc that many, though not all, of his subsequent *Metro Éireann* stories would follow. New and native Irish characters encounter one another; foibles ensue, usually the stuff of comedy; and in those moments when racism does surface, it is either quickly vanquished or else relegated to the background. In Doyle's fictional world, intolerance is conquered at the level of the individual. Larry's acceptance of Ben does not require that he abandon his broader associations of Africa with AIDS, poverty, criminality, "machetes and machine-guns, and burning car tyres draped around people's necks, the savagery," nor that the Irish state reform its immigration policies and improve its integration efforts.[16] There is no difference between Larry and his dinner guest that cannot be overcome through a shared appreciation of the latter's "Towering Ebony" cologne. As Maureen T. Reddy has suggested, stories like "Guess Who's Coming for the Dinner" reflect the difficulty that Doyle and other contributors faced in the early 2000s in addressing *Metro Éireann*'s two very different implied audiences: Irish nationals sympathetic to multiculturalism who wanted to believe the best about themselves and their conationals, and new migrants who were witness to the racism and inequality that persisted. In his serialized fiction, Reddy argues, Doyle tends to cater to the former audience, thereby reinforcing the paper's adherence to "an integrationist, celebrate-difference racial discourse that is centrist and reformist, not radical or revolutionary."[17]

Doyle's second story for *Metro Éireann*, "The Deportees," which was serialized in 2001 and 2002, also privileges its readership of Irish nationals insofar as it builds on the immense popularity of his breakout novel-turned-film *The Commitments*. The sequel opens as wunderkind Jimmy Rabbitte, the visionary youth who created a north Dublin soul band in *The Commitments*, attempts to enliven

16. Doyle, *Deportees*, 9.

17. Maureen T. Reddy, "Reading and Writing Race in Ireland: Roddy Doyle and 'Metro Éireann,'" *Irish University Review* 35, no. 2 (Autumn–Winter 2005): 378–79.

the tedium of married life and parenthood by forming a new band, this time comprised of Dublin's recent immigrants. "White Irish," he jokes, "need not apply," though he does include a few in the end.[18] As Jimmy assembles the band, which he calls the Deportees—comprised of African, Spanish, Black American, and Traveler vocalists; a Russian drummer, Nigerian djembe drummer, and Romanian accordionist; his trumpet-player son; and two quirky white Irish musicians on guitar and bass—history appears to be repeating itself with a colorful twist. The optimism of "The Deportees" hinges on a form that I am calling the "immigrant-as-sequel," wherein newcomers are envisioned as later iterations of those who preceded them. In identifying the immigrant-as-sequel as a form, I draw on Caroline Levine's useful distinction between genre and form. Whereas *genres* are categories that classify artworks into historically specific groupings, *forms* "are organizations or arrangements that afford repetition and portability across materials and contexts."[19] Malleable, mobile, and multivarious, forms both make and disrupt the political order.[20] It is the *form* of the immigrant-as-sequel that enables the ideological work performed by the *genre* of the Irish multicultural sequel or adaptation. Yet, this form also exceeds literary genre, appearing in sites as diverse as political rhetoric, immigration policy, education, and urban development, both in Ireland and well beyond.[21] While I focus here on its specific role in Celtic Tiger and post–Celtic Tiger era literature and theater, it is important to remember that the immigrant-as-sequel draws its power precisely from its vast diffusion.

18. Doyle, *Deportees*, 36.

19. Caroline Levine, *Forms: Whole, Rhythm, Hierarchy, Network* (Princeton, NJ: Princeton Univ. Press, 2015), 14.

20. For more on form's relationship to political life, see Levine, *Forms*, 11–19.

21. I examine its appearance in mid-twentieth-century journalism and urban planning documents about the Irish neighborhood of Corktown in Detroit, Michigan, in my article "The 'New Irish' Neighborhood: Race and Succession in Ireland and Irish America," in *The Routledge International Handbook of Irish Studies*, ed. Renée Fox, Mike Cronin, and Brian Ó Conchubhair (London: Routledge, 2021).

Through peddling difference as a variation on the familiar, the immigrant-as-sequel form lent stability to the first wave of multicultural literature and theater, which came to a close in 2008 with the financial crash. During the Celtic Tiger years, it worked to the benefit of artists, who were guaranteed audiences that otherwise might not have sought out material about Ireland's immigrant communities. In particular, "The Deportees" and *The Playboy of the Western World—A New Version* capitalized on two of the most globally successful Irish works to date. The immigrant-as-sequel also served readers and audiences by providing an affective inoculation against the perceived strangeness of the "foreigner," allowing them to broach stories about Ireland's newcomers because they were situated comfortably within well-known narrative worlds. The most crucial function of the immigrant-as-sequel form during this period, though, was its ability to generate the congratulatory sense of progress that rested at the heart of the Celtic Tiger multicultural sequel or adaptation. Jimmy Rabbitte's joke that "white Irish need not apply" is funny only because the histories of emigration and anti-Irish discrimination that it references lay firmly in the past, eclipsed by Ireland's newfound prosperity in the 1990s and 2000s. In Jimmy's privileging of immigrant musicians, "The Deportees" implicitly suggests that the white Irish no longer require any such affirmative action. The Celtic Tiger-era multicultural sequel/adaptation ceded the condition of striving to the so-called New Irish who succeeded the native Irish. By bestowing on recent immigrants the opportunity to refashion themselves in the image of Hibernian success—and what are *The Commitments* and *The Playboy of the Western World* if not narratives of unlikely success?—these works invited longtime citizens to imagine themselves as having crossed the finish line of historical development.

Both "The Deportees" and *The Playboy of the Western World—A New Version* center on inchoate fantasies about fame, ones that originate not with the immigrant characters themselves but with the white Irish characters who aspire on their behalf. In Adigun and Doyle's adaptation, the local girls imagine Christopher as a minor celebrity and tabloid star in the making, drawing on mostly African

American pop culture references, including basketball players, Akon, and R. Kelly. During one scene, the girls, who, Pegeen notes, "all tried for Eurovision, and they were shite," declare that Christopher "should be in a group" and proceed to sing "I Believe I Can Fly" behind him as if they are his backup singers. Meanwhile, in "The Deportees," Jimmy fashions his multiracial cover band into a dungaree-and-fedora-clad emblem of Irish diversity. As they play their first real gig amid prop suitcases and a banner that reads "BOUND FOR GLORY,"[22] Jimmy sees their potential anew—"God, they were good, the real thing," he muses, "they were happy, sexy; they were cooking and Irish"—and predicts the band's successful future.[23] Yet, for all their optimism, the two works also intimate the high unlikeliness that these fantasized scenarios will come to fruition. By foisting white Irish ambitions on immigrant characters while simultaneously undercutting them, "The Deportees" and *The Playboy of the Western World—A New Version* encapsulate the ideological handiwork of the immigrant-as-sequel form, which defuses the threat of pluralism in Celtic Tiger era literature and theater. Through its operation, tolerance is made safe and satisfying. Irish progress is confirmed in the passing of the aspirational baton to new arrivals, and the predictable repetition of late capitalist prosperity is enlivened by an amusing bit of variation that, importantly, never threatens to upend the social order. Even the works' divergences from their source texts err on the side of reassurance. In Doyle's world, the Black man coming for the dinner has no interest in marrying your daughter. The patricidal playboy, whom Pegeen accuses of being "a sponger, milking the system," turns out to have an MBA and a job as managing director of his father's thriving import business back home. And the Deportees will not overtake the Irish airwaves anytime soon: their big break is a comically modest gig at the twenty-first birthday party for the daughter of the owner of the local takeaway Celtic Tandoori.

22. Doyle, *Deportees*, 65.
23. Doyle, *Deportees*, 67, 69.

Doyle attempts to be optimistic at the end of "The Deportees," and Jimmy predicts the group's longevity: "They were happy up there. And Jimmy knew: they were staying."[24] At this point, an omniscient narrator takes over, foretelling the group's prospective fame. Throughout the denouement, the narrator noticeably employs the future tense: "Jimmy's right. . . . The Deportees will stay together. . . . For years and albums. . . . They'll get better and quite well known. They'll tour Wales and Nigeria."[25] The fantasy about their musical success spirals into other forecasts about their fate. They will cycle in and out of the country, the narrator predicts; they will gain legal status through marriage; they will not be deported. As the fantasizing goes into overdrive in the story's closing moments—the narrator envisions the band sharing pizza and tea with the Wu-Tang Clan, Lauryn Hill, Bono, Eminem and his mother, and Yo-Yo Ma—it becomes clear just how hard Doyle is working to end on a hopeful note. The decidedly speculative conclusion of "The Deportees" betokens the fragility of Celtic Tiger integration, which would become especially apparent during the recession when funding cuts severely hampered migrant-oriented state efforts and nongovernmental organizations,[26] as well as intercultural arts initiatives.[27] The turn away from multicultural priorities in the post–Celtic Tiger years is also apparent in Doyle's subsequent literary output. In 2013, eleven

24. Doyle, *Deportees*, 74.

25. Doyle, *Deportees*, 75.

26. For instance, the National Consultative Committee on Racism and Interculturalism was closed in 2008, and its functions were absorbed by the minister for integration, a position subsequently eliminated in 2011. In addition, organizations like the Human Rights Commission and the Equality Authority (which merged in 2014), as well as smaller migrant-oriented and migrant-led nongovernmental organizations, received significant cuts in funding. See Theophilus Ejorh, "The Challenge of Resilience: Migrant-led Organizations and the Recession in Ireland," *Journal of International Migration and Integration* 16, no. 3 (August 2015): 683, 696–97.

27. Jason King, "Contemporary Irish Theatre, the New Playboy Controversy, and the Economic Crisis," *Irish Studies Review* 24, no. 1 (2016): 67–78.

years after the serialization of "The Deportees" in *Metro Éireann* and six years after its republication in the short story collection of the same title, Doyle published another sequel to *The Commitments*, titled *The Guts*. In the novel, a middle-aged Jimmy battles stomach cancer, runs a music website, and manages gigs for washed-up punk bands. All of the characters are explicitly or implicitly white, and while Jimmy reminisces about the Commitments and other previous bands he managed, no reference is made to either the Deportees or the changing Ireland they heralded. Ireland's migrant communities are simply written out. The novel's only allusions to foreignness, in fact, take the form of a racist metaphor (Jimmy likens a music festival tent city to Darfur—a "kind o' Southside Darfur," his companion counters) and a joke (Jimmy's son and friends impersonate a Bulgarian band to bolster his career).[28] Doyle's erasure of immigrants in *The Guts*, and the more general retreat from integration-related priorities during the recession, operate not unlike the turn in popular culture from gender equity to renewed discourses of manliness, which Diane Negra has analyzed. In each instance, progressive politics is regarded as "a luxury that [Ireland] can no longer afford under [the] straitened circumstances" of austerity.[29]

Doyle's *Metro Éireann* stories, like Adigun and Doyle's adaptation of Synge's play, attempt to tell an optimistic story about the multicultural generosity of the Irish citizenry who, having reached the telos of prosperity, benevolently offer new immigrants the opportunity to work themselves up the socioeconomic ladder. For instance, early in act 2 of *The Playboy of the Western World—A New Version*, the newly employed Christopher admires the "First World" amenities of his workplace (not to mention his own reflection in the mirror), declaring, "Henceforth, it's forward ever, backward never."[30] Like its

28. Roddy Doyle, *The Guts* (Toronto: Knopf Canada, 2013), 265.

29. Diane Negra, "Adjusting Men and Abiding Mammies: Gendering the Recession in Ireland," *Gender, Sexuality and Feminism* 1, no. 2 (December 2014): 44.

30. The play neglects to credit the line, which was coined by Kwame Nkrumah and adopted by his revolutionary Ghanaian Convention People's Party. This

counterpart in Synge's original, the scene suggests a causal relationship between the Playboy's new location and his enhanced future
prospects. But in order to sustain the fiction of Irish beneficence, one
must overlook both Michael's blatant exploitation of Christopher's
undocumented status and the glaring fact that Christopher enjoys
a far more privileged life back home in Nigeria than do any of his
benefactors in Ireland. Indeed, amid the strained optimism of Celtic
Tiger multicultural sequels and adaptations lurks a profound sense of
loss. For Jimmy Rabbitte, in particular, Ireland's new immigrants stir
in him a youthful working-class ambitiousness that he can now only
seem to access by proxy. It is as if the native Irish are no longer fitting
subjects for stories of upward mobility, and thus the immigrant must
stand in as surrogate for a bygone, reckless kind of Irish longing.
Joseph Cleary has identified an "'end of history' structure of feeling"
that, he argues, "weighs upon" Celtic Tiger literary production.[31]
Cleary is drawing on Francis Fukuyama's influential pronouncement
in 1989 that the end of history had arrived, by which he meant the end
of viable alternatives to capitalism. Events may continue to unfold,
but for Fukuyama, the window in which vast epochal transformation
might transpire had already closed.[32] The Celtic Tiger multicultural
sequel/adaptation is one site where this sense of an ending plays out.
These wistful works at once celebrate and mourn the completed development of the native Irish social body, whose youthful pursuit of
Bildung appears to have drawn to a close. This is why the narrative
energy shifts in these works to the still-developing corporate body of
Ireland's new immigrant population.

---

omission is symptomatic of the play's broader tendency to limit reflection on African politics. For instance, earlier Christopher alludes to his father's profiteering
from the political corruption of the First Republic, but trails off when he "sens[es]
that he is losing Pegeen's interest."

31. Joseph Cleary, *Outrageous Fortune: Culture and Capital in Modern Ireland* (Derry: Field Day, 2006), 2.

32. Francis Fukuyama, "The End of History?" *National Interest* 16 (Summer
1989): 3–18.

The aesthetic effects of repetition, familiarity, and optimism afforded by the immigrant-as-sequel have significant implications for the formation or forestalling of political solidarities. During the Celtic Tiger, the form tended to serve conservative ends, performing and rewarding Irish tolerance all the while relieving citizens of their ongoing responsibility to migrant individuals and communities. By peddling the soon-debunked fantasy of Ireland's definitive socioeconomic advancement, the immigrant-as-sequel cultivated a misplaced faith in the permanence of upward mobility and the reproducibility of Irish success. Meanwhile, anti-immigrant sentiment and incidents of racism were on the rise.[33] The most significant outcome of this backlash was the 2004 citizenship referendum, in which a majority of Irish voters elected to rescind automatic birthright citizenship.[34] It is no accident that the opening of the Irish canon to immigrant artists, characters, and storylines coincided with the contraction of political rights. These conflicting developments present divergent responses to a shared predicament: how to secure a state of predictable prosperity that one hopes is permanent, but suspects to be entirely fleeting.

Adigun and Doyle's adaptation premiered in the autumn of 2007 amid early warning signs of the impending global financial crisis. While it evinces some of the strategic optimism that characterizes Celtic Tiger multiculturalism, the play also anticipates the self-reckoning that would suffuse post–Celtic Tiger sequels and adaptations. *The Playboy of the Western World—A New Version* unfolds

---

33. Paul Cullen, *Refugees and Asylum-Seekers in Ireland* (Cork: Cork Univ. Press, 2000); Steve Garner, *Racism in the Irish Experience* (London: Pluto, 2004); Ronit Lentin and Robbie McVeigh, eds., *Racism and Anti-Racism in Ireland* (Belfast: Beyond the Pale, 2002).

34. As scholars have shown, anti-immigrant rhetoric about anchor babies and maternity tourism escalated in the lead-up to the referendum. See Michael Breen, Amanda Haynes, and Eoin Devereux, "Citizens, Loopholes and Maternity Tourists: Irish Print Media Coverage of the 2004 Citizenship Referendum," in *Uncertain Ireland: A Sociological Chronicle, 2003–2004*, ed. Mary P. Corcoran and Michel Peillon (Dublin: Institute of Public Administration, 2006), 59–72.

at the fringes of the Irish boom, both figuratively and literally: the action occurs at a remove from the city-center concentration of financial capital, in a suburban Dublin pub that also serves as a front for Michael's criminal activities. And unlike Doyle's stories, where the connections between upstanding natives and newcomers are forged electively through the familiar rituals of hospitality or collaboration, the adaptation examines the dangerous symbiosis that develops underground between marginalized citizens who have everything to gain and coercible undocumented migrants who have nothing to lose. Adigun and Doyle's play operates as a pivot between first-wave and second-wave multicultural literature and theater. Whereas the former employs the immigrant-as-sequel form to temper the shock of the new, the latter uses it to underscore Ireland's responsibility to new immigrants, whose journeys echo those undertaken by its own citizens in the not-so-distant past. As Irish and non-Irish histories of migration and trauma converge in these second-wave works, they ameliorate what Pilar Villar-Argáiz has termed the "butterfly effects of globalization" by opening unexpected points of transnational empathy and alliance.[35]

Post–Celtic Tiger multicultural theater enacts the immigrant-as-sequel form in a number of different and innovative ways. In Dermot Bolger's 2006 play *The Townlands of Brazil*, which was produced before the financial crash, but which registers a prescient skepticism about Irish prosperity, the use of dual roles facilitates the parallel stories of a pregnant Irish emigrant who departs for England in the 1960s and a Polish immigrant who arrives to Celtic Tiger Ireland in search of work and opportunity for herself and her young daughter. The mirroring effect generated by the actors, who play Irish characters in act 1 and New Irish migrants in act 2, grants bodily shape to the immigrant-as-sequel form, channeling it into a mode of critique rather than a mechanism for reinforcing consensus. *The Townlands*

---

35. Pilar Villar-Argáiz, "Introduction: The Immigrant in Contemporary Irish Literature," in *Literary Visions of Multicultural Ireland*, ed. Pilar Villar-Argáiz (Manchester: Manchester Univ. Press, 2014), 9.

of Brazil is the second in a trilogy of plays commissioned from Bolger by the axis: Ballymun Arts Centre to mark the demolition and regeneration of Ballymun, a 1960s housing project that had fallen into disrepair during the latter decades of the twentieth century, and it focuses attention on the migrant workers whose underrecognized and undercompensated labor fueled the utopianism of postwar British urbanization and Celtic Tiger–era construction alike. Although the play does not fit within the genre of the multicultural sequel, it generates the sequel's logic through alternate dramatic means.

Adigun's 2013 play, *The Paddies of Parnell Street*, also draws together the painful history of Irish emigration and the experiences of Ireland's recent immigrants, albeit in a more oblique manner. The play was adapted from Jimmy Murphy's 2000 play, *The Kings of the Kilburn High Road*, which depicts a reunion of aging, mostly disappointed, Irish emigrants a quarter century after their arrival in London during the 1970s. *The Paddies of Parnell Street* reimagines Murphy's Irish expatriates as contemporary Dublin-based Nigerian immigrants who arrived during the early Celtic Tiger years. While the interplay of the source text and the adaptation invites comparisons between Ireland's past departures and its present arrivals, these insights are reserved mostly for scholars and theater aficionados. *The Paddies of Parnell Street* does not make the analogy explicit like Bolger does in *The Townlands of Brazil*, nor can it depend (as could Adigun and Doyle with *The Playboy of the Western World—A New Version*) on an audience familiar enough with Murphy's play to recognize its traces. Rather, the immigrant-as-sequel form is manifested in the play's production history. *The Paddies of Parnell Street* was the third version of *The Kings of the Kilburn High Road* produced by Adigun and Arambe Productions. The first version, which premiered in Dublin in 2006, was a straightforward production of Murphy's play with an important twist: West African–Irish actors were cast in the roles of Irish emigrants living in London. The second version, which was staged in Lagos in 2010 under the title *Home, Sweet Home*, also took place in London but replaced the Irish expats of *The Kings of the Kilburn High Road* with contemporary West

African immigrants. These prior productions inform *The Paddies of Parnell Street*, amplifying its palimpsestic meaning.[36] The layered genesis of *The Paddies of Parnell Street* distinguishes it from earlier multicultural adaptations like *The Playboy of the Western World—A New Version*. Whereas the latter frames the phenomenon of multiculturalism as a one-and-done endeavor, the former supplies a theatrical model for approaching migration as an ongoing process of relocation, revision, and readjustment.

Another multicultural adaptation, *The Hijabi Monologues Ireland*, premiered in 2013 at axis: Ballymun Arts Centre. The production was based on the American theater project *The Hijabi Monologues*, founded in 2006 by University of Chicago graduate students Sahar Ullah, Zeenat Rahman, and Daniel Morrison as a Muslim response to Eve Ensler's 1996 fringe-theater-production-turned-international-sensation, *The Vagina Monologues*. While *The Hijabi Monologues Ireland* included a number of the monologues from the original American script, the production also featured several new Irish-authored monologues that addressed the specific nature of Muslim integration in Ireland.[37] Serving as the launch for *The Hijabi Monologues Europe*, a British Council project, the 2013 Irish production established a model of adaptation that would be employed by future licensed productions in Europe.[38] A contest was held to solicit stories from Muslim women in Ireland, winning entries were incorporated into the script, Irish actors were cast, and a

---

36. For a reading of the interplay between the different versions, see Jason King, "Three Kings: Migrant Masculinities in Irish Social Practice, Theoretical Perspective and Theatre Performance," *Irish Journal of Applied Social Studies* 16, no. 1 (2016): 20–34.

37. The site-specific elements of *The Hijabi Monologues Ireland* distinguish it from a preliminary production staged a year earlier in Ireland as the project's European premiere. The 2012 production followed the American script and featured an American cast.

38. The Irish production was followed by the *Hijabi Monologen Nederland*, which toured the Netherlands in 2014, and the *Hijabi Monologues London*, which premiered at the Bush Theatre in September 2017.

variety of local and national partnerships were forged to support and promote the production. *The Hijabi Monologues Ireland* enacts the immigrant-as-sequel form in certain parts in the production, such as the monologue "Light on My Face," which describes the social ostracizing faced by an unwed woman who becomes pregnant. The monologue recalls the historical treatment of unwed Irish mothers, drawing into silent relation the rigid patriarchal norms of Islamic and Catholic conservatism. Yet, it is in the work's production model that the sequelized logic of the multicultural adaptation begins to give way to something more synchronic and circuitous. By licensing *The Hijabi Monologues* script and then building a locally based community theater coalition to adapt it, the Irish production established a portable model for staging many such productions around the globe. The routes of influence that inform any given production of this theatrical work (say, the 2014–15 production of *Hijabi Monologen Nederland*, which came to the Netherlands by way of Ireland, by way of the United States) more closely enact the peripatetic nature of contemporary migration.[39] In *The Hijabi Monologues Ireland* and other second-wave multicultural adaptations, the immigrant begins to look less like a sequel and more like a diasporic franchise.[40]

As a critical mass of immigrant and second-generation voices has emerged in Irish writing and theater during more recent years, a wide array of genres and media have come to supplant the multicultural sequel and adaptation, and for good reason. These creators have original stories to tell, and not simply variations on a theme. *The Playboy of the Western World—A New Version* reflects a specific historical moment, when the optimism of early Celtic Tiger multiculturalism began to fray amid escalating signs of the economic

39. The *Hijabi Monologen Nederland* was launched after the British Council invited artist Rajae El Mouhandiz to attend the 2012 European premiere of *The Hijabi Monologues* in Dublin, along with other European Union–based guests.

40. For more on *The Hijabi Monologues Ireland*, see Sarah L. Townsend, "Muslim Integration and the *Hijabi Monologues Ireland*," *Irish University Review* 51, no. 2 (2021): 209–26.

catastrophe that would follow. The play manages to forestall serious reservations about the finality of prosperity and the prospect of a multiracial future only through the deus ex machina of its hero's considerable privilege, which far outstrips anything enjoyed by his Syngean predecessor. Christopher Malomo's wealth and the global mobility it affords is not simply reassuring; it threatens to invalidate the role of the striving Playboy altogether. This is a necessary tradeoff, perhaps, for a more realistic version of Adigun and Doyle's adaptation—a play about a poor uneducated Nigerian father-killer who nearly scams his way into a white Irish family and a criminal enterprise, only to be executed and disappeared—is one not easily staged as a comedy.

4

The Intercultural Theater Wars and *The Playboy of the Western World—A New Version*

Emer O'Toole

In theater and performance studies, there exists a long-running debate over the politics and ethics of Western intercultural artists—such as Richard Schechner, Peter Brook, Jerry Grotowski, and Ariane Mnouchkine—looking to Othered cultures, often in developing countries, in search of artistic collaboration and inspiration. Many of these artists see the Western canon as moribund and in need of reinvigoration. For example, Mnouchkine explains that in deciding to perform Shakespeare with Théâtre du Soleil "a recourse to Asia became a necessity" in order to avoid "the realistic and the prosaic."[1] She makes Asian theater a "voyage of research" because "Western theatre offers little in this way"[2] and realism bores her.[3] But postcolonial and cultural materialist critics—such as Rustom Bharucha, Una Chaudhuri, Helen Gilbert, Jaqueline Lo, Gautam Dasgupta, and Ric

---

1. Ariane Mnouchkine, "The Theatre Is Oriental," in *The Intercultural Performance Reader*, ed. Henry Bial (London: Routledge, 1996), 93–98.

2. Mnouchkine, "Theatre Is Oriental," 96.

3. See also Peter Brook, "The Deadly Theatre," in *The Empty Space: A Book about the Theatre: Deadly, Holy, Rough, Immediate* (New York: Scribner, 1968), 9–41, which designates the theater one sees most often as "excruciatingly boring" and laments the infection of grand opera, classical tragedy, Molière, Bertolt Brecht, and William Shakespeare with this deadly disease.

Knowles—decry the paternalistic and often exploitative nature of these intercultural interactions.[4]

In Ireland, with the change in cultural demographics that accompanied and extended beyond the Celtic Tiger years (1994–2008)—a new multiculturalism, which Ronit Lentin's work for the Trinity Immigration Initiative indicates is now a lasting part of Irish society—there has been a proliferation of intercultural theater, some aimed at reinvigorating the Irish canon. In this chapter, I reflect on the lessons to be learned from the history of what Ric Knowles calls the "intercultural wars"[5] as they pertain to the controversy surrounding Bisi Adigun and Roddy Doyle's high-profile intercultural adaptation of John Millington Synge's *The Playboy of the Western World*, performed at the Abbey Theatre in 2007 and 2008–9. Irish artists and arts institutions have much to gain from considered engagement with the tensions that have bristled under the banner of theatrical interculturalism since the 1980s, namely those surrounding the use of Othered cultures to reanimate the Western canon, attempts to elide difference in intercultural exchanges, and attention to historically inscribed power dynamics in collaborative exchanges. The rise of the field of performance studies in the 1980s and its central debates pertaining to intercultural theater practice in many ways lie at the heart of the dispute between Adigun, Doyle, and the Abbey Theatre concerning *The Playboy of the Western World—A New Version*. I

4. See Rustom Bharucha, "A View from India," in *Peter Brook and the Mahabharata: Critical Perspectives*, ed. David Williams (London: Routledge, 1991), 228–52; Rustom Bharucha, "Reply to Richard Schechner," *Asian Theatre Journal* 1, no. 2 (1984): 254–60; Una Chaudhuri, "Working Out (of) Place: Brook's Mahabharata and the Problematics of Intercultural Performance," in *Staging Resistance*, ed. Jenny Spencer (Ann Arbor: Univ. of Michigan Press, 1998); Jacqueline Lo and Helen Gilbert, "Toward a Topography of Cross-Cultural Theatre Praxis," *Drama Review* 46, no. 3 (2002): 31–53; Gautam Dasgupta, "Peter Brook's 'Orientalism,'" in *Peter Brook and the Mahabharata: Critical Perspectives*, ed. David Williams (London: Routledge, 1991), 262–67; and Ric Knowles, *Theatre and Interculturalism* (London: Palgrave Macmillan, 2010), 2–5, 21–41.

5. Knowles, *Theatre and Interculturalism*, 13.

spend the first part of this chapter describing the rise of intercultural theater scholarship and practice, and its attendant ethical debates, in the two decades prior to Adigun and Doyle's production of *The Playboy of the Western World—A New Version*. I then argue that the Abbey Theatre's public framing and ultimate staging of *The Playboy of the Western World—A New Version* reproduced these inequitable power dynamics by marginalizing Adigun's role and vision within its intercultural collaborative exchange.

Intercultural theater practice is, at base, any theatrical fusing of two or more cultures, whereas intercultural theater scholarship tends to focus primarily, though not exclusively, on theatrical encounters between members of different nation-states. While intercultural theater practice is often driven by a search for new and exciting aesthetic interactions, intercultural theater scholarship is largely concerned with how material inequalities and Orientalist relationships resulting from colonial pasts inform many such collaborations, creating ethical and political challenges for those involved. Intercultural theater practice can be read as a continuation of Orientalist dynamics of the West speaking for the East, or of Europe speaking for Africa, or even of Dublin speaking for the Aran Islands, which is something of the case in Synge's *Playboy of the Western World*. Such interculturalism can be seen as cultural piracy, specifically the appropriation of Othered cultural artifacts for economic or symbolic profit. This polarized debate between the dichotomous ways of reading intercultural theater—broadly cast as the universalist and aesthetic versus the materialist and political[6]—is what Knowles refers to as the "intercultural wars."

Many theorists tread a middle path on this contested ground. For example, Brian Singleton warns that "the danger of following [Edward] Said's politics and Bharucha's prescriptions is to produce hermetically sealed metacultures which do not exchange, trade, or evolve,"[7] but Singleton equally advises "the unequal distribution of

6. Knowles, *Theatre and Interculturalism*, 20.

7. Brian Singleton, "The Pursuit of Otherness for the Investigation of Self," *Theatre Research International* 22, no. 2 (1997): 96.

wealth, power, and access to other cultures means that a 'culture of choice' might only ever be a first-world postmodern possibility."[8] Lo and Gilbert locate theater productions on a spectrum between collaborative interculturalism and imperialist interculturalism,[9] while Daphne Lei uses the term *Hegemonic Intercultural Theatre* to distinguish "a specific artistic genre and state of mind that combines First World capital and brainpower with Third World raw material and labor" from more egalitarian fare.[10] In short, scholars and artists have long recognized that intercultural theater practice has both ethical problems and positive potential, sometimes simultaneously. As I argue elsewhere,[11] the position that Western practitioners should not assume, but can earn the right, to represent Othered nations, cultures, and people—dependent on adequate engagement with the materialities of history, global power dynamics, economics, politics, language, class, and gender informing intercultural productions—might be said to constitute a contemporary morality of the academic field.

Perhaps the most (in)famous focal point for tensions surrounding the intercultural theater wars is Peter Brook's *Mahabharata* (1985). Finding Western theater culture "deadly" and "moribund,"[12] Brook looked to Asia and Africa for inspiration, material, and even "ideal" audiences.[13] Informed by a universalist doctrine Brook designates the "culture of links," the British director and his international ensemble

8. Singleton, "Pursuit of Otherness," 96.

9. Lo and Gilbert, "Toward a Topography of Cross-Cultural Theatre Praxis," 31–53.

10. Daphne Lei, "Interruption, Intervention, Interculturalism: Robert Wilson's HIT Productions in Taiwan," *Theatre Journal* 63, no. 4 (2011): 571.

11. Emer O'Toole, "Cultural Capital in Intercultural Theatre: A Study of Pan Pan Theatre Company's *The Playboy of the Western World*," *Target* 25, no. 3 (2013): 407–26; Emer O'Toole, "Towards Best Intercultural Practice: An Analysis of Tim Supple's Pan-Indian *A Midsummer Night's Dream*," *Journal of Adaptation in Film and Performance* 4, no. 3 (2011): 289–302.

12. Peter Brook, *The Empty Space: A Book about the Theatre: Deadly, Holy, Rough, Immediate* (New York: Scribner, 1968).

13. Peter Brook, *Threads of Time* (London: Counterpoint, 1999).

of actors created a retelling of the Indian religious epic about the origins of the world. Brook and adaptor Jean-Claude Carrière spent time in India researching the production, studying ancient texts and observing folk and traditional performances of the epic. The acting ensemble also traveled to India in preparation for the performance. The resultant production, which gave the great epic an accessible Western teleology and theatrical format, toured the world to great critical acclaim, but never played in India. "*The Mahabharata* for thousands of years had belonged to its soil, India," Brook said, "but now, just like Shakespeare, it demanded to be opened to all humanity."[14]

For scholars such as Dasgupta, Pradip Bhattacharya, Bharucha, and Marvin Carlson, however, Brook's production glossed over the religious and cultural significance of the *Mahabharata* to many Indian people, its universalism representing an unapologetic neocolonialism and Orientalism. Carlson asserts: "The universal, like the unmediated, can be and has been a dangerous and self-deceptive vision, denying the voice of the Other in an attempt to transcend it."[15] Dasgupta regrets that while, in India, performances of the *Mahabharata*, through heterogeneous enactments, address "a deeply engrained structure of ritual beliefs and ethical codes of conduct intrinsic to its audience," the epic becomes "nothing, an empty shell, if it is read merely as a compendium of martial legends of revenge, valour and bravura," as "is the reading attributed to *The Mahabharata* by Carrière and Brook."[16] Bharucha locates Brook's interculturalism in a colonial tradition: the British took Indian raw

14. Peter Brook, quoted in Saumya Ancheri, "'The Mahabharata Does Not Leave You': Notes from Peter Book's Third Play about the Epic," *Scroll.in*, February 15, 2016, https://scroll.in/article/803515/the-mahabharata-does-not-leave-you-notes-from-peter-brooks-third-play-about-the-epic.

15. Marvin Carlson, "Brook and Mnouchkine: Passages to India?" in *Peter Brook and the Mahabharata: Critical Perspectives*, ed. David Williams (London: Routledge, 1991), 91.

16. Dasgupta, "Peter Brook's 'Orientalism,'" 264.

materials, transported them to factories in England where they were transformed into commodities, then "forcibly" sold these back to India; Brook acts similarly, as a "maestro" who converts the cultural artifacts of the Orient "into raw material for his own intercultural experiments."[17] Even Richard Schechner, who usually champions the potential for productive exchange in intercultural theater, chides Brook's attempts to "elide difference" in *The Mahabharata*.[18]

Similar debates also raged in relation to practices within the academy itself, particularly about the ideologies and methodologies of intercultural performance studies. In the early 1980s, Schechner became entangled in a heated and personal public debate over his own intercultural theater practices with Bharucha, who questioned his ethics of representation. Schechner, while taking care to acknowledge that there can be some dubious forces at work in cultural exchange, believes intercultural practice, including reenactments and borrowings, should be celebrated insofar as it allows people to influence one another and learn from one another.[19] For Schechner, it is patronizing not to acknowledge that cultural exchange is a two-way street, especially because, as he sees it, "traditional boundaries not only between peoples and nations but also within nations and cultures are being transformed if not abolished."[20] Bharucha, conversely, sees intercultural exchange conducted by many Western scholars and practitioners, Schechner included, as appropriative, exploitative, and ethnocentric. He demands that intercultural exchanges be "confronted within the particularities of a specific historical condition";[21] for Bharucha, "it should be acknowledged that the implications of interculturalism are very different for people in impoverished,

17. Bharucha, "View from India," 229.

18. Richard Schechner, *The Future of Ritual: Writings on Culture and Performance* (London: Routledge, 1993), 17.

19. Richard Schechner, "A Reply to Rustom Bharucha," *Asian Theatre Journal* 1, no. 2 (1984): 252.

20. Schechner, "Reply to Rustom Bharucha," 248.

21. Bharucha, "Reply to Richard Schechner," 255.

'developing' countries like India, and for people in technologically advanced capitalist societies like America."[22] He takes umbrage at the idea that one can perform the cultures of others in the same way that one can perform one's own culture. Bharucha writes, "I believe a distinction should be made between 'performing your own culture' and 'performing other peoples' cultures.' Even if these performances were possible, they would be two totally different propositions demanding totally disparate degrees of absorption, knowledge, and commitment. Schechner's writings do not sufficiently acknowledge the implications of this distinction. The predominant thrust of his thought is directed towards the synthesis of cultures, or more precisely, in his words, towards the 'elision' of the differences that exist between 'them' and 'us.'"[23] As the postnational "intercultural phase of human history"[24] foretold by Schechner in 1985 failed to materialize, and as intercultural artists and scholars continued to operate in ways that did not sufficiently acknowledge the effects of material inequalities on their exchanges, intercultural performance studies found it increasingly difficult to defend itself against the slew of postcolonial, material, and political voices asking it to account for its cultural privilege and bias.

By the time Schechner's edited volume *By Means of Performance: Intercultural Studies of Performance and Ritual* came out in 1990, with Edith Turner's analyses of Yakui deer dances and Phillip Zarrilli's writing on the Asian body, objections were increasingly vocal regarding the moral authority of scholars to subject cultural practices that were not their own to the same deconstructionist airs as Western cultures, as well as the neocolonial implications of recasting Othered cultural practices as performances to be observed, reenacted, and explained by the Western scholar. The well-intentioned project of admitting performances outside the Western canon to university

22. Bharucha, "Reply to Richard Schechner," 255.

23. Bharucha, "Reply to Richard Schechner," 255–56.

24. Richard Schechner, *Between Theatre and Anthropology* (Philadelphia: Univ. of Pennsylvania Press, 1985), 149.

curriculums could equally be read as a self-interested attempt to reinvigorate those curriculums, keeping Western arts and humanities programs profitable through cultural appropriation. Subjecting the religions, rituals, and cultural practices of Othered peoples, often those without their own academic voices, to anthropological study and performative reenactment risked exoticism and "speaking for the Other," aspects of cultural colonialism that postcolonial critics in parallel fields were busy deriding. It would seem that while Schechner, Brook, and other practitioners of intercultural theater practice and scholarship saw themselves as leaders of an antihegemonic movement dedicated to resisting the lionization of the Western canon through the celebration of formerly colonized or denigrated cultures, their critics saw them as something like neocolonial, patriarchal exploiters.

This history of intercultural theater practice is urgently relevant to Ireland, to Irish theater studies, and to the performance of Irish cultural identity. The movement of intercultural theater that began with the Celtic Tiger is largely cosmopolitan, humanistic, and born out of interest in Othered cultures. Having said that, many Irish practitioners and scholars have yet to learn the lessons apparent from the fate of Brook and Schechner's generation of interculturalists, and could benefit from careful consideration of the place of the Western canon in intercultural exchanges, the politics and ethics of attempts to elide difference, and the effects of historically inscribed power dynamics on contemporary intercultural collaborations.

Jason King, who has been at the forefront of documenting the representation of asylum seekers, refugees, and other immigrants on the Irish stage, calls for greater use of the wider debate surrounding intercultural theater in the Irish setting. In an attempt to move beyond Irish theater discourse dominated by the challenges to postcolonial-focused models of scholarship posed by globalization, King traces the beginnings of an intercultural theater movement in Ireland. King's proposal to apply the wider debate surrounding intercultural theater to the Irish context has radical potential, but I think this potential has not been recognized, as it can be read simply as a plea for greater attention to the increasingly culturally and ethnically diverse productions the Irish stage has to offer. Looking at the oftentimes fraught yet potentially productive discourse about intercultural theater and performance studies, however, it becomes clear that intercultural analysis in the Irish context has a deeper potential, specifically, to destabilize the fixities of performances of Irishness—both canonical and everyday—while dealing respectfully with cultural difference. Intercultural discourse can help us recognize the privilege inherent in being able to declare one's canon open to reimaginings, as well as in declaring one's cultural practices "performance." It reveals a set of provocations regarding how to collaborate and deal with cultural difference. And it offers a valuable and productive set of historical precedents that can enable us to think through the power dynamics at play in Ireland's intercultural milieu.

Indeed, nuanced intercultural consideration may well have avoided the situation wherein, in 2013, Ireland's national theater, the Abbey, paid out €600,000[25] to settle a copyright case with Bisi Adigun, the Nigerian cowriter of *The Playboy of the Western World—A New Version*. Adigun and Roddy Doyle's adaptation was produced at the Abbey Theatre on the centenary of Synge's original production. The adaptation is set in a west Dublin suburb in 2007, amongst gangland criminals, and Christy Mahon becomes Christopher Malomo, a Nigerian asylum seeker. The script follows the bends and twists of Synge's plot precisely and beautifully, updating each event with humour and an urban edge. The dark brown oaks of the set on the Abbey Theatre stage invoked the earthy, rustic furnishings of traditional productions of *The Playboy of the Western World*, while the walls of O'Flaherty's pub are hung with pictures of Mary Robinson, Michael Flatley, and Roy Keane, modern icons representative of a certain type of cosmopolitan Irishness, marking the space as a site of globalized encounters. Guinness signs and an ornamental bale

---

25. Ronan McGreevy, "Abbey 'to Pay €600,000' in Dispute over Play Copyright," *Irish Times* January 31, 2013, http://www.irishtimes.com/news/abbey-to-pay-600-000-in-dispute-over-play-copyright-1.1255531.

of turf beside an artificial fire draw our attention to what the script calls "an invented form of Irishness," a form that seems outdated when juxtaposed with markers of rough reality—CCTV, Lycra-clad women, leather-clad men, drugs, and the constant threat of violence.

The impulse to reimagine *The Playboy of the Western World* sprang from Adigun's desire to use theater to contribute to Ireland's emergent "discourse of migration, otherness, diversity."[26] In choosing to collaborate, Doyle and Adigun sought to make the production an intercultural one by fusing their respective experiences, traditions, and creative talents from distinct cultural milieux. Both authors brought knowledge and intimacy of their cultural, racial, and class-based constituencies, allowing rich characterizations based in two distinct cultures, even while they wrote each line together. The result was so successful that the Abbey Theatre programmed the play for a second run starting in December 2008.

But behind the scenes, and especially in the lead-up to and during the second production, rifts had started to form. Adigun withdrew his support from the second production (2008–9) over a dispute with the Abbey Theatre about how the royalties would be paid, and he initiated a number of legal proceedings in relation to it. Following the second mounting of *The Playboy of the Western World—A New Version*, Adigun sued the Abbey, Doyle, and director Jimmy Fay for breach of contract and infringement of his copyright, claiming that 120 changes had been made to the script without his consent. This action went to the High Court, and resulted in an admission of failure to pay royalties and violation of Adigun's moral rights on behalf of the Abbey, who settled the case at great expense. Adigun was awarded €200,000, including €40,000 in royalties to Arambe Productions, and €60,000 to cover some of his legal costs—thus the Abbey's €600,000 payout, which included its own legal fees, to address and settle the case.

---

26. Bisi Adigun, interview, January 13, 2009, in Emer O'Toole, "Rights of Representation: An Ethics of Intercultural Theatre Practice" (PhD diss., Royal Holloway, Univ. of London, 2012), 301.

In an interview with me, Adigun took issue with how the Abbey framed the play in its preproduction marketing, pointing out that the theater did not use the word *intercultural* in any of its publicity.[27] Indeed, the emphasis in the promotional material on the Abbey Theatre website focused on the play as a "contemporary reimagining" of "the most famous and infamous play in The Abbey Theatre's repertoire."[28] The promotional images highlight the blackness of the stranger on the CCTV screen, but the accompanying text does not suggest that the audience engage with the cultural difference that blackness might imply. Rather, we are told by the Abbey's marketing that in "this vivid retelling Synge's play rediscovers its ability to tell the truth of a contemporary Irish experience and continues its legacy, vibrant as ever."[29] And the outreach resources issued by the Abbey for students wishing to engage with the production—comprised of performers' diaries, interviews with Adigun and Doyle, extensive notes on the production, and guidelines for writing a review of the show—do not mention the words *intercultural* or *multicultural* at all. Although the sixty-four-page guidance notes do touch on issues of national identity, refugees and asylum seekers, contemporary Nigeria, and the significance of being an outsider, in the main, the focus is on Synge's play reimagined and the Abbey as a prominent cultural institution. The concern of national identity is simply one of many themes outlined in this material, and Nigerian affairs are listed alongside violence and "happy-slapping" under "Contemporary Issues." The absence of multicultural and intercultural handles in its promotional and outreach material raises the issue of the increasing complexity of the role of the Abbey Theatre as a national theater in a multicultural state. The framing of *The Playboy of the Western*

27. Adigun, interview, 304.

28. "The Playboy of the Western World," Abbey Theatre, 2007, last modified December 10, 2008, http://www.abbeytheatre.ie/whatson/playboy.html.

29. "Playboy of the Western World"; "What's On: The Playboy of the Western World," Abbey Theatre, 2008, last modified March 14, 2012, http://www.abbey theatre.ie/whats_on/event/the_playboy_of_the_western_world/.

World—A New Version clearly invokes the intense schisms playing out in intercultural theory and theater practice since the 1980s, where there was widespread critique of the use of exotic-Other elements by Western practitioners and institutions to reinvigorate moribund, "deadly" canons while failing to treat collaborators with respect, or to represent Othered cultures appropriately, or to be aware of the ways in which these cultures might be consumed by an Irish audience.

In 2010, when Adigun's copyright suit was made public, Fintan O'Toole observed, "There is an inherent tension between the nature of theater—open, collaborative, fluid—on the one hand and the closed, precise notion of legal ownership on the other."[30] O'Toole points out that the production itself is an adaptation and asks where Synge's moral rights are "when his famous closing line, Pegeen Mike's 'My grief, I've lost him surely. I've lost the only playboy of the western world' becomes, in the Adigun/Doyle version, 'Fuck!'"?[31] Placed in this framework, O'Toole suggests that Adigun's allegations of substantial alterations to the script are hypocritical. But I would note that there are significant differences between Adigun and Doyle adapting Synge's play, and in the process creating a new work, and the Abbey Theatre making unauthorized changes to Adigun and Doyle's play and presenting it under their names as if both authors had approved those changes. The first is an adaptation, a widely practiced form of dramatic writing. The second is a violation of the playwright's legal right to integrity. Playwrights and theaters sign contracts preventing this sort of thing from happening, and when it does, the playwright can sue for damages, as Adigun did successfully in this case.

While the legal aspect of this issue has been decided in the courts, O'Toole gestures toward broader ethical implications of artistic collaboration. Like Brook, O'Toole seems to indicate that the fact that an Othered person has used the Western canon in a revisionary,

30. Fintan O'Toole, "Theatre Has Nothing to Declare but an Innate Uncertainty," *Irish Times*, May 22, 2010, https://www.irishtimes.com/life-and-style/people/theatre-has-nothing-to-declare-but-an-innate-uncertainty-1.668749.

31. O'Toole, "Theatre Has Nothing to Declare," 9.

deconstructionist, or radical manner gives Western artists and institutions the right to similarly use Othered cultural products. He puts forth the argument that since we all borrow material from each other all the time, such borrowings are not ethically or politically problematic, even if, as his nod to author's moral rights suggests, they might be legally bound. But, as the intercultural wars should illustrate, these deconstructionist airs, embraced by Schechner's generation of interculturalists and given voice by O'Toole here, take on troubling ethical overtones in intercultural situations.

If studying cultural practices as performance can destabilize fixities of identity, including national identity, then considering Synge's *Playboy of the Western World* as a performance of Irishness allows us to see the constructed nature—linguistic, regional, denominational—of Synge's play, and this opens up the potential for new modes of performing national identity, modes that speak to modern realities. This is exactly how the Abbey marketed Adigun and Doyle's *Playboy of the Western World—A New Version*. Yet, one of the lessons of intercultural theater is that we cannot demand of the people with whom we choose to collaborate that they adopt our airs of deconstruction. Adigun understood his play to be finished, and while his moral rights as an author are not in question, ethically and politically, his commitment to representational precision is given added heft when one considers the limiting ways in which Black African subjects are usually represented in Irish arts and media,[32] and the concurrent need for representations by African artists to do the work of countering stereotypes and Orientalist modes of "speaking for." Moreover, Adigun clearly understood the purpose of his and Doyle's *Playboy of the Western World—A New Version* differently from the Abbey—it was not a vehicle to reinvigorate a moribund Irish canon, but rather to create intercultural collaboration and even criticism of Irish society. To this effect, his involvement within the creative process, as

32. Bisi Adigun, "Arambe Productions: An African's Response to the Recent Portrayal of the Fear Gorm in Irish Drama," in *Performing Global Networks*, ed. Karen Fricker and Ronit Lentin (Newcastle: Cambridge Scholars, 2007), 52–65.

an immigrant to Ireland and a Black man, was key. Respectful collaboration must be a part of ethical interculturalism, otherwise the same critiques—speaking for Others, using the cultural artifacts of Othered people for the gain of the dominant culture in a so-called collaborative context—will return again and again.

Much as Schechner and other intercultural performance studies practitioners and theorists had good intentions—to give Othered cultures due respect on university curriculums, to create intercultural understanding, to break down the toxic fixities that give rise to hegemony—so, too, have the Abbey Theatre and, particularly, Roddy Doyle given time, passion, and resources to reimagining the Irish canon in ways that give voice to Ireland's new multiculturalism. I am aware from having spoken to Doyle on this topic that Adigun does not have the monopoly on personal hurt in this story. However, when you adopt intercultural ways of working you need to be cognizant of how the status and celebrity of one collaborator may function in the relationship; if that person acts from a position of power within a given intercultural exchange, this needs to be acknowledged so that it can be offset with care, thus—hopefully—achieving for both the equitable working conditions and due dispersal of cultural capital required of ethical practice. There needs to be acknowledgment that different parties are entitled to invest differently in how their cultures and cultural products are represented. And the primacy of the canon in both making and framing the production must be open to renegotiation and change. Otherwise, as the intercultural wars show and the Adigun/Abbey controversy exemplifies, the outcome of intercultural collaborations will not be utopian cross-cultural fertilizations and understandings, but rather a sense that those already disempowered by structural oppressions have been further taken advantage of, however difficult this is for their well-intentioned collaborators to hear.

5

Contemporary Irish Theater, the New *Playboy of the Western World* Controversy, and the Economic Crisis

Jason King

"There's a huge difference—right?—between a big story and a dirty deed," Pegeen proclaimed on the opening night of Bisi Adigun and Roddy Doyle's second production of *The Playboy of the Western World—A New Version* at the Abbey Theatre on December 16, 2008.[1] Similar sentiments had been expressed the day before by David Drumm, CEO of the play's main sponsor, Anglo Irish Bank, albeit with more expletives. "You've told the fuckin' world we're all solvent," he exclaimed, in mock conversation with Irish finance minister Brian Lenihan.[2] "Now you can protect your hundred billion [euro] guarantee of us by writing a two or three billion cheque and get on with it." Drumm was alluding to the Irish bank guarantee

---

An earlier version of this chapter was published as "Contemporary Irish Theatre, the new *Playboy* Controversy, and the Economic Crisis," *Irish Studies Review* 24, no. 1 (2016): 67–78, https://www.tandfonline.com/. I am grateful to Taylor and Francis for permission to republish it here.

1. Bisi Adigun and Roddy Doyle, *The Playboy of the Western World—A New Version*, 117.

2. Colin Gleeson, "Drumm Said He Would 'Punch' Lenihan," *Irish Times*, July 1, 2013. David Drumm was sentenced to six years in prison for conspiracy to defraud and false accounting in the Dublin Circuit Criminal Court after being unanimously convicted by a jury on June 7, 2018.

two and a half months earlier, on September 30, 2008, which he expected would lead to the state's recapitalization of Anglo Irish Bank without "having to go through due diligence." This great gap between the gallous story of Irish solvency and the dirty deed of lost sovereignty and economic collapse was exposed not only in the ensuing nationalization of Anglo Irish Bank on January 15, 2009, but also in the controversy surrounding the second run of *The Playboy of the Western World—A New Version* that it sponsored.

Since 1907, *Playboy of the Western World* productions have served to reveal Ireland's shifting cultural fault lines and to contest its national self-images. "Both nationally and internationally, the performance history of the play over the last century has allowed theatre-makers to assert the relationship of *Playboy* to Irish cultural realities. Indeed, it has become *the* definitive play in the Irish theatre canon," Sara Keating claims.[3] According to Patrick Lonergan, it revealed that "the gallous story of the Celtic Tiger period was a fantasy designed to mask the 'dirty deeds' of bankers, politicians, property developers, and regulators. Synge's warnings about the dangers of self-delusion seemed more pertinent than ever."[4]

Yet the Irish theater industry was no less implicated in this culture of self-deception. The controversy surrounding the second run of *The Playboy of the Western World—A New Version* between December 16, 2008, and January 31, 2009, not only coincided with the resignation of David Drumm (December 19) and the nationalization of its sponsor, Anglo Irish Bank (January 15), but it also raised questions about whether the Abbey Theatre itself had employed due diligence in its choice to proceed with the play despite the objections of coauthor Bisi Adigun, who instigated legal proceedings against

3. Sara Keating, "Evolving *Playboys* for the Global World," in *Synge and His Influences: Centenary Essays from the Synge Summer School*, ed. Patrick Lonergan (Dublin: Carysfort Press, 2011), 245–57.

4. Patrick Lonergan, "Introduction," in *Synge and His Influences: Centenary Essays from the Synge Summer School*, ed. Patrick Lonergan (Dublin: Carysfort Press, 2011), 4.

the theater. Ultimately, the case was resolved out of court in Adigun's favor in January 2013 at a cost of approximately €600,000 to the Abbey, most of which was comprised of legal fees.[5] As we will see, the Irish culture industry could ill afford such expenditures in a context of arts-funding cutbacks that were suffered disproportionately by its most vulnerable members.

It is my contention that this new *Playboy of the Western World* controversy epitomizes the cultural condition of post–Celtic Tiger Ireland in economic collapse. Broadly speaking, this dispute did not simply reflect but also reinforced the social effects of the economic crisis, through its prolonged litigation, enormous expense, and especially the missed opportunity that it represented to position the multicultural and migrant-themed *Playboy of the Western World—A New Version* within the Irish theatrical mainstream. More specifically, the *Playboy of the Western World—A New Version* controversy provides a case study of how professional theater productions that dramatized stories of immigrant empowerment during the Irish economic boom were profoundly inhibited by the bust that followed. Since the economic downturn in 2008, Arts Council funding cuts, as well as the fallout from the *Playboy of the Western World—A New Version* legal dispute, have resulted in fewer stories of immigrant empowerment on the professional Irish stage. Before then, professional Irish theater companies were increasingly featuring immigrant characters in the development of their plotlines, which culminated in the performance of Adigun and Doyle's adaptation of *The Playboy of the Western World* in Ireland's national theater, the Abbey, in 2007, where it became a commercial success. Since 2008, many of these companies have lost their funding and closed, and fewer immigrant storylines have featured in professional theater productions. This diminishing visibility of the figure of the migrant in mainstream Irish theater is particularly exemplified by the fate

---

5. Ronan McGreevy, "Abbey 'to Pay €600,000' in Dispute over Play Copyright," *Irish Times*, January 31, 2013.

of the African-Irish theater company Arambe Productions and its subsequent staging of its founder Bisi Adigun's adaptation of Jimmy Murphy's play *The Kings of the Kilburn High Road* (2001), with an African immigrant cast, which he transformed into *The Paddies of Parnell Street* in 2013.

My second point is that both Arambe adaptations, *The Playboy of the Western World—A New Version* and *The Paddies of Parnell Street*, epitomize what Ric Knowles defines as "intercultural reappropriation,"[6] based on the reclamation of Irish historical memories of migration from the perspective of Ireland's immigrants. According to Adigun, Arambe's mission is "to create an avenue through which African immigrants can express themselves . . . by producing African plays as well as reinterpreting relevant plays in the Irish canon."[7] I also want to suggest that community theater performances like *The Paddies of Parnell Street* tend now to be more empowering, inclusive, and participatory for their immigrant casts than the earlier professional productions about them.

This tension between professional and community theatrical (self-)representations of migrants in Ireland, as well as the rise and fall of the Celtic Tiger, are implicated in the performance histories of *The Playboy of the Western World—A New Version* and *The Paddies of Parnell Street*. According to Christopher Murray, "The Adigun-Doyle *Playboy* opened at the Abbey on 29 September 2007 and ran to packed houses for two months; the following year it was revived, this time during the Christmas period, running from 16 December 2008 to 31 January 2009. It could readily be described as a major hit."[8] Adigun claims that he was originally struck by the idea

6. Ric Knowles, *Theatre and Interculturalism* (New York: Palgrave, 2010), 67.

7. Bisi Adigun, "Re-Writing Synge's *Playboy*—Christy's Metamorphosis, A Hundred Years On," in *Synge and His Influences: Centenary Essays from the Synge Summer School*, ed. Patrick Lonergan (Dublin: Carysfort Press, 2011), 262.

8. Christopher Murray, "Beyond the Passion Machine: The Adigun Doyle Playboy and Multiculturalism," in *Irish Drama: Local and Global Perspectives*, ed. Nicholas Grene and Patrick Lonergan (Dublin: Carysfort Press, 2012), 109.

of adapting a "modern version of the play with a Nigerian Christy Mahon" after he first saw *The Playboy of the Western World* performed and then read the script in 1998. "It occurred to me that Synge's Christy is the archetypal 'asylum seeker,'" he recalls. "Like Christy, an asylum seeker must have a story to back up his/her refugee application . . . [that] must be compellingly convincing."[9] Adigun then approached Doyle, whom he had worked with in the past, to help dramatize this premise. In the program for the second version of *The Playboy of the Western World—A New Version*, their collaborative process of adapting the play is described as follows: "To coincide with the centenary of the first production of his Irish classic in the Abbey in 1907, Arambe commissioned its founder and artistic director, Bisi Adigun, and Irish award winning author Roddy Doyle . . . to work collaboratively for ten months in 2006 to adapt the *Playboy*. In October 2007, the Abbey produced the premiere of the new version to critical and commercial success."[10]

Their production of this new version of *The Playboy of the Western World* was indeed a commercial success, but actually garnered mixed reviews. It was set in "a modern, suburban pub, on the west side of Dublin"[11] where Christopher Malomo, like Synge's original Christy Mahon, ingratiates himself into the family of a Dublin crime lord through his physical prowess and prodigious feats of storytelling. Although thoroughly adapted to a contemporary Dublin setting, the plotline of the play closely adhered to Synge's script. By equating asylum seekers with the archetypal figure of the itinerant storyteller, Adigun and Doyle represented them to be the most recent incarnation of the shanachie, whose claim to hospitality was deeply rooted in Irish culture. According to Luke Gibbons, the adapted play provided a "dress rehearsal [for] a future multi-ethnic Ireland, a western world

9. Adigun, "Rewriting Synge's *Playboy*," 262.

10. Abbey Theatre, *At the Abbey: The Playboy of the Western World in a New Version by Bisi Adigun and Roddy Doyle*, program (Dublin: Abbey Theatre, 2008), 6.

11. Adigun and Doyle, *The Playboy of the Western World—A New Version*, 17.

renewed through contact with other wider worlds."[12] On the other hand, critics such as Peter Crawley, Karen Fricker, and Susan Conley found fault with both the language and the politics of the play, which they felt were insufficiently evocative of either Synge's poetic lyricism or the reality of racism in contemporary Ireland. In particular, Conley objected to its seemingly naïve portrayal "of mixed race romance" as a plot device that appeared devoid of "dramatic racial tension."[13] The play's treatment of celebrity culture and colorful criminality also generated controversy. The ultimate transformation of Christopher Malomo from Synge's "likely gaffer in the end of all"[14] into a "*hard* man"[15] was interpreted as trivializing the original *Playboy of the Western World* as a popular cultural stereotype.

More recently, critics have debated whether the play should be regarded as a "genuinely intercultural creative collaboration," as Adigun contends.[16] "What is important for me," he suggests, is "for Synge's iconic Christy to metamorphose into a Nigerian Christopher Malomo a hundred years on. Now a black character can come on stage tired and timid and leave at the end brave and bold."[17] The question of whether the play's final plot device appears empowering or disempowering for Ireland's immigrants has divided critics, including its two most perceptive interpreters, Emer O'Toole and Charlotte McIvor.

O'Toole offers a positive appraisal of Adigun and Doyle's adaptation of *The Playboy of the Western World* in terms of their intercultural collaborative process and product, which, she claims, "contains

12. Luke Gibbons, "Finding Integration through Engaging with Our Past," *Irish Times,* October 29, 2007.

13. Susan Conley, review of *The Playboy of the Western World: A New Version* by Bisi Adigun and Roddy Doyle, *Irish Theatre Magazine*, October 5, 2007.

14. John Millington Synge, *The Playboy of the Western World*, in *Irish Writing in the Twentieth Century: A Reader,* ed. David Pierce (Cork: Cork Univ. Press, 2000), 194.

15. Adigun and Doyle, *The Playboy of the Western World—A New Version*, 121.

16. Adigun, "Rewriting Synge's *Playboy*," 261.

17. Adigun, "Rewriting Synge's *Playboy*," 267.

the cultural and individual experiences of both authors, destabilizing hierarchies of representation."[18] In her doctoral dissertation, "Rights of Representation: An Ethics of Intercultural Theatre Practice" (2012), O'Toole argues that *"Playboy* presents both an African reaction to Irishness and an Irish reaction to Africanness, which should be understood as not representative of either culture, but as a Janus-faced collaborative artefact in which all representations bear the imprint of two distinct voices and two distinct cultures."[19] It is precisely the play's accessibility that explains not only its popularity but also its versatility as a medium of intercultural exchange, she suggests. In her own words: "Adigun and Doyle's funny, entertaining, accessible and populist adaptation of Synge's classic reached wide audiences, including working-class and youth audiences who would not usually go to the theatre."[20] Moreover, O'Toole agrees with Adigun that the departure of the protagonist at the end of the play appears empowering for immigrants, because "he leaves the stage as master of his own destiny, with his head held high."[21] In short, she suggests that "this production seems to represent ethical intercultural practice" and "a wonderful example of an intercultural collaboration" prior to the litigation it gave rise to.[22]

By contrast, Charlotte McIvor does not regard Adigun and Doyle's adaptation as an exemplary model of Irish intercultural theater. In her view, it "falls victim to the dramaturgy of Synge's play, not gathering enough courage to push convincingly against the text or break past its proscribed ending. The project breaks down, therefore, from the moment Christopher appears as an outsider with no real claim to the space he enters, whether Pegeen's bar or the Abbey Theatre stage, because there is no way he will be permitted to stay

---

18. Emer O'Toole, "Rights of Representation: An Ethics of Intercultural Theatre Practice" (PhD diss., Royal Holloway, Univ. of London, 2012), 255.

19. O'Toole, "Rights of Representation," 217.

20. O'Toole, "Rights of Representation," 225.

21. O'Toole, "Rights of Representation," 226.

22. O'Toole, "Rights of Representation," 234, 308.

at the end of three acts. Christopher and Chief Malomo leave at the conclusion of the play in order to spread the news about the 'villainy of Ireland,' and Christopher's earlier plan to remain lingers as nothing more than the far-fetched fantasy of a cocky would-be murderer . . . [not] truly present within Irish society."[23] McIvor contends that Adigun and Doyle's adaptation remains too faithful to Synge's original plotline and thereby consigns the protagonist to inevitable departure not only from "the villainy of Ireland," but the audience's normative frame of reference. Whereas Adigun and O'Toole interpret his final displacement as a gesture of defiance and immigrant self-determination—leaving "brave and bold," "master of his own destiny, with his head held high," McIvor sees it as confirmation of his lack of acceptance in the first place. Far from challenging audience preconceptions about Ireland's immigrants, the very familiarity of the plot confirms expectations that they will go home again. Indeed, its sheer repetition compounds the impression that migrants like Christopher will leave of their own volition. According to McIvor, "Adigun and Doyle ultimately stage a version of interculturalism that continues to isolate Irish-born, African, and other minority-ethnic communities from one another, barely capable of acknowledging each other's existence, let alone working towards a mutually transformative co-existence."[24] Hence, it is not just the *Playboy of the Western World—A New Version* controversy but the play itself that exemplifies the gap between intercultural aspiration and its successful realization.

The play's intercultural aspirations were also undermined by its coauthors' collaborative breakdown. During her doctoral research, O'Toole interviewed both Doyle and Adigun at a crucial moment on January 13 and 14, 2009, a week after Adigun initiated legal proceedings. In these early days of the *Playboy of the Western World—A New Version* controversy, O'Toole elicited comments from both

---

23. Charlotte McIvor, "Staging the New Irish: Interculturalism and the Future of the Post–Celtic Tiger Irish Theatre," *Modern Drama* 54, no. 3 (2011): 319–20.

24. McIvor, "Staging the New Irish," 319.

Adigun and Doyle about their intercultural collaborative process and the deterioration of their working relationship. "The authors wrote the play line by line together, meaning that they both had agency and equality within the collaboration, if not, as the legal controversy that arose from the production might indicate, within the production process," she contends.[25] "The play was co-written. It was written line by line together," Doyle confirmed.[26] "We collaborated and wrote a very good play," Adigun claimed, "and if The Abbey had given Arambe even a little bit of the kind of respect that Roddy Doyle gave Bisi, this production" may not have resulted in legal proceedings.[27] In describing the origins of their legal dispute, O'Toole observed that "Adigun feels that, due to his race, he has not received appropriate credit and monetary recompense for, nor adequate control over, his ideas and work; Doyle feels used for his celebrity, then unfairly attacked for media responses beyond his control."[28] Ultimately, their legal dispute was settled out of court. On January 31, 2013, the *Irish Times* reported that the board of the Abbey Theatre convened an emergency meeting to approve the settlement, which would cost €600,000 when its own legal fees were taken into account—€500,000 according to the *Sunday Times*.[29] A spokeswoman issued the statement that "the Abbey Theatre is satisfied with this outcome. It is the best possible outcome for us from a financial point of view."[30]

All previous analysis of Adigun and Doyle's collaboration had been written before the case was settled. The cultural implications of the *Playboy of the Western World—A New Version* controversy can now be more fully considered. One of the more perceptive observations of the legal dispute is from the County Kerry law firm of

25. O'Toole, "Rights of Representation," 241.

26. O'Toole, "Rights of Representation," 319.

27. O'Toole, "Rights of Representation," 308.

28. O'Toole, "Rights of Representation," 236.

29. John Burns, "Abbey in €500,000 Legal Drama," *Sunday Times*, February 3, 2013.

30. McGreevy, "Abbey 'to Pay €600,000.'"

Healy, Crowley, Ahern. In its view, "The case does . . . raise questions [about] the strategy adopted by the Abbey Theatre. The costs do far outweigh the ultimate payment in damages. . . . One would have thought, a case of this nature, where, it seems on the reading of the reports the Abbey Theatre would have been aware of its breach of contractual rights from the outset, that the Abbey should not have allowed costs to increase to such a high degree."[31] Indeed, newspaper reports indicate that the Abbey Theatre spent up to ten times more in legal fees than the amount of royalties it was liable for in the first place.[32] According to Kevin Myers, "Such an absurd amount of money could only have been squandered so frivolously in the knowledge that the bill would ultimately be paid by that brainless dupe, the taxpayer, from whom The Abbey gets €7m a year, via the Arts Council."[33]

In my view, this legal controversy offstage was more symptomatic of the cultural condition of Ireland in economic collapse than the content of the play itself, or many works produced during the era of the Celtic Tiger and its aftermath. Its main beneficiary was not necessarily Adigun nor Arambe Productions, who arguably have won a pyrrhic victory, but rather the legal industry which enjoyed a hidden subsidy from the cultural sector and its ever-diminishing proportion of taxpayer funding. It seems unlikely that there will ever be a third production of the new version of *The Playboy of the Western World* in Ireland, or future artistic collaborations between the Abbey Theatre and Arambe Productions. The momentum that was generated by Ireland's most commercially successful intercultural play during the Celtic Tiger period in 2007 was abruptly halted by the legal proceedings it gave rise to the following year. More broadly, the question that

---

31. "Abbey Theatre in Dramatic Copyright Case," Healy, Crowley, Ahern Law, last modified January 30, 2013, http://hcalaw.ie/copyright-play-abbey-theatre-infringement-costs-county-kerry-solicitor/ (link no longer valid).

32. McGreevy, "Abbey 'to Pay €600,000.'"

33. Myers, "Making Synge's Great Comedy 'Relevant' Ended in Costly Farce," *Irish Independent*, February 5, 2013.

Healy, Crowley, Ahern raises about the legal "strategy adopted by the Abbey Theatre," when it should "have been aware of its breach of contractual rights from the outset" and "not have allowed costs to increase to such a high degree," seems especially pertinent in light of its other budgetary pressures and "Arts Council funding [being] reduced by almost 30% since 2008" following the economic crash.[34] It was not only elite politicians and bankers but also arts managers and practitioners who faced questions about due diligence in taking stock of their situation in 2008 as the crisis unfolded around them.

Yet, as in the financial sector, Ireland's cultural elite was largely insulated from the consequences of its poor decision-making. The litigation surrounding the unauthorized second production of *The Playboy of the Western World—A New Version* bears no resemblance to previous Abbey controversies: the riots that broke out during Synge's opening night in 1907 and Sean O'Casey's *The Plough and the Stars* in 1926; the principled disputes that arose between William Butler Yeats, Lady Gregory, and Annie Horniman over the Abbey's subsidy in 1909; Sean O'Casey's artistic vision for *The Silver Tassie* in 1928; or even the cost overruns for Ben Barnes's "overambitious [2004 *Playboy of the Western World*] production that would soon come to symbolize the Abbey's faltering centenary celebrations and its looming bankruptcy."[35] It was simply financially ruinous with no compensatory artistic gain. The €600,000 expense of the Abbey's legal dispute pales in comparison, of course, with the estimated tens of billions it has cost the Irish taxpayer to cover the losses of the play's sponsor, Anglo Irish Bank, but in the context of arts sector cutbacks it was proportionally devastating. It is certainly far more than the Arts Council ever spent on the Irish intercultural artistic and theatrical productions either before or since.

On the surface, there appears to be a veneer of continuity in the Irish arts and culture industries between the period of the Celtic

---

34. "Review of Abbey Theatre's Funding," *Irish Examiner*, November 7, 2013.
35. Lonergan, "Introduction," 3.

Tiger and the present as the mainstream players seem to have survived the financial crisis largely unscathed. Beneath the surface, however, emergent immigrant and minority-ethnic arts practitioners have been devastated by the economic collapse and largely disappeared from the Irish professional theater scene. The consequence has been a kind of cultural atrophy in which community and nonprofessional theater productions largely fill the void.

Thus, there can be no doubt that the collapse of the Celtic Tiger and the *Playboy of the Western World—A New Version* controversy represented a profound setback for the professionalization of migrant and minority ethnic theater in Ireland and the portrayal of immigrants on mainstream Irish stages. It is also profoundly ironic that the escalation of the legal dispute coincided with the publication of a groundbreaking Arts Council–funded report, *Cultural Diversity and the Arts* (2009), which signaled a new commitment by the Irish state to be more inclusive in its arts resource allocations. The report recognized "the scarcity of opportunities for professional development for practitioners from minority backgrounds [which] creates a system of perpetuated exclusion."[36] Moreover, it found that "minority ethnic arts practitioners born in Ireland have limited opportunities to present work as 'Irish,' and are often restricted to descriptions of their heritage."[37] The lack of cultural diversity in Irish artistic production was thus attributed both to blocked mobility and restricted pathways for the professionalization of minority artists and a broader lack of engagement in arts management with minority communities and their various forms of cultural expression.

The publication of the *Cultural Diversity and the Arts* report coincided, however, with the collapse of Ireland's Celtic Tiger economy in 2009, which occasioned drastic cuts in the country's arts budget rather than the targeted support for minority ethnic artists and

36. Daniel Jewesbury, Jagtar Singh, and Sarah Tuck, *Cultural Diversity and the Arts: Final Report* (Dublin: Create—National Development Agency for Collaborative Arts and Arts Council, 2009), 45.

37. Jewesbury, Singh, and Tuck, *Cultural Diversity and the Arts*, 58.

communities it had recommended. The eruption of the *Playboy of the Western World—A New Version* controversy also significantly undermined its impact. If the Arts Council had invested the same half million euros that the Abbey spent in settling the *Playboy of the Western World—A New Version* case, then the report's recommendations would not be mere aspirations but an enduring reality. Moreover, if Adigun had formerly been a poster boy for cultural diversity in the arts, then his experiences belied its claims to inclusivity. As Colin Murphy notes, the commercial success of *Playboy of the Western World—A New Version* "should have propelled Adigun to further high-profile stage work."[38] Instead, he was "leaving to take up a position as a university lecturer in Nigeria." "The fact that the *Playboy* proved the high point of his theatrical career here, rather than a launching point" was a source of regret, said Adigun. More broadly, the *Playboy of the Western World—A New Version* controversy represents a missed opportunity to tour and consolidate the place of the migrant and minority-themed play within the Irish theater canon. Adigun's career trajectory appears to be one of blocked mobility, of arrested development for minorities who are perpetually excluded from the Irish cultural mainstream.

This blocked mobility is especially apparent in the disparity of resources between Arambe and the Abbey's professional production of *The Playboy of the Western World—A New Version* in 2007 and Arambe's community theater performance of *The Paddies of Parnell Street* in 2013. Whereas *The Playboy of the Western World—A New Version* was performed on Ireland's national stage, *The Paddies of Parnell Street* appeared in the Teachers' Club with honorariums for its five cast members that were a tiny fraction of the former's budget. *The Paddies of Parnell Street* was also Adigun and Arambe's most recent adaptation of Jimmy Murphy's 2001 play *The Kings of the Kilburn High Road*—a play that featured a cast of five embittered

38. Colin Murphy, "Our Stage Will Be a Poorer Place after Losing One of Its Few African Voices," *Irish Independent*, August 25, 2013.

Irish emigrants in London whom Arambe replaced with African immigrants, but otherwise left the script unchanged.

The premise of *The Kings of the Kilburn High Road* is that these long-term Irish laborers have gathered to mourn the loss of their friend, Jackie Flavin, who was killed in an accident on the London Underground. As the plot develops, tensions arise while they drink to Jackie's memory in a pub and gradually reveal their struggles with alcoholism, domestic violence, discrimination, varying degrees of poverty, and poor living conditions. They also harbor illusions about returning to Ireland, which they left decades ago. The two alpha males in the play are Jap Kavanagh, who is accused of leading his friends astray to London, and Joe Mullen, the only one of them to achieve prosperity by breaking their fellowship to strike out on his own many years beforehand. The play's climax is precipitated by the revelation that Jackie Flavin's death was, in fact, not accidental, which leads to mutual recriminations and a final confrontation between Jap Kavanagh and Joe Mullen. Both of them are revealed to be failed mentors for Jackie Flavin, and Jap Kavanagh, in particular, overcompensates for his sense of social failure through expressions of false bravado that only partially mask his utter destitution. Thus, the characters in *The Kings of the Kilburn High Road* embody competing conceptions of hegemonic masculinity marked by cultural loyalty and economic prosperity that come into conflict at the culmination of the plot's development.

These outbursts of emigrant bravado and hypermasculine performances are ironically reversed in Adigun and Arambe's version of *The Kings of the Kilburn High Road* (2006). As noted, Adigun recast the play with West African immigrants in Ireland reenacting the roles of Irish emigrants in London. "By producing this play we hoped," Adigun claims, "that it would remind Irish people that many immigrants who had recently arrived in Ireland would rather have remained in their country of origin. On the other hand, it was our hope that the play would remind our African brothers and sisters why they left home in the first place, by borrowing a leaf from Joe Mullen, the only character in the play who becomes successful in London, because he refuses to be distracted from achieving his personal goals."[39] Thus, the character of Joe Mullen becomes more of an exemplary figure and masculine role model than a culprit in Arambe's version of the play. His resilience, ruthlessness, and refusal to countenance the idea of failure at the expense of cultural, familial, and social ties stand in stark contrast with his fellow migrant characters. Whether African or Irish, the migrant must struggle mightily to succeed rather than wallow in self-pity, Adigun suggests.

Arambe's version of *The Kings of the Kilburn High Road* appears most powerful, however, in its reversal of the setting of immigrant adversity from England to Ireland. If Adigun and Doyle's adaptation lacked the "courage to push convincingly against the text or break past its proscribed ending," as McIvor contends,[40] then *The Paddies of Parnell Street* is a more ambitious "intercultural re-appropriation" of *The Kings of the Kilburn High Road*. Adigun took liberties in his adaptation of both the ending and the genre of the play that he transformed from a tragic lament for Irish migrants in London into a cautionary tale about immigrant self-assertion and community formation. Thus, he changes the jaded entrepreneur Joe Mullen into an unambiguous mentor and positive role model in the character of Victor, who learns from the misfortunes of his Nigerian compatriots to lend them a helping hand and find employment. Indeed, whereas the Irish emigrant characters at the end of *The Kings of the Kilburn High Road* wallow in self-pity and regret their fate, *The Paddies of Parnell Street* concludes with Victor offering his friend Dapo a job. His sense of compassion for his fellow migrants counterpoints Joe Mullen's repudiation of them in *The Kings of the Kilburn High Road*. Victor does, of course, recognize the reality of Irish racism, but insists that it is not an insurmountable barrier to success: "As a black man in Ireland you must always double, triple, or quadruple your effort to

39. Bisi Adigun, "Arambe Productions: An African's Response to the Recent Portrayal of the Fear Gorm in Irish Drama," in *Performing Global Networks*, ed. Karen Fricker and Ronit Lentin (Newcastle: Cambridge Scholars, 2007), 52–66.

40. McIvor, "Staging the New Irish," 319.

get the same result as your Irish colleagues," he avows.[41] His compatriots learn to follow his example of resilience and self-reliance, and instead of succumbing to self-pity and despair like the characters in *The Kings of the Kilburn High Road*, they renew their determination to struggle to succeed. Ultimately, whereas their Irish predecessors ruefully acknowledge that they have no home left outside of London, Adigun's African characters embrace Ireland as their "home, sweet home."[42]

Yet as a community theater production, *The Paddies of Parnell Street* could provide only a limited vehicle for the professional development of its minority-ethnic cast. Two of the actors in the play, Uche Gabriel Akujobi (Dapo) and Bola Ogundeji (Pete), had begun their careers with Calypso Productions' Tower of Babel youth theater project a decade earlier. As described by Calypso's artistic director Bairbre Ní Chaoimh, "The Tower of Babel programme came about [in 2002] as a result of a growing awareness of all of the artistic talent within the new minority ethnic communities for which there was no suitable outlet. We were keen to use our imaginative resources as a professional theatre company to devise an integrated cross-cultural arts programme that would develop and showcase the talent and skills of young people from minority ethnic communities living in Dublin side by side with their Irish counterparts. We also wanted to provide recreational opportunities for some vulnerable young people, especially separated children seeking asylum, who were at risk of isolation or exclusion."[43] As a talented minority ethnic actor, Uche Gabriel Akujobi went on from Tower of Babel to join Dublin Youth Theatre in 2003 and then receive professional training in the

41. Bisi Adigun, "The Paddies of Parnell Street" (unpublished manuscript, 2013).

42. Adigun, "Paddies of Parnell Street."

43. Bairbre Ní Chaoimh, interview by Charlotte McIvor and Matthew Spangler, in *Staging Intercultural Ireland: New Plays and Practitioner Perspectives*, ed. Charlotte McIvor and Matthew Spangler (Cork: Cork Univ. Press, 2014), 345.

Gaiety School of Acting. He performed in Calypso's *Bones* (2007), almost all of Arambe's productions, and a variety of other works, before landing a role on RTÉ's *Fair City*. He is extraordinarily talented and was riveting to watch as Dapo in *The Paddies of Parnell Street*. When he declared, "So what, if we've never made it big?,"[44] he could have been speaking in or out of character.

The most important changes that Adigun and Arambe wrought to *The Kings of the Kilburn High Road* script occurred offstage rather than on. Their adaptation, *The Paddies of Parnell Street*, has provided a vehicle for the development of migrant and minority-ethnic community theater in the absence of significant resources or state support. Their reclamation of Irish stories of migration also inscribed the figure of the immigrant rather than the departed emigrant at the center of contemporary Irish theater. In the aftermath of the *Playboy of the Western World—A New Version* controversy, and economic recession, the pathways to professionalization for minority-ethnic artists envisioned in the *Cultural Diversity and the Arts* report had largely disappeared, and *The Paddies of Parnell Street* helped to fill the void. Even now in an era of economic recovery, it remains questionable whether the report's recommendations will ever be implemented. Indeed, the *Playboy of the Western World—A New Version* controversy would appear to provide a case study of the deprofessionalization of one of Ireland's most prominent minority-ethnic artists and theater companies.

Nevertheless, it should be recognized that not just Arambe but a wide variety of community theater groups have embraced immigrant participants and have found new outlets to adapt and devise plays and to perform them in unconventional theater settings. As Charlotte McIvor and Matthew Spangler note in their introduction to *Staging Intercultural Ireland*, "While Adigun and Doyle's *The Playboy of the Western World* may be the most high profile and

---

44. Adigun, "Paddies of Parnell Street," 63.

indeed controversial Irish theatre production on the theme of inward migration and interculturalism, it is far from the only one."[45] Indeed, Charlotte McIvor leads the way in studying these intercultural Irish theater productions in *Migration and Performance in Contemporary Ireland: Towards A New Interculturalism*.[46] She observes that the *Playboy of the Western World—A New Version* controversy brought "an end to any fast-tracked hopes for the integration of minority-ethnic and migrant artists into the institutionalised professional Irish theatre, represented at its zenith by the Abbey, the nation's most highly funded theatre and its designated 'national theatre.'"[47] Even so, she also notes that "the existence of migrant and minority-ethnic artists and companies with professional aspirations, if not wholly professional production histories, did continue post-2008," including Adigun and Arambe's adaptations of *The Kings of the Kilburn High Road* in *Home, Sweet Home* and *The Paddies of Parnell Street*.[48] McIvor argues that these more recent, precariously funded migrant-led adaptations have been more successful than *Playboy of the Western World—A New Version* in exemplifying "interculturalism-from-below" and reconceptualizing "Ireland as a national space that supports minority-ethnic inclusion in the 'Irish' imaginary," although they faced "very real material constraints that should not be romanticized."[49] As such, they set a very high standard for cultural diversity in the arts that remains largely lacking at the professional level.

45. Charlotte McIvor and Matthew Spangler, "Introduction," in *Staging Intercultural Ireland: New Plays and Practitioner Perspectives*, ed. Charlotte McIvor and Matthew Spangler (Cork: Cork Univ. Press, 2014), 2.

46. See Charlotte McIvor, *Migration and Performance in Contemporary Ireland: Towards A New Interculturalism* (London: Palgrave Macmillan, 2016), esp. chaps. 4 and 5.

47. McIvor, *Migration and Performance in Contemporary Ireland*, 68.

48. McIvor, *Migration and Performance in Contemporary Ireland*, 95–101.

49. McIvor, *Migration and Performance in Contemporary Ireland*, 85–86.

6

A New *Playboy of the Western World* at the Abbey Theatre

A Catalyst for Change or a Change for Catalyst?

Bisi Adigun

Claire Conceison identifies two poles of intercultural collaboration: "Interculturalism at its best is a reinforcement of international understanding and friendship, a celebration of common bonds of creativity; at its worst, it is a tangled web of false assumptions and distorted images, a reinforcement of the very hegemonic relationship it desires to eradicate."[1] There's "understanding and friendship . . . a celebration of common bonds," on one hand, and on the other, a "web of false assumptions" that reinforces the hegemonic relationships the intercultural collaboration seeks to displace. My aim here is to subject my process of coadapting *The Playboy of the Western World* with Roddy Doyle and Arambe Productions' subsequent collaboration with the Abbey Theatre in producing the world premiere of the play in 2007 to Conceison's framework of intercultural collaboration. My collaboration with Doyle epitomizes interculturalism at its best—a "celebration of common bonds"—whereas Arambe's collaboration with the Abbey presents an example of the "false assumptions and distorted images" that mark interculturalism at its worst.

---

1. Claire Conceison, "Translating Collaborations: *The Joy Luck Club* and Intercultural Theatre," *Drama Review* 39 (Fall 1995): 151–66.

But first, I must declare my point of view. I am not only the originator and coauthor of *The Playboy of the Western World—A New Version*, I am also the founder and artistic director of Arambe Productions, the theater company that commissioned the cowriting of the play and enabled its premiere production at the Abbey. So any reader of this chapter, particularly one familiar with the protracted controversy and legal quagmire that the second production of the play at the Abbey in 2008–9 left in its wake, may be right to conclude that my discussion here is bound to be tainted by a degree of subjectivity. However, it needs to be borne in mind, too, that "even a tear veiled eye still preserves its function of sight," to borrow a proverb from Wole Soyinka's play *Death and the King's Horseman*. Or as Edward Said has eloquently put it in the introduction to *Orientalism*, "No one has ever devised a method for detaching the scholar from the circumstances of life, from the fact of his [or her] involvement (conscious or unconscious) with a class, a set of beliefs, a social position or member of a society."[2] It is my hope, therefore, that my direct corporeal experience, as a Nigerian immigrant theatermaker, of cowriting *The Playboy of the Western World—A New Version* with Doyle and my subsequent involvement in its premiere production at the Abbey (2007) should stand me in good stead and afford me a unique vantage point from which to engage critically with a cross-cultural and collaborative theater practice in Ireland.

I have already written in great detail elsewhere about how the idea of *The Playboy of the Western World—A New Version* came to me, as well as about the joy of cowriting it with Doyle.[3] As with any

2. Edward Said, *Orientalism* (London: Penguin Books, 1978), 10.

3. See, for example, Bisi Adigun, "Re-Writing Synge's *Playboy*—Christy's Metamorphosis, a Hundred Years On," in *Synge and His Influences: Centenary Essays from the Synge Summer School*, ed. Patrick Lonergan (Dublin: Carysfort Press, 2011), 259–68, and Bisi Adigun, "To Adapt or Not to Adapt: The Question of Originality in a Nigerian Rewrite of Two Irish Classics," in *Where Motley Is Worn: Transnational Irish Literatures*, ed. Moira Casey and Amanda Tucker (Cork: Cork Univ. Press, 2014), 27–42.

seed that is planted, for the idea of the play to germinate, grow, and yield a tangible fruit, it needed fertilization. In other words, to metamorphose from a mere concept to a readable text on the page and then into a tangible, corporeal performance on the Abbey stage, *The Playboy of the Western World—A New Version* passed through a series of complex interpersonal as well as intercultural collaborations and was subjected to what I would term *interorganizational permutations*. Upon coming up with the idea while writing the essay "An Irish Joke, A Nigerian Laughter," which I contributed to the book of essays *The Power of Laughter* (2004), edited by Eric Weitz, I mentioned, at an Arambe Productions board meeting sometime in the summer of 2004, that I would like to adapt John Millington Synge's *The Playboy of the Western World* and make Christy Mahon an African immigrant to Ireland. The board members, including Weitz, thought it was a good idea, and Rupert Murray apprised me of the fact that 2007 would be the centenary of the premiere of *The Playboy of the Western World* at the Abbey. It was also Murray who suggested that I speak to Doyle to ask him if he would be willing to cowrite the adaptation with me.

I had known of Doyle as an Irish writer, but I was not familiar with his work until the year 2000, when I participated in the weeklong workshop that Calypso Productions organized to test whether the series of short stories *Guess Who's Coming for the Dinner*, which Doyle was at the time writing for the multicultural newspaper *Metro Éireann*, could be adapted for the stage. Doyle and I subsequently became friends. I interviewed Doyle for the second series of *Mono*, the intercultural television program I copresented on RTÉ between 2000 and 2003; he was also the chief speaker when Arambe was formally launched as an incorporated theater company at the O'Reilly Theatre in Dublin in February 2004.

Meanwhile, pursuant to an interview that I gave to a newspaper sometime in 2003 where I said that it was high time that the Abbey began to reflect Ireland's increasing diversity, Ali Curran, who was then the artistic director of the Peacock Theatre, contacted me and said she was open to my ideas. It was against this backdrop that, soon after the aforementioned Arambe board meeting, I set up a meeting with Curran and discussed the idea of the adaptation with her.

Having gotten the Abbey at least interested in staging the premiere of *The Playboy of the Western World—A New Version* in 2007 and having convinced Doyle to cowrite it with me, the next issue was to secure the required funds for Arambe to commission Doyle and me. That was how the Arts Council came into the picture. Below is the brief description of the proposal in the application that I made to the Arts Council in 2005, in my capacity as the artistic director of Arambe.

> Arambe proposes to commission its Artistic Director, Nigerian dramatist Bisi Adigun, and acclaimed Irish writer Roddy Doyle to jointly create a new work by adapting John Millington Synge's comic masterpiece *The Playboy of the Western World*.
>
> Designed to commemorate, and to coincide with, the centenary of the first production of the *Playboy* at the Abbey Theatre on 26 January 1907, this proposed adaptation is intended to, in the context of the recent phenomenon of refuge seeking in Ireland, explore the original play's theme of identity construction through the narrative of self-invention.
>
> By reworking Christy Mahon's role, the crucial power of storytelling in a situation where acceptance is dependent on narrative credibility, will be demonstrated. While reception of the stranger demands a clear differentiation between truth and fiction, the central insight to be developed is how the relations between a refugee and a host community could hinge upon conflicting interpretations of heroism and victimhood.
>
> The adaptation will also reflect how notions of virtue decorum have changed so dramatically in Ireland since the *Playboy* riots of 1907, so that the spectacle of females standing in their shifts—deemed scandalous a century ago—has now become an accepted feature of our urban shopscape.

Arambe's Arts Council grant application for the sum of €10,000 was successful, and with it Arambe commissioned Doyle and me to write the play.

We began work on February 6, 2006. We worked every Tuesday and Thursday thereafter from about 9:00 a.m. to 4:00 p.m. in Doyle's attic: writing, rewriting, editing, brainstorming, adding, and changing. It was a creative experience that I will never forget. No doubt, I felt challenged by the unique opportunity. Emer O'Toole is correct when she asserts that "the authors wrote the play line by line together, meaning that they both had agency and equality within the collaboration."[4]

Let me cite two examples from the play text of our version of *The Playboy of the Western World* to describe this point. The first one is at the point when the three girls—Sarah, Honor, and Susan—arrive in the pub after learning from Sean Keogh that a Black man who killed his dad in Nigeria is boarding at the O'Flaherty's pub. Before the girls' arrival, Christopher has noticed them on the closed-circuit television and has gone into hiding behind the bar counter, so when the girls enter they cannot find him. After a while, one of the girls notices Christopher's shoes:

SUSAN: God, yeah. (*Seeing CHRISTOPHER's shoes under the table*) Hang on, but. They're his shoes; I bet they are.
SARAH: There should be blood on them.
SUSAN: Why should there be?

SARAH goes down on her knees, examining the shoes, not touching them yet.

SARAH: Did you never see in the films how murdered men bleed and drip?
HONOR: He'd have washed them. You couldn't get through all that airport security with blood on your shoes.
SUSAN (*agreeing*): Yeah.
SARAH (*picking up one of the shoes, looking at it*): No blood.
HONOR: Told you.
SARAH (*smelling the shoe*): No.
SUSAN: Nice shoes, though.

4. Emer O'Toole, "Rights of Representation: An Ethics of Intercultural Theatre Practice" (PhD diss., Royal Holloway, Univ. of London, 2012), 207.

HONOR: They're a bit wrecked.

SUSAN: What size are they?

SARAH: Why?

SUSAN: You can tell a lot about a fella by the size of his shoes.

SARAH: It's a nine, I'd say.

HONOR: Wow!

They laugh. SARAH drops the shoe to the floor, slips off her own, and puts CHRISTOPHER's shoe on.

Bearing in mind the double entendre about a man's shoe size, Doyle and I deliberated for a long time before we agreed to make Christopher's shoe size a nine. My view was that the average shoe size of a Nigerian male is eight, which happens to be my own shoe size. The humor of the moment is in Honor's line, "Wow!," after Sara announces that he wears size nine.

The second example I would give is the point at which Christopher and Pegeen have decided to get married, and out of jealousy Sean, to whom Pegeen is already engaged, moves toward her:

CHRISTOPHER: One more step from you, sir, and murder will be added to my list of deeds today.

MICHAEL (*standing up*): Murder?! Are you fuckin' mad?! The Guards will be sniffing all over the place, upstairs and all. (*To PEGEEN*) You won't be marrying anyone if they find some of the stuff we have here. Not for a long time, missis. (*To the men*) Go outside or somewhere else if you want to fight and kill each other.

He pushes SEAN towards CHRISTOPHER. SEAN shakes himself free and gets behind MICHAEL. They struggle.

SEAN: Fight him yourself, or all deals are off. I'm phoning me ma.

MICHAEL: Go on; be a fuckin' man.

SEAN: No way am I fighting him. I'd prefer to stay a bachelor than face that savage.

CHRISTOPHER pulls a crutch away from MICHAEL. MICHAEL falls. CHRISTOPHER holds the crutch like a weapon he intends using.

CHRISTOPHER (*to SEAN*): What did you say?!

He follows SEAN as SEAN retreats. MICHAEL, from the floor, holds up the second crutch for SEAN.

MICHAEL: There you go, Sean.
PEGEEN: Da!

PEGEEN takes the crutch from MICHAEL, and slides it across the floor, away from the action. CHRISTOPHER still holds the crutch, ready, but he does not strike.

PEGEEN (*to SEAN*): Get out.
SEAN: I didn't say anything.
PEGEEN: Get out.
SEAN: I didn't mean—
PEGEEN: No. Out.

SEAN exits. CHRISTOPHER lowers the crutch and steps towards MICHAEL. He offers his hand to help him up.

We decided that if we made Pegeen stop Christopher from hitting Sean, it could render Christopher as the noble savage, which we did not want to do. Instead, we made Christopher stop himself, rather than being stopped by Pegeen.

These two examples illustrate the strategy that Doyle and I adopted in cowriting *The Playboy of the Western World—A New Version* word by word, scene by scene, and act by act. These are only two examples, but with everything in the play, we created it together, from debating something as small as Christopher's shoe size to careful consideration of physical gestures like whether Christopher or Pegeen should stop Christopher from hitting Sean. It is against this backdrop that I would consider my collaboration with Doyle the epitome of an intercultural theater initiative. O'Toole echoes the same sentiments: "The intercultural work of Adigun and Doyle allowed two artists with significant social and symbolic capital and with strong liberal commitments to Irish multicultural and immigration issues to create a hybrid containing cultural and individual vantage points and perspectives made only through collaboration."[5] Unfortunately, the intercultural collaboration between Arambe and the Abbey was more difficult.

I founded Arambe in 2003 with the aim of diversifying Irish theater and affording African immigrants living in Ireland the opportunity to express themselves through the art of theater. Bearing in mind August Wilson's statement in "On the Ground on Which I Stand" that theater can educate the miseducated and Peter Brook's view as articulated in *The Shifting Point* about theater's responsibility to bring into our understanding that which cannot be conveyed in a book or truly explained by a philosopher, Arambe's aim was to employ the medium of theater to educate audiences in Ireland about Africa and how we Africans living in Ireland perceive ourselves against the notion of how we are perceived by others.[6] To achieve this aim, Arambe produced traditionally written or devised plays in the African tradition as well as reinterpretations of relevant plays in the Irish canon. But regardless of the specific play Arambe presented, interculturalism was at the core of the company's artistic and strategic policy. Since its inception, one of the company's main objectives has been to attract and grow audiences from diverse cultural backgrounds by facilitating and presenting works that afford African budding actors the opportunity to collaborate with their Irish counterparts. This policy was supported by the simple logic that people of diverse cultural backgrounds coming together to work toward the achievement of a common goal, more often than not, brings about cross-cultural understanding.

Soon after Fiach MacConghail replaced Ben Barnes as artistic director of the Abbey, I met with him on August 17, 2005, to discuss the idea of staging *The Playboy of the Western World—A New Version*. I had worked with MacConghail in 2000, when he curated the Irish pavilion at the World Expo 2000 in Hanover, Germany. I

5. O'Toole, "Rights of Representation," 211–12.
6. August Wilson, "The Ground on Which I Stand," *American Theatre Magazine*, September 1996, 225; Peter Brook, *The Shifting Point* (London: Methuen Drama, 1994), 164.

was part of the contingent of eight musicians drawn from the Afro-Irish band De Jimbe and Afro-Celtic band Kila that featured at the pavilion every day for a week. In contrast with the Barnes era at the Abbey, MacConghail was appointed as the artistic director of both the Abbey and the Peacock, while Aideen Howard was appointed the literary director for both theaters. On March 1, 2006, Doyle and I met with Howard at the Abbey to discuss our adaptation of *The Playboy of the Western World*. When we completed the first draft of the play in May of that year, we delivered it to the Abbey on June 8, and a reading, directed by Jimmy Fay, was soon held.

I had worked with Fay as an actor in Bedrock Theatre's production of *Quay West* in 1998 at the Project Mint Theatre in Dublin. We kept in touch and also had the opportunity to work together again when I produced Ola Rotimi's *The Gods Are Not to Blame*, in which I played the lead role at the 2003 Dublin Fringe Festival. Although the production was supported by the Project Arts Theatre under the directorship of Willie White and Vallejo Gantner, then director of the Dublin Fringe Festival, Fay gave time and financial support to ensure the success of the production, which required more than twenty actors, the majority of whom were not professionally trained. Hence, Fay was my first choice of director for the reading. My sense was that MacConghail and Doyle were also admirers of Fay's work.

The reading, which took place on June 29, 2006, was a private affair for an invited small audience.[7] Doyle and I suggested the actors who participated in the reading. It was fascinating to hear the play read aloud for the first time by live actors who, at appropriate times, were directed by Fay to stop and pose questions for me and Doyle to address. Then the actors read the play again from beginning to end, uninterrupted for all of us, so that we could feel the flow and rhythm of the play. Afterward, some of us, including Howard

---

7. As per Arambe's commissioning grant application to the Arts Council, the original plan was to hold a public reading of the first draft of *The Playboy of the Western World—A New Version* before a carefully selected audience not exceeding fifty in number.

and Doyle, retired to the Flowing Tide pub across the street from the Abbey for a mini celebration of a major milestone on the journey of *The Playboy of the Western World—A New Version*. Overall, we thought the script was in good shape, though some of the notes that came out of that first reading are as follows:

- Pages 1–4 need a lot of work
- Get two or all leather-jacket MEN to snort a line/lines of cocaine without comment
- Do a bit more work on SUSAN's speech to make it more convincing
- We need to think about why the WIDOW is not in jail
- Need a new name for the VIPER
- Clearer emphasis on the world of the GANGSTERS
- WIDOW's various deals etc. have to be clearer
- CHRISTOPHER needs to react to the reference to PEGEEN's engagement
- No need to make PEGEEN tougher but more clued-in at the start of act 1
- The GIRLS are, overall, fine

These notes were central in our minds as we commenced the process of writing the second draft, which we submitted to the Abbey on October 27, 2006. I was of the view that Doyle and I had done what we had to do to ensure that our adaptation was as good as it could be. So both of us had no doubt in our minds that the Abbey would produce the play come 2007, at least until I received Howard's email on December 19, 2006. The email stated that MacConghail had decided not to produce the play after all and gave no reason why. And so it was, my long-held dream of having the play staged at the Abbey was shattered.

So in early 2007, I started work to ensure that Arambe produced the play. First, I made contact with Loughlin Deegan, who was then the newly appointed director of the Dublin Theatre Festival, to see if he would be interested in including a production of the play in the 2007 Dublin Theatre Festival program. Then I decided to make a production-funding application to the Arts Council. The play had been accepted in principle by the Dublin Theatre Festival, and the Arts Council was willing to grant Arambe the sum of €90,000 to produce it, when, suddenly, in April 2007, MacConghail changed his mind. He decided to produce the play after all. It would be directed by Fay on the Abbey main stage for seven weeks at the Dublin Theatre Festival that autumn. I immediately called Doyle to share the good news, and thereafter I abandoned all plans by Arambe to produce the play, including a formal rejection of the grant the Arts Council had earmarked for Arambe to produce the play—that is, after I confirmed with the Abbey that the licensing agreement to permit the Abbey to produce the play would be between Arambe and the Abbey.

It was in my capacity as Arambe's artistic director that I signed the agreement Arambe entered into with the Abbey on May 22, 2007, after which the premiere production of the play at the Abbey started in earnest. To many observers, I must have been in an enviable position, both as a coauthor and as Arambe's artistic director. But "uneasy lies the head that wears the crown" is the way I now would describe my situation. No sooner had I signed the agreement on behalf of Arambe than I began to have misgivings, for while my aim was to bring to the Abbey the same kind of collaborative energy that I had experienced with Doyle, the Abbey did not appear keen to frame the play as an intercultural collaboration. At times, I felt that, as far as the Abbey was concerned, *The Playboy of the Western World—A New Version* was an opportunity to celebrate their association with a well-known Irish writer, often at the expense of the critical commentary and intercultural possibilities of the play. To a certain extent, this celebration carried over to the Irish media. For example, the *Sunday Independent*'s Emer O'Kelly described *The Playboy of the Western World—A New Version* as "pure Doyle," and Christopher Murray suggested "Doyle must have written the Dublin characters' dialogue as it was clearly in his style."[8]

---

8. Quoted in O'Toole, "Rights of Representation," 235.

Nonetheless, that *The Playboy of the Western World—A New Version* turned out to be a theatrical phenomenon was due largely to the play's intercultural and collaborative roots. Frist, it was a modern version of one of the most important plays in the Irish canon, and it was appearing on the Abbey stage, where the source material had appeared one hundred years previously. Second, the production took place at a time in Ireland of heightened concern for immigration, particularly that of refugees and asylum seekers. Third, the production was directed by Jimmy Fay, one of Ireland's most innovative directors. And last, but not least, the play was commissioned by Arambe, the same company that was behind the critically acclaimed all-Black-cast production of Jimmy Murphy's powerful play *The Kings of the Kilburn High Road*, which was produced at the 2006 Dublin Fringe Festival. For these reasons, the first production of the new *The Playboy of the Western World—A New Version* drew large audiences night after night, so much so that the Abbey remounted the play just over a year later (2008–9). As my people would say, it is not possible for one to sight an elephant and describe the experience as merely catching a glimpse of something. When one sees an elephant, one knows one has seen an elephant.

But there were tensions during the process of producing the premiere of *The Playboy of the Western World—A New Version*, particularly between myself and the bureaucracy of the Abbey. While I was fully aware, as Conceison reminds us, that "no intercultural project is without its challenges and these challenges provide opportunity for growth and experimentation," I also knew, as Conceison hastens to add, "there are also misunderstandings that can be avoided, setbacks to the progress of a production that can be prevented and harsh repercussions among participants and in the theater-going public that can be softened."[9] Issues arose during the production of the play at the Abbey that I feel likely would not have arisen had Arambe been a white, Irish-led theater company. Things came to a boiling point

9. Conceison, "Translating Collaborations," 164.

when the Abbey sent a letter to Arambe, dated November 26, 2008, saying that the Abbey was withholding the balance of royalties of more than €20,000 that were due to Arambe because the Abbey wanted to reconsider the initial contract that would have paid Arambe a portion of the royalties, in addition to royalties paid to myself and Doyle. Perhaps if the Abbey had been more interculturally inclined toward this project, it would have been more circumspect in this regard and would not have tried to kill a mosquito with a hammer by breaching the initial licensing agreement with Arambe.

Declan Kiberd offers the following words of wisdom in his article "After Ireland?," published in the *Irish Times* on August 29, 2009:

> Sometimes when a people are about to surrender a culture, outsiders come to its rescue. It was Eliot, a young man from St Louis, Missouri, who saved English poetry in the 1920s, abetted ably by other outsiders like Pound and Yeats. In the previous generation, the English novel had been reconfigured by an American named James and a Pole named Conrad. . . . All cultures which survive strongly do so because they are open to injections of new life from without. It would not therefore be altogether surprising if immigrant writers from Africa or Eastern Europe reopened dialogue with Cuchulain and Deidre. They may well find inspiration and new meaning in these marginal figures, who exist still as buried memories of that landscape in which these newcomers are choosing to live.[10]

What Kiberd describes here is precisely what Arambe set out to achieve with *The Playboy of the Western World—A New Version* as well as other plays, such as *The Paddies of Parnell Street* and my adaptation of *The Kings of the Kilburn High Road*. Luke Gibbons echoed these sentiments in his closing address, "Ireland, Immigration, and Memory," delivered at the international conference Immigration in the New Ireland, held in October 2007 at the University of Notre Dame: "One of the biggest hits at this year's Dublin Theatre

---

10. Declan Kiberd, "After Ireland?" *Irish Times*, August 29, 2009.

Festival was a rewriting of Synge's play by Bisi Adigun and Roddy Doyle in which the playboy is re-cast as a Nigerian refugee in contemporary Dublin. At the end of the play, the local community is brought to its senses through an encounter with the outsider, but the immigrant's relationship with his own Nigerian background is also restored with a sense of purpose and independence. . . . It would be fitting if this staging of the play was a dress rehearsal of a future multi-ethnic Ireland, a western world renewed through contact with other, wider worlds."[11] It is ironic, therefore, that *The Playboy of the Western World—A New Version* at the Abbey, which could have opened more doors for Arambe and Ireland's other immigrant-centric theater companies, has turned out to be the biggest reason for the near extinction of Arambe today and for what Jason King describes in chapter 5 as "the diminishing visibility of the figure of the migrant in mainstream Irish theater."

The Playboy of the Western World—A New Version was meant to be a catalyst for positive change in the development of immigrant theater in Ireland, but it turned out to be a change of catalyst. Charlotte McIvor might be right then when she posits that Doyle and I should have considered parting ways with Synge by ensuring that Christopher Malomo remains in Ireland—and on the Abbey stage—at the end of our new version, rather than returning to Nigeria with his father. That way, McIvor reckons, the Irish preconception that immigrants will one day return to wherever they came from would have been truly challenged. Whether the Abbey would have been interested in staging an adaptation with such an ending is a consideration for another day. In any event, the intercultural collaborations discussed in this chapter are now in the past. The challenge now is to focus on the future and ensure that African immigrant actors who want to play the part of Christy Mahon, Pegeen Mike, or, indeed, Public or Private Gar are afforded the same opportunities as their

---

11. Luke Gibbons, "Finding Integration through Engaging with Our Past," *Irish Times*, October 29, 2007.

Irish counterparts to tread the mainstream Irish boards, rather than being labeled mere "community theater artists." Unlike Christopher Malomo, who returned home after dazzling his listeners with the tale of how he killed his father, diversity in Ireland is here to stay, and it needs to be visible and on the mainstream Irish stage in the same way that ethnic and racial diversity is noticeably visible in almost every nook and cranny of Ireland. It is high time immigrant theater artists were woken up in the same way that the Abbey inadvertently and forever awakened feminists and their supporters in 2015 and beyond. The future will tell.

Bibliography

Contributors

Bibliography

Abbey Theatre. *At the Abbey: The Playboy of the Western World in a New Version by Bisi Adigun and Roddy Doyle.* Program. Dublin: Abbey Theatre, 2008.

Adigun, Bisi. Address. Create IHREC (Irish Human Rights and Equality Commission), Collaborative Arts, Interculturalism and Human Rights Seminar, Dublin, April 6, 2017. https://vimeo.com/216565070.

———. "Arambe Productions: An African's Response to the Recent Portrayal of the Fear Gorm in Irish Drama." In *Performing Global Networks*, edited by Karen Fricker and Ronit Lentin, 52–66. Newcastle: Cambridge Scholars, 2007.

———. Interview by Emer O'Toole, January 13, 2009. In "Rights of Representation: An Ethics of Intercultural Theatre Practice," by Emer O'Toole. PhD diss., Royal Holloway, Univ. of London, 2012.

———. "Nigerian *Playboy of the Western World.*" Interview by Colin Murphy. *Le Monde Diplomatique*, November 2007, 13.

———. "The Paddies of Parnell Street." Unpublished manuscript, 2013.

———. "Re-Writing Synge's *Playboy*—Christy's Metamorphosis, A Hundred Years On." In *Synge and His Influences: Centenary Essays from the Synge Summer School*, edited by Patrick Lonergan, 259–68. Dublin: Carysfort Press, 2011.

———. "To Adapt or Not to Adapt: The Question of Originality in a Nigerian Rewrite of Two Irish Classics." In *Where Motley Is Worn: Transnational Irish Literatures*, edited by Moira Casey and Amanda Tucker, 27–42. Cork: Cork Univ. Press, 2014.

Ancheri, Saumya. "'The Mahabharata Does Not Leave You': Notes from Peter Book's Third Play about the Epic." *Scroll.in*, February 15, 2016. https://scroll.in/article/803515/the-mahabharata-does-not-leave-you-notes-from-peter-brooks-third-play-about-the-epic.

Ashcroft, Bill, Gareth Griffiths, and Helen Tiffin. *The Empire Writes Back: Theory and Practice in Post-Colonial Literatures*. London: Routledge, 1989.

Babbage, Frances, Robert Neumark Jones, and Lauren Williams. "Adapting Wilde for the Performance Classroom: 'No Small Parts.'" In *Redefining Adaptation Studies*, edited by Dennis Cutchins, Laurence Raw, and James M. Welsh, 1–16. Lanham, MD: Scarecrow Press, 2010.

Bhabha, Homi. *The Location of Culture*. London: Routledge, 1994.

Bharucha, Rustom. "A Reply to Richard Schechner." *Asian Theatre Journal* 1, no. 2 (1984): 255. In *Theatre and the World: Performance and the Politics of Culture*, 13–90. London: Routledge, 1983.

———. "A View from India." In *Peter Brook and the Mahabharata: Critical Perspectives*, edited by David Williams, 228–52. London: Routledge, 1991.

Bhattacharyya, Gargi. "Riding Multiculturalism." In *Multicultural States: Rethinking Difference and Identity*, edited by David Bennett, 252–66. London: Routledge, 1998.

Boynton, T. J. "'The Fearful Crimes of Ireland': Tabloid Journalism and Irish Nationalism in *The Playboy of the Western World*." *Éire-Ireland* 47, nos. 3/4 (Fall/Winter 2012): 230–50.

Breen, Michael, Amanda Haynes, and Eoin Devereux. "Citizens, Loopholes and Maternity Tourists: Irish Print Media Coverage of the 2004 Citizenship Referendum." In *Uncertain Ireland: A Sociological Chronicle, 2003–2004*, edited by Mary P. Corcoran and Michel Peillon, 59–72. Dublin: Institute of Public Administration, 2006.

Brook, Peter. *The Empty Space: A Book about the Theatre: Deadly, Holy, Rough, Immediate*. New York: Scribner, 1968.

———. *The Shifting Point*. London: Methuen Drama, 1994.

———. *Threads of Time*. London: Counterpoint, 1999.

Burns, John. "Abbey in €500,000 Legal Drama." *Sunday Times*, February 3, 2013.

Carlson, Marvin. "Brook and Mnouchkine: Passages to India?" In *Peter Brook and the Mahabharata: Critical Perspectives*, edited by David Williams, 79–92. London: Routledge, 1991.

Capell, Kerry. "Ireland: A Nation of Immigrants?" *Businessweek*, July 25, 2004.

"Census of Population 2016—Profile 7 Migration and Diversity." Central Statistics Office, 2016. https://www.cso.ie/en/releasesandpublications /ep/p-cp7md/p7md/p7anii/.

Chaudhuri, Una. "Working Out (of) Place: Brook's Mahabharata and the Problematics of Intercultural Performance." In *Staging Resistance*, edited by Jenny Spencer, 77–97. Ann Arbor: Univ. of Michigan Press, 1998.

Cleary, Joseph. *Outrageous Fortune: Culture and Capital in Modern Ireland*. Derry: Field Day, 2006.

Conceison, Claire. "Translating Collaborations: *The Joy Luck Club* and Intercultural Theatre." *Drama Review* 39 (Fall 1995): 151–66.

Conley, Susan. Review of *The Playboy of the Western World—A New Version* by Bisi Adigun and Roddy Doyle, Abbey Theatre, Dublin. *Irish Theatre Magazine*, October 5, 2007.

Conquergood, Dwight. "Performance Studies: Interventions and Radical Research." *Drama Review* 46, no. 2 (2002): 145–56.

Crawley, Peter. Review of *Playboy of the Western World—A New Version*, by Bisi Adigun and Roddy Doyle, Abbey Theatre, Dublin. *Irish Times*, October 5, 2007.

Cullen, Paul. *Refugees and Asylum-Seekers in Ireland*. Cork: Cork Univ. Press, 2000.

Cummins, Steve. "*The Playboy of the Western World*." Review of *The Playboy of the Western World—A New Version*, by Bisi Adigun and Roddy Doyle, Abbey Theatre, Dublin. RTÊ, October 8, 2007.

Cutchins, Dennis. "Introduction to the Companion." In *The Routledge Companion to Adaptation*, edited by Dennis Cutchins, Katja Krebs, and Eckart Voigts, 1–4. London: Routledge, 2018.

Dasgupta, Gautam. "Peter Brook's 'Orientalism.'" In *Peter Brook and the Mahabharata: Critical Perspectives*, edited by David Williams, 262–67. London: Routledge, 1991.

Diamond, Suzanne. "Whose Life *Is* It, Anyway? Adaptation, Collective Memory, and (Auto)Biographical Processes." In *Redefining Adaptation Studies*, edited by Dennis Cutchins, Laurence Raw, and James M. Welsh, 95–110. Lanham, MD: Scarecrow Press, 2010.

Doyle, Roddy. *The Deportees and Other Stories*. New York: Viking, 2008.

———. *The Guts*. Toronto: Knopf Canada, 2013.

Ejorh, Theophilus. "The Challenge of Resilience: Migrant-Led Organizations and the Recession in Ireland." *Journal of International Migration and Integration* 16, no. 3 (August 2015): 679–99.

Fanning, Bryan. *Migration and the Making of Ireland*. Dublin: Univ. College Dublin Press, 2018.

———. "Racism, Rules and Rights." In *Immigration and Social Change in the Republic of Ireland*, edited by Bryan Fanning, 6–26. Manchester: Manchester Univ. Press, 2007.

Frazier, Adrian. "'Quaint Pastoral Numbskulls': Siobhán McKenna's Playboy Film." In *Playboys of the Western World: Production Histories*, edited by Adrian Frazier, 59–74. Dublin: Carysfort Press, 2004.

Fricker, Karen. Review of *The Playboy of The Western World—A New Version*, by Bisi Adigun and Roddy Doyle, Abbey Theatre, Dublin. *Variety*, October 9, 2007. https://variety.com/2007/legit/reviews/the-playboy -of-the-western-world-8-1200555477/.

Fricker, Karen, and Ronit Lentin, eds. *Performing Global Networks*. Newcastle: Cambridge Scholars Publishing, 2007.

Fukuyama, Francis. "The End of History?" *National Interest* 16 (Summer 1989): 3–18.

Garner, Steve. *Racism in the Irish Experience*. London: Pluto, 2004.

Gibbons, Luke. "Finding Integration through Engaging with Our Past." *Irish Times*, October 29, 2007.

Gilbert, Helen, and Joanne Tompkins. *Post-Colonial Drama: Theory, Practice, Politics*. London: Routledge, 1996.

Gilroy, Paul. *Against Race: Imagining Political Culture beyond the Color Line*. Cambridge, MA: Harvard Univ. Press, 2000.

Gleeson, Colin. "Drumm Said He Would 'Punch' Lenihan." *Irish Times*, July 1, 2013.

Green, Steph. *New Boy*. Dublin: Zanzibar Films, 2007. https://www.you tube.com/watch?v=FdeioVndUhs.

Gregory, Augusta. *Our Irish Theatre: A Chapter of Autobiography*. New York: G. P. Putnam's Sons, 1913.

Grene, Nicholas. *The Politics of Irish Drama: Plays in Context from Boucicault to Friel*. Cambridge: Cambridge Univ. Press, 1999.

Gussow, Mel. "Stage: 'Christy,' Musical." *New York Times*, October 16, 1975, https://www.nytimes.com/1975/10/16/archives/stage christy musical .html.

Halsing, Donald. "Representing Populations of Change." Undergraduate paper, Framingham State Univ., 2019.

Hamilton, Margaret. "Hayloft's *Thyestes*: Adapting Seneca for the Australian Stage and Context." *Theatre Journal* 66, no. 4 (2014): 519–40.

Harrington, John. "The Playboy IN the Western World: J. M. Synge's Play in America." In *Playboys of the Western World: Production Histories*, edited by Adrian Frazier, 46–58. Dublin: Carysfort Press, 2004.

Hutcheon, Linda. *A Theory of Adaptation*. New York: Taylor and Francis, 2013.

Hyde, Douglas. "The Necessity for De-Anglicising Ireland." In *Language, Lore and Lyrics*, edited by Breandán Ó Conaire, 153–70. Dublin: Irish Academic Press, 1986.

Jellenik, Glenn. "Adaptation's Originality Problem: 'Grappling with the Thorny Questions of What Constitutes Originality.'" In *The Routledge Companion to Adaptation*, edited by Dennis Cutchins, Katja Krebs, and Eckart Voigts, 182–93. London: Routledge, 2018.

Jewesbury, Daniel, Jagtar Singh, and Sarah Tuck. *Cultural Diversity and the Arts: Final Report*. Dublin: Create—The National Development Agency for Collaborative Arts and Arts Council, 2009.

Keating, Sara. "Evolving *Playboys* for the Global World." In *Synge and His Influences: Centenary Essays from the Synge Summer School*, edited by Patrick Lonergan, 245–57. Dublin: Carysfort Press, 2011.

Kenny, Patrick. "That Dreadful Play." Review of *Playboy of the Western World*, by J. M. Synge. *Irish Times*, January 30, 1907. In *The Playboy Riots*, edited by James Kilroy, 37–40. Dublin: Dolmen, 1971.

Kiberd, Declan. "After Ireland?" *Irish Times*, August 29, 2009.

———. *Inventing Ireland: The Literature of the Modern Nation*. Cambridge, MA: Harvard Univ. Press, 1995.

———. "Strangers in Their Own Country: Multi-Culturalism in Ireland." In *Multi-Culturalism: The View from the Two Irelands*, by Edna Longley and Declan Kiberd, 45–78. Cork: Cork University Press, 2001.

Kilroy, Thomas. "Adaptation: A Privileged Conversation with a Dead Author." *Irish Times*, February 13, 2010. https://www.irishtimes.com/culture/stage/adaptation-a-privileged-conversation-with-a-dead-author-1.62 1741.

King, Jason. "Contemporary Irish Theatre, the New Playboy Controversy, and the Economic Crisis." *Irish Studies Review* 24, no. 1 (2016): 67–78.

———. "Three Kings: Migrant Masculinities in Irish Social Practice, Theoretical Perspective and Theatre Performance." *Irish Journal of Applied Social Studies* 16, no. 1 (2016): 20–34.

Knowles, Ric. *Performing the Intercultural City.* Ann Arbor: Univ. of Michigan Press, 2017.

———. *Theatre and Interculturalism.* London: Palgrave Macmillan, 2010.

Krebs, Katja. "Adapting Identities: Performing the Self." In *The Routledge Companion to Adaptation,* edited by Dennis Cutchins, Katja Krebs, and Eckart Voigts, 207–17. London: Routledge, 2018.

Lally, Conor. "Gangland 2021: A World Veronica Guerin Would Not Recognise." *Irish Times,* June 25, 2021. https://www.irishtimes.com/news /crime-and-law/gangland-2021-a-world-veronica-guerin-would-not -recognise-1.4603561.

Lei, Daphne. "Interruption, Intervention, Interculturalism: Robert Wilson's HIT Productions in Taiwan." *Theatre Journal* 63, no. 4 (2011): 571–86.

Leitch, Thomas. "Twelve Fallacies in Contemporary Adaptation Theory." *Criticism* 45, no. 2 (2003): 149–71.

Lentin, Ronit, and Robbie McVeigh. *After Optimism? Ireland, Racism and Globalisation.* Dublin: Metro Éireann Publications, 2006.

Lentin, Ronit, and Robbie McVeigh, eds. *Racism and Anti-Racism in Ireland.* Belfast: Beyond the Pale, 2002.

Levine, Caroline. *Forms: Whole, Rhythm, Hierarchy, Network.* Princeton, NJ: Princeton Univ. Press, 2015.

Lo, Jacqueline, and Helen Gilbert. "Toward a Topography of Cross-Cultural Theatre Praxis." *Drama Review* 46, no. 3 (2002): 31–53.

Lonergan, Patrick. "Introduction." In *Synge and His Influences: Centenary Essays from the Synge Summer School,* edited by Patrick Lonergan. Dublin: Carysfort Press, 2011.

———. *Irish Drama and Theatre since 1950.* London: Bloomsbury-Methuen, 2019.

———. *Theatre and Globalization: Irish Drama in the Celtic Tiger Era.* London: Palgrave Macmillan, 2009.

"*Love/Hate* Tops the 2012 Ratings." RTÊ Archives, n.d. https://www.rte .ie/archives/exhibitions/681-history-of-rte/709-rte-2010s/482242-love hate tops the ratings/.

McGreevy, Ronan. "Abbey 'to Pay €600,000' in Dispute over Play Copyright." *Irish Times*, January 31, 2013. http://www.irishtimes.com/news/abbey-to-pay-600-000-in-dispute-over-play-copyright-1.1255531.

McGuire, Matt. "Dialect(ic) Nationalism?: The Fiction of James Kelman and Roddy Doyle." *Scottish Studies Review* 7, no. 1 (Spring 2006): 80–94.

McIvor, Charlotte. *Migration and Performance in Contemporary Ireland: Towards a New Interculturalism*. London: Palgrave Macmillan, 2016.

———. "Staging the 'New Irish': Interculturalism and the Future of Post-Celtic Tiger Irish Theatre." *Modern Drama* 54, no. 3 (Fall 2011): 310–32.

McIvor, Charlotte, and Jason King, eds. *Interculturalism and Performance Now: New Directions?* London: Palgrave Macmillan, 2019.

McIvor, Charlotte, and Matthew Spangler, eds. *Staging Intercultural Ireland: New Plays and Practitioner Perspectives*. Cork: Cork University Press, 2014.

Meany, Helen. "*The Playboy of the Western World*." Review of *The Playboy of the Western World—A New Version*, by Bisi Adigun and Roddy Doyle, Abbey Theatre, Dublin. *Guardian*, October 6, 2007. https://www.theguardian.com/stage/2007/oct/06/theatre1.

Mnouchkine, Ariane. "The Theatre Is Oriental." In *The Intercultural Performance Reader*, edited by Henry Bial, 93–98. London: Routledge, 1996.

Morash, Christopher. *A History of Irish Theatre, 1601–2000*. Cambridge: Cambridge Univ. Press, 2002.

Mukherjee, Ankhi. *What Is a Classic? Postcolonial Rewriting and Invention of the Canon*. Stanford, CA: Stanford Univ. Press, 2014.

Murphy, Colin. "Our Stage Will Be a Poorer Place after Losing One of Its Few African Voices." *Irish Independent*, August 25, 2013.

Murray, Christopher. "Beyond the Passion Machine: The Adigun-Doyle Playboy and Multiculturalism." In *Irish Drama: Local and Global Perspectives*, edited by Nicholas Grene and Patrick Lonergan, 105–20. Dublin: Carysfort Press, 2012.

———. *Twentieth-Century Irish Drama: Mirror Up to Nation*. Manchester: Manchester Univ. Press, 1997.

Murray, Simone. *The Adaptation Industry: The Cultural Economy of Contemporary Literary Adaptation*. London: Routledge, 2012.

Myers, Kevin. "Making Synge's Great Comedy 'Relevant' Ended in Costly Farce." *Irish Independent*, February 5, 2013.

Negra, Diane. "Adjusting Men and Abiding Mammies: Gendering the Recession in Ireland," *Gender, Sexuality and Feminism* 1, no. 2 (December 2014): 42–58.

Ní Chaoimh, Bairbre. Interview by Charlotte McIvor. In *Staging Intercultural Ireland: New Plays and Practitioner Perspectives*, edited by Charlotte McIvor and Matthew Spangler, 341–49. Cork: Cork Univ. Press, 2014.

O'Kelly, Emer. "Playboy of the Badlands a Riot." *Sunday Independent*, October 7, 2007. https://www.pressreader.com/ireland/sunday-independent -ireland/20071007/282205121518890.

O'Toole, Emer. "Cultural Capital in Intercultural Theatre: A Study of Pan Pan Theatre Company's *The Playboy of the Western World.*" *Target* 25, no. 3 (2013): 407–26.

———. "Rights of Representation: An Ethics of Intercultural Theatre Practice." PhD diss., Royal Holloway, Univ. of London, 2012.

———. "Theatre Has Nothing to Declare but an Innate Uncertainty." *Irish Times*, May 22, 2010. https://www.irishtimes.com/life-and-style/people /theatre-has-nothing-to-declare-but-an-innate-uncertainty-1.668749.

———. "Towards Best Intercultural Practice: An Analysis of Tim Supple's Pan-Indian *A Midsummer Night's Dream.*" *Journal of Adaptation in Film and Performance* 4, no. 3 (2011): 289–302.

Pribisic, Milan. "The Pleasures of 'Theater Film': Stage to Film Adaptation." In *Redefining Adaptation Studies*, edited by Dennis Cutchins, Laurence Raw, and James M. Welsh, 147–59. Lanham, MD: Scarecrow Press, 2010.

Reddy, Maureen T. "Reading and Writing Race in Ireland: Roddy Doyle and 'Metro Éireann.'" *Irish University Review* 35, no. 2 (Autumn–Winter 2005): 374–88.

"Review of Abbey Theatre's Funding." *Irish Examiner*, November 7, 2013.

Said, Edward. *Orientalism*. London: Penguin Books, 1978.

Salis, Loredana. *Stage Migrants: Representations of the Migrant Other in Modern Irish Drama*. Newcastle: Cambridge Scholars Publishing, 2010.

Sanders, Julie. *Adaptation and Appropriation*. London: Routledge, 2007.

Schechner, Richard. *Between Theatre and Anthropology*. Philadelphia: Univ. of Pennsylvania Press, 1985.

———. *The Future of Ritual: Writings on Culture and Performance*. London: Routledge, 1993.

———. "A Reply to Rustom Bharucha." *Asian Theatre Journal* 1, no. 2 (1984): 252.

Severn, John. "*All Shook Up* and the Unannounced Adaptation: Engaging with *Twelfth Night*'s Unstable Identities." *Theatre Journal* 66, no. 4 (2014): 541–57.

Singleton, Brian. *Masculinities and the Contemporary Irish Theatre*. London: Palgrave Macmillan, 2011.

———. "The Pursuit of Otherness for the Investigation of Self." *Theatre Research International* 22, no. 2 (1997): 93–97.

Spangler, Matthew. "Winds of Change: Immigration, Bloomsday, and 'Aeolus' in Dublin Street Theatre." *James Joyce Quarterly* 45, vol. 1 (2007): 47–68.

Sunday Tribune. "The Big Issues." Unsigned review of *The Playboy of the Western World—A New Version*, by Bisi Adigun and Roddy Doyle, Abbey Theatre, Dublin, October 7, 2007.

Synge, John Millington. *The Aran Islands*. In *The Collected Plays and Poems and "The Aran Islands."* London: Everyman, 1996.

———. *The Playboy of the Western World*. In *Collected Works of J. M. Synge: Plays*, vol. 4, book 2, edited by Ann Saddlemyer. Gerrards Cross: Colin Smythe, 1982.

———. *The Playboy of the Western World*. In *The Complete Plays*. New York: Vintage, 1960.

———. *The Playboy of the Western World*. In *Irish Writing in the Twentieth Century: A Reader*, edited by David Pierce, 171–94. Cork: Cork Univ. Press, 2000.

———. *The Playboy of the Western World: A Comedy in Three Acts*. Boston: John W. Luce, 1911.

Townsend, Sarah L. "Cosmopolitanism at Home: Ireland's Playboys from Celtic Revival to Celtic Tiger." *Journal of Modern Literature* 34, no. 2 (Winter 2011): 45–64.

———. "Muslim Integration and the *Hijabi Monologues Ireland*." *Irish University Review* 51, no. 2 (2021): 209–26.

——. "The 'New Irish' Neighborhood: Race and Succession in Ireland and Irish America." In *The Routledge International Handbook of Irish Studies*, edited by Renée Fox, Mike Cronin, and Brian Ó Conchubhair, 220–29. London: Routledge, 2021.

Villar-Argáiz, Pilar. "Introduction: The Immigrant in Contemporary Irish Literature." In *Literary Visions of Multicultural Ireland*, edited by Pilar Villar-Argáiz, 1–34. Manchester: Manchester Univ. Press, 2014.

——, ed. *Literary Visions of Multicultural Ireland: The Immigrant in Contemporary Irish Literature*. Manchester: Manchester Univ. Press, 2014.

Wilson, August. "The Ground on Which I Stand." *American Theatre Magazine*, September 1996.

Contributors

Bisi Adigun, before joining Bowen University (of the Baptist Convention), Iwo, Osun State, Nigeria, as a Senior Lecturer in October 2019, was an adjunct lecturer of African theater and performance studies at Trinity College, Dublin, Ireland, where he earned his PhD in drama in 2013. Between 2000 and 2003, Adigun was a co-presenter of *MONO*, RTÊ's intercultural television magazine program. He founded Arambe Productions in 2003, Ireland's first African theater company, for which he produced and directed over twenty-five productions in Ireland, Nigeria, and the United States. Adigun's first volume of plays, *An Other Playboy, The Butcher Babes*, and *Home, Sweet Home (Three Plays)*, was published by Universal Books in 2018. He is the coeditor of *The Soyinka Impulse: Essays on Wole Soyinka* (BookCraft, 2019). Adigun also edited *Remembering Ola Rotimi: A Complete Man of the Theatre*, a book of essays about Ola Rotimi, the renowned Nigerian playwright and director (Bowen University Press, 2022). Currently, Adigun is working on his adaptation of Brian Friel's *Philadelphia Here I Come!!* as well as coediting *Nigerian Directors: Philosophies, Styles and Aesthetics*, which will feature interview and essay contributions by thirty living Nigerian stage directors, scheduled for release by Cambridge Scholars in 2024.

Roddy Doyle is the author of eleven acclaimed novels, including *The Commitments, The Snapper, The Van* (finalist for the Booker Prize), *Paddy Clarke Ha Ha Ha* (winner of the Booker Prize), *The Woman Who Walked into Doors, A Star Called Henry*, and *Smile*. Doyle has also written two collections of stories, several works for children and young adults, and *Rory & Ita*, a memoir of his parents, and has contributed to the *New Yorker, McSweeney's*, and *Metro Éireann*, among other publications. Doyle's stage plays include *Brownbread, War, Guess Who's Coming for the Dinner*, and adaptations of *The Commitments* and *The Woman Who Walked into Doors*, co-adapted with Joe O'Byrne.

Jason King is academic coordinator of the Irish Heritage Trust and National Famine Museum at Strokestown Park, County Roscommon, Ireland. He has held previous appointments at the National University of Ireland, Galway; the University of Limerick; the Université de Montréal; Concordia University; the National University of Ireland, Maynooth; and University College Cork. He has an extensive track record of teaching and publications in the areas of contemporary Irish interculturalism, migration, and theater and performance, as well as nineteenth-century Irish literature and the cultural memory of the Great Famine in Ireland and North America. His recent publications include *Performance and Interculturalism Now: New Directions?* (Palgrave, 2018) and *Irish Famine Migration Narratives: Eyewitness Testimonies* (Routledge, 2018).

Kelly Matthews is professor of English at Framingham State University in Massachusetts. She is the author of *"The Bell" Magazine and the Representation of Irish Identity* (Four Courts Press, 2012), and she is the coeditor of *The Country of the Young: Interpretations of Youth and Childhood in Irish Culture* (Four Courts Press, 2013). Her current research focuses on the first decade of Brian Friel's career (1956–66), drawing upon new archival material from the *New Yorker* and the BBC.

Emer O'Toole is associate professor of Irish performance studies at the School of Irish Studies, Concordia University, Montreal. She is also a fellow of Concordia's Simone de Beauvoir Institute and an affiliate associate professor at the Mel Hoppenheim School of Film. She is author of *Girls Will Be Girls* (Orion, 2015), and coeditor of *Ethical Exchanges in Translation, Adaptation and Dramaturgy*. Her current project illuminates the relationship between contemporary Irish theater and social change. Her academic work has appeared in international journals, including *LIT: Literature Interpretation Theory*, *Sexualities*, *Éire-Ireland*, and *Target*. She is also a regular contributor to the *Guardian* and the *Irish Times*, among other publications.

Matthew Spangler is professor of performance studies and chair of the Film, Theatre, and Dance Department at San José State University. His articles have appeared in *James Joyce Quarterly, Text and Performance Quarterly*, the *New Hibernia Review, Theatre Journal, Theatre Annual*, the *South Atlantic Review, Nineteenth Century Literature*, and *Crossroads: Performance Studies and Irish Culture* (Palgrave, 2009). He is the coeditor of *Staging Intercultural Ireland: New Plays and Practitioner Perspectives* (Cork University Press, 2014). He is also an award-winning playwright. His plays have been produced on Broadway, in London's West End, off-Broadway, at the Gaiety Theatre in Dublin, Dubai Opera House, Carthage Theatre Days in Tunisia, as well as at many other theaters worldwide. His widely produced stage adaptation of Khaled Hosseini's novel *The Kite Runner* was published by Bloomsbury (2016) and Penguin Press (2018). More on his plays can be found at: www.matthwspangler.org.

Maria Szasz (notes to the play text) teaches theater history in the University of New Mexico Honors College, where she specializes in comedy, musical theater, American and Irish drama, and theater and human rights. Her publications include *Brian Friel and America* (Glasnevin Press, 2013), and "Lyra McKee (1990–2019): How Uncomfortable Conversations Can Save Lives," in *The Rose and Irish Identity: Seeding, Blooming, Piercing & Withering* (Cambridge Univ. Press, 2021). She is currently working on a history of the Irish Repertory Theatre Company in New York City.

Sarah L. Townsend is associate professor of English at the University of New Mexico, where she specializes in modern and contemporary Irish fiction and drama. Her scholarship explores the relationship between economic globalization, immigration, and literary form. She has published articles and chapters in *New Literary History*, the *Journal of Modern Literature*, the *Journal of Commonwealth Literature*, and a number of edited collections. She is completing her first monograph on modern Irish drama's radical transformation of the *Bildungsroman*. Her next project examines the interlinked histories of transatlantic Irish migration, white racial striving, and the term *new Irish*, from Ellis Island to contemporary Irish multiculturalism.